The Definitive Christian D. Larson Collection

6 Volumes
30 Titles

Compiled and Edited
by
David Allen

Volume 5 of 6

Copyright © 2014 by David Allen / Shanon Allen
All rights reserved. No part of this publication may be reproduced, distributed, or transmitted in any form or by any means, including photocopying, recording, or other electronic or mechanical methods, without the prior written permission of the publisher, except in the case of brief quotations embodied in critical reviews and certain other noncommercial uses permitted by copyright law.
Printed in the United States of America

Reprint

First Printing November 2014

ISBN: 978-0-9909643-4-6

Visit Us At **NevilleGoddardBooks.com** for a complete listing of all our books and **1000's of Free Books to Read online and download.**

Books include: The Power of I AM 1, 2, 3, The Neville Goddard Collection, Neville Goddard's Interpretation of Scripture, The Money Bible, The Creative Power of Thought, The Secrets, Mysteries & Powers of The Subconscious Mind, Your Inner Conversations are Creating Your World, The World is At Your Command - The Very Best of Neville Goddard, Imagining Creates Reality - 365 Mystical Daily Quotes, Imagination: The Redemptive Power in Man, Assumptions Harden Into Facts: The Book, David Allen - Your Faith Is Your Fortune, Your Unlimited Power

First Printing
Copyright © 2014

Foreword

The Definitive Christian D. Larson Collection is a 6 volume set of 30 titles from one of the most renowned and prolific new thought authors and lecturers of his day. No metaphysical, new thought, law of attraction collection would be complete without Christian D. Larson's books. Before Neville Goddard, before Ernest Holmes, before Joseph Murphy and Napoleon Hill and a host of many of the great authors and teachers of today, there was Christian D. Larson (1874 – 1954) who was credited by Horatio Dresser as being a founder in the New Thought movement.

Christian D. Larson books contain hidden secrets (hidden from the conscious minds of those not prepared to receive them) and treasures that you are unlikely to find anywhere else and if you do it is likely it originated from Christian D. Larson.

David Allen

All Christian D. Larson's books are in the public domain.

* Editors note: Some Christian D. Larson books were originally published without chapter titles. They were later added by other editors of Mr. Larson's works. To my knowledge none of them are copyrighted.

Christian D. Larson Titles
Volume - Original Year Published - Title

Vol. 1	1913	Brains and How to Get Them
Vol. 1	1912	Business Psychology
Vol. 1	1907	How Great Men Succeed
Vol. 1	1912	How the Mind Works
Vol. 2	1920	Concentration
Vol. 2	1912	How to Stay Well
Vol. 2	1908	How to Stay Young
Vol. 3	1908	The Great Within
Vol. 3	1912	The Mind Cure
Vol. 3	1912	What is Truth
Vol. 3	1912	Your Forces and How to Use Them
Vol. 4	1916	The Good Side of Christian Science
Vol. 4	1912	The Ideal Made Real
Vol. 4	1910	Mastery of Fate
Vol. 4	1907	Mastery of Self
Vol. 4	1916	My Ideal of Marriage
Vol. 4	1916	Nothing Succeeds Like Success
Vol. 4	1916	Steps in Human Progress
Vol. 5	**1918**	**Healing Yourself**
Vol. 5	**1912**	**Just Be Glad**
Vol. 5	**1940**	**Leave it to God**
Vol. 5	**1908**	**On the Heights**
Vol. 5	**1910**	**Perfect Health**
Vol. 5	**1922**	**Practical Self-Help**
Vol. 5	**1912**	**Scientific Training of Children**
Vol. 5	**1912**	**Thinking for Results**
Vol. 6	1912	The Hidden Secret
Vol. 6	1916	In Light of the Spirit
Vol. 6	1912	The Pathway of Roses
Vol. 6	1907	Poise and Power

Volume 5

Healing Yourself	6
Just Be Glad	88
Leave it to God	107
On the Heights	124
Perfect Health	154
Practical Self-Help	202
Scientific Training of Children	369
Thinking for Results	415

Healing Yourself

Healing Yourself

Table of Contents

Introductory Statement	8
Chapter 1 - Full Supply of Vital Energy	9
Chapter 2 - The Super-Physical Breath	14
Chapter 3 - Psychological Equilibrium	20
Chapter 4 - Nourishing the Body	25
Chapter 5 - Nourishing the Mind	30
Chapter 6 - The Will to Be Well	36
Chapter 7 - Interior Relaxation	41
Chapter 8 - Imagine Yourself Well	46
Chapter 9 - The Real Living of Life	51
Chapter 10 - The Right Use of Body, Mind and Soul	55
Chapter 11 - The Finer Curative Forces	65
Chapter 12 - Living in the Absolute	75

Introductory Statement

There are many states and conditions of mind, and many stages in human development. Also, there are many special personal needs. Therefore, it is necessary to have many methods of healing and many ways to open the doors to personal emancipation and well being.

Upon the following pages many methods are presented, each one of which has proven its own efficacy and power in no uncertain manner; in-deed, each one of these methods has helped its thousands and its tens of thousands, and will continue to do so.

The reader is advised, therefore, to study each chapter carefully so as to become thoroughly familiar with the place, the possibility and the application of each method, and selecting, for the present, those methods that make the deepest and most positive appeal.

Later, when needs arise for healing or physical and personal upbuilding, the best methods for the occasion will readily suggest themselves; and definite results may be secured in the least time with the least effort.

The larger purpose should be, however, to gain that wider consciousness through which we may combine, harmoniously, all worthy methods — the psychological, the metaphysical and the spiritual — causing all good things to work together for greater and greater good.

Chapter 1

Full Supply of Vital Energy

The Great Law. — It is absolutely impossible for any form of disease, physical or mental, organic or functional, to enter the human system so long as that system is abundantly supplied with vital energy. And it is absolutely impossible for any form of disease to remain in the human system after a full supply of vital energy has been provided for every part of that system.

The First Essential. — Recognizing the validity and the certainty of the law just presented, we realize that the first essential in the attainment of health, in the regaining of health, or in the maintenance of health, must necessarily be to supply the human system with all the vital energy that mind and body can appropriate and employ. In brief, if we have good health, and wish to continue in good health, we must take immediate steps to keep the system brim full of vital energy under every circumstance; or, if we wish to regain health, we must proceed to recharge and revitalize the entire system until the full supply of energy has been secured.

How to Proceed. — Our purpose must be, to so live, think and act that all waste of vital energy may be prevented absolutely; and also, to adopt such methods as may prove directly conducive to the increase of vital energy; that is, we must learn to retain what energy we have, and learn to produce more and more as growth and advancement may demand.

Practical Methods. — The first and simplest rule to observe is that of moderation in all things. Act only in conformity with present capacity; and aim to increase your capacity before you increase your activity. Believe that you can do as much as you like; then do only as much as you know you have the available energy to do at present. Take good care of the energy you have. Permit no waste; but do not permit the least to lie dormant. Use all the energy you have every day. Live and work to full capacity. But do not live and work beyond your present capacity. First, increase your capacity; and know that you can.

Revitalization. — When all the energy in the system has been used for the day, in wholesome living and constructive work, proper methods must be taken to revitalize and recharge the system. And this is accomplished in the natural way, through change of activity, recreation and sleep. Should you feel the energy of the system running low, the simplest and quickest way to recuperate is to go and do something else, or to turn thought and attention into some other channel. In brief, permit the muscles and the faculties you have been using to relax, and call into action muscles and faculties that have not been used for a time. The practice of turning thought and attention into other channels for thirty minutes several times every day is one of the best methods known for recharging the system with energy, and thus keeping mind and body fully supplied at all times.

Source of Energy. — The real source of vital energy is found in the subconscious mind; and we enter the subconscious whenever we go to sleep, largely for the purpose of gaining a new supply of life, force and energy. It is highly important, therefore, to go to sleep with the expectation of gaining a larger supply of energy than we ever possessed before, because it is always the law everywhere that the more we expect the more we receive. However, we must never permit anxiety to accompany our expectations; we must, in all things, be calm and serene, and make it our purpose to live and act in the full faith that all our expectations will be realized. The fact is, that there is more power in a calm, serene faith than in anything else in the world.

How to Live. — In order that the system may be full of life and energy at all times, live the serene life, but turn on the full current. Give full, harmonious and constructive expression to all the power there is in you, but see that every action is calm, orderly and in perfect poise. Live a large life and a powerful life, but invariably combine the expression of power with a deep feeling of peace. Try to feel serene and strong at the same time, and at all times. This is most important if you would have an abundance of energy, and retain it all, with full force, in your own system. And you will find that this simple practice of trying to feel serene and strong at the same time will work wonders for you.

How to Work. — Under every circumstance, work in poise. Work with all the energy you have, but apply that energy in poise; and never permit yourself to violate this rule. Avoid nervous rush, regardless of conditions or demands; and also avoid the habit of doing less than you can do; for remember that we always lose what energy we do not use. Use all the energy you have; use it constructively; use it in poise; and use it in the full conviction that you will immediately receive more. Again, we should consider the great law of expectation. Expect more; expect much; expect everything you want; then live in the absolute faith that all your expectations will be realized.

Very Important. — All waste of energy must be prevented if we wish to have continuous and perfect health. And, therefore, everything must be avoided that may tend to produce such waste, be the action physical or mental. We must not only avoid the misuse of the body, but also the misuse of the mind. Such states therefore as anger, fear or worry, or similar states of mind must never be tolerated for a single moment. The fact is, that one hour of severe mental depression may lower your vital energy down to a point where you have less than one-fourth as much as you had before. If one hour of such a state of mind can destroy more than three-fourths of your energy, we have something here that must not be ignored for a moment. And it is too true that mental depression, or similar states, will have this very effect. We must therefore eliminate such states absolutely, and keep the mind in a clean, lofty, harmonious condition at all times. Remember this: Do nothing to lower your vitality and you will always be well.

Special Exercise. — We find in every human system a tendency to lose energy. In fact, most people are losing vital energy, unconsciously, most of the time. But this loss we must prevent; and we can. We can learn to hold, in our own system, all the energy we generate; and this may be accomplished in a very short time through the following exercise:

Take a few moments several times every day, and turn attention upon the energy that fills your physical and mental system. Then try to feel that you are holding all of this energy in your own system through the power of your mind. In fact, try to take conscious hold of this energy and keep it all in yourself. In a moment, you will feel more and more energy accumulating in every part of your being until you actually feel as if you were recharged. And you are. You have, for the time being, prevented all loss; and you are beginning to realize what a power you would become if you could always retain all the energy you generate. Repeat the exercise several times every day until it becomes second nature for your mind to hold within your own system all the energy you generate. Thus you prevent all loss permanently, and you will feel far stronger, both in mind and body, than ever before.

Full Supply. — Realizing the fact that the sub-conscious mind is the real source of energy, and that the subconscious will invariably respond to our conscious directions, we should make it a point to direct the subconscious every day to keep the system, physical and mental, absolutely full of vital energy every moment. This may be accomplished by turning attention upon the subconscious at frequent intervals, and actually declaring to the subconscious that this full supply be maintained. Results will positively follow.

Increase of Energy. — The permanent increase of vital energy may be secured by directing the subconscious to express, in mind and body, a larger supply. The subconscious can. The amount of latent energy in the great within is limitless; and, therefore, we may secure more and more as we desire. Turn the positive will upon the subconscious, and will to arouse more and more vital energy from within. Proceed calmly, and with determination; and fully expect to receive the increase that you have in mind.

The Aim in View. — We know the great law, that no ailment whatever can enter the human system, so long as that system is brim full of vital energy. Our aim in view therefore must be to possess, at all times, this full and abundant supply. And as we learn this great art, we shall always be well; we shall always be strong; we shall live a long, active life, and enjoy every moment to the highest degree.

Chapter 2

The Super-Physical Breath

Important Fact. — The physical atmosphere with which we are surrounded, and portions of which we inhale with every breath, is not composed of physical elements alone. And when we breathe, we take into the system something more besides the air that enters the lungs. The fact is, that the physical atmosphere is charged with certain vital forces, or life energies, that are drawn more or less into the physical system when we breathe; and that invariably tend to increase the vital energy of the system. In some localities the atmosphere contains more of this vital force than elsewhere; and we always find that the population of such localities feel stronger, more energetic and more alive, and accomplish a great deal more, both in the physical and the mental fields of activity. We also find that certain individuals have the happy faculty of drawing into their systems a greater supply than usual of this atmospheric life force, regardless of where they may live; and, in consequence, have far more energy, under every circumstance, than the majority.

The Energizing Breath. — It is not always convenient to select those localities where the atmosphere has the most energy; besides, the atmosphere in every locality may change its energy-producing power with every change in climatic conditions. We cannot depend, therefore, upon conditions as they come and go in the external; but we can depend upon our own power to extract from the atmosphere all the life energy we may desire; for the fact is, that there is an abundance of this life energy in the atmosphere of any locality, regardless of climatic conditions; and we can, through the energizing breath, or the super-physical breath, draw into our systems as much of this force as we can hold or apply. This must become our purpose, therefore, because the human system does require a certain amount of this atmospheric energy in order to maintain perfect health. And when we can draw into the system a great deal more of this energy than is required for perfect health, we may increase remarkably both our working capacity and our joy of living. This latter fact is most evident, because it is when we feel as if we were literally charged with these highly re-4 fined life energies that life becomes nothing less than supreme joy. And it is then that we want to live for an indefinite period, and achieve wonderfully upon this planet.

The New Way. — In the usual way of breathing, we inhale what we can appropriate of the physical atmosphere, so as to supply certain demands of nature; and if the atmosphere happens to be well charged at the time, we draw into the system considerable life energy with every inhalation; but if the atmosphere does not happen to be well charged, we receive but a scant supply of this energy, and in consequence do not feel as strong or as well as usual. In the new way of breathing, however, we do not rely merely upon what energy may be received in the usual manner; we make a special effort to draw into the system an extra supply of life energy with every inhalation. And this we can readily do if we observe a few important laws in connection with general breathing and special exercises in breathing.

How to Begin. — Realize that the atmosphere you breathe is charged with certain vital energies and that a certain supply of these energies is taken into the system with every breath. Then realize that you can draw into your system a far greater supply of these energies; and that your body will have greater vitality and better health with every increase of this supply that you receive. The fact is, that, although your body may be too weak to move around, you can, by drawing more energy from the atmosphere into your system, make your body so strong and so vigorous that you will actually feel as if you were electrically charged through and through. You can, through the super-physical breath, restore your physical system to full health and vigor, no matter how low your vitality may be. And you can, in the same manner, increase your physical and mental power remarkably every year for an indefinite period.

General Exercise. — Whenever you breathe consciously, think deeply of the vital energy of the atmosphere; and as you inhale, desire with depth of feeling to draw more and more of this energy into your system with every breath. In ordinary physical breathing, the object is simply to secure oxygen for the lungs; but in super-physical breathing, the object is to secure a greater and a greater supply of that finer life energy that permeates the atmosphere everywhere. And as you make a special and a conscious effort, in your general breathing, to attract more of this finer energy, you will soon develop the faculty of attracting more of this energy at all times, with every breath, whether you think of your breathing or not. The result will be that you will always have more energy than usual, and in every kind of atmosphere or climatic condition.

Special Exercise. — Be seated in a comfortable position, a position that will permit of a free and easy exercise of the lungs. See that there is an abundance of fresh air in the room. Then begin to breathe, gently and deeply, inhaling and exhaling slowly, holding the breath a few seconds after each inhalation, and being particular to note that the lungs are filled comfortably, through and through, with each succeeding inhalation. Continue this mode of breathing for ten or fifteen minutes, and as you do so turn your attention upon the finer life currents of the atmosphere. Try to get into conscious touch with the finer forces of these currents, and try to draw a goodly supply of those forces into your system with every inhalation. In this connection, it is most important to realize that the finer forces of the atmosphere that surround you will obey the desires of your mind. Therefore, if you place your mind and thought in touch with those forces, and deeply desire to draw them into your system as you inhale, those forces will actually obey; and you will receive a far greater supply of life energy from the atmosphere than usual.

The Chief Secret. — In order to draw more and more of this life force into your system as you breathe, the chief secret is to get your mind into such close contact with the finer side of that force, that you can actually feel it coming into every atom of your body with every breath. And this closer contact may be secured, by thinking deeply and frequently of the finer energies of the atmosphere, concentrating attention, as much as possible, upon that finer feeling in yourself that can feel the finer forces within you and about you. With practice and perseverance this finer feeling will come; and by using the mind in the attitude of that finer feeling, you can get into perfect touch with that finer force, thereby mastering the chief secret in the super-physical breath.

Further Information. — During this special exercise, try to draw an extra supply of atmospheric energy into your system with every inhalation; then as you hold your breath for a few seconds, try to feel that this finer energy is penetrating every fiber in your being, giving new life and vitality to every nerve and cell; and as you exhale, try to feel that all the extra energy received is retained in the system, as a permanent addition to your physical and mental power. Then inhale again, as before, repeating the entire process again and again, gently and in poise, for ten or fifteen minutes. At the close of this exercise, you will feel that you have a great deal more vitality in your system than you ever felt before, even though you did not get fully into the real secret of the exercise. But when you do get fully into the real secret of this exercise, you will actually feel like a "live wire," and you will feel strong enough "to move the world." However, do not permit yourself to be carried away. Be calm and continue in poise.

Positive Results. — This special exercise may be taken twice a day, preferably in the morning and early in the afternoon; but it is an excellent practice to employ the same process for a minute or two any time during the day when you have the opportunity. The result will be a steady increase of energy and vitality; and where the body is ailing, this increase of energy will soon provide you with sufficient health-giving vitality to eliminate completely every trace of disease, and restore your system absolutely to full health and vigor. And here it is well to repeat the great fact, that whenever the physical system becomes thoroughly filled with vital energy, it is impossible for any form of disease to remain in that system any more. When the room is filled with light, all darkness must entirely disappear. One of the great secrets to perfect health, therefore, is to fill the system thoroughly with vital energy; and super-physical breathing can positively do this under every circumstance.

Further Application. — The reason why we speak of this process as super-physical breathing is found in the fact that it deals with the attraction and appropriation of forces that are finer than the usual physical forces; and that it is a higher form of breathing added to the ordinary physical breathing. It is in every sense super-physical in its application; but it provides those finer life energies that alone can give the physical system that greater measure of vitality and force required for the highest state of vigorous health and power. It is "therefore physical breathing extended, advanced and perfected to a much greater degree of effectiveness, and lifted up, so to speak, to a plane of action where we may draw upon the tremendous forces of nature in its finer and inexhaustible domains. This being true, we realize that the further application of the super-physical breath holds, within itself, most remarkable possibilities. We find that we may, through the simpler application of this breathing, supply the physical system with more and more vital energy until the body becomes strong enough to put every form of disease out of the way. And this is indeed a great achievement in itself. But when we find that we are surrounded with a limitless sea of inexhaustible energy, that permeates the atmosphere everywhere, and that we can learn to draw, more and more, upon this vast sea of energy through what we speak of as the super-physical breath, we realize what the further application of this great secret will mean. And our conclusion must be, that we will not delay this practice or study an-other day, but proceed at once to master this remarkable secret in every form and manner.

Chapter 3

Psychological Equilibrium

A Remarkable Fact. — If every man, woman and child in the world would attain to what we shall here speak of as psychological equilibrium, and would continue to live in that equilibrium, we should find, in less than a year, that more than ninety per cent of all the ailments of mankind would have disappeared completely.

The Reason Why. — The majority of all the ills that come to the human family have their origin, either in loss of vital energy, or in nervous conditions; that is, interior discord. But psychological equilibrium means interior harmony and balance; and therefore, when such an equilibrium is maintained, all nervous conditions and every form of nervousness will cease to exist in the system.

Wonderful Remedy. — Learn to live continually in a state of psychological equilibrium, and you will cure yourself absolutely of any and every nervous ailment you may have; and this is of vast importance, as there are very few people to be found that are not addicted to nervousness of some kind. And more than this: continue to live in this equilibrium, and you will avoid all nervous or mental ailments in the future. Your nerves will always be strong, and your mind in perfect harmony and balance. And here we should remember, that when the mind is always well the body will always be well.

A Personal Experiment. — Watch yourself closely for one whole day, with a view of ascertaining whether or not every element in your being has continued to act in perfect harmony and balance. In brief, ask yourself if you can actually feel harmonious in the within during that entire day. Then note the answer. If you do not feel harmonious in the within all through the day, you are addicted to nervousness; you are troubled with interior discord; and interior discord may, at any time, work itself out into all kinds of functional or organic ailments. But if you do feel harmonious in the within all through the day, you are living in a state of psychological equilibrium; and the spirit of health is abroad in every part of your system.

Remember This. — If you wish to be well, every organ in your body must perform its function perfectly; but no physical organ can perform its function perfectly unless it can act continually in a state of interior harmony and poise. The very moment you feel nervous, restless, agitated, disturbed or discordant in the within, you are undermining the natural and harmonious actions of your physical organs; and they will fail to do their duty. The result is that adverse conditions will arise, which, if not checked, may develop into serious ailments. It is absolutely necessary therefore to maintain interior harmony at all times, and such harmony may be realized through the attainment of psychological equilibrium.

The Two Sides. — There are two sides to the human system: the physiological and the psycho-logical. And the latter governs the former. The physiological side is that part of the human system that can be weighed and measured. The psychological side is the interior, the intangible, the invisible; and, in brief, the sum total of all the forces, undercurrents, feelings, emotions, chemical processes and interior activities that live and act and work in the body, but that are finer than the body, being composed, not of physical substance or matter, but of energies proceeding from mind and soul. And whenever the psychological side is disturbed, there will be a corresponding disturbance in the physiological; that is, any disturbance that you may feel in the within will produce a similar disturbance in the organs of the body, thereby preventing those organs from doing their work as they should.

The Ideal in View. — In the attainment of perfect health, our ideal in view must ever be to maintain that deep interior harmony and calm, wherein we feel that we are inwardly strong and inwardly serene at the same time — and at all times. Our aim must be to keep all the psychological factors within us in harmony and in balance, because this is indispensable to the highest degree of perfect health. The within must be charged with power, and alive through and through with perfect peace.

First Experiment. — Try for one whole day to feel exceedingly strong, and perfectly serene in the within. However active you may be with mind or body, try to feel this interior peace and power combine in your system every moment. But do not try hard. Simply know what you want to do; then know that you can. The experiment will be extremely interesting, and will mark a most important turning point in your life.

An Even Temper. — We all realize the value of an even temper if we wish to gain or retain perfect health; but an even temper is a state of mind that exists merely on the surface; it is a mere effect of deeper states of poise within. When we speak of the state of psychological equilibrium, however, we are dealing with the deepest state of feeling and life that we possess.

We are dealing with those factors and forces within us that govern all physical conditions absolutely. And, therefore, we must have equilibrium, balance and harmony among the psychological factors before we can have equilibrium, balance and harmony among the physical factors. The body can be in order only when those finer and deeper forces within us, that govern the body, are in order. Physical health invariably proceeds from interior harmony; and when all the psychological or interior factors are in harmony, every cell in the body will be in perfect health.

General Exercise. — Form in your mind a clear idea of what the psychological factors really are. Then proceed to picture in your mind a state of being wherein all those factors are in harmony and equilibrium. Dwell deeply and constantly upon this mental picture until you can actually feel the spirit of this harmony and equilibrium gaining a deeper and deeper foothold in your system. In brief, try to live in the very soul of this interior state of perfect equilibrium; and try to realize the active presence of this state in every atom of your being. You will soon begin to feel the harmony you have in mind; and this feeling will become deeper and stronger every day until it becomes a permanent part of your consciousness.

Special Exercise. — Take ten minutes two or three times every day for the purpose of establishing permanently absolutely equilibrium, among the psychological factors, through the power of concentration; and proceed as follows:

Turn attention upon all the psychological factors in your system, including your feelings, your emotions, the undercurrents of all the physical processes, the creative forces of mind and body, the interior workings of your system, the finer forces and elements in your personality, the mental life of every fiber and cell, the mentalities of all the organs in your body, and, briefly, everything in your system that you can think of as being psychological. Then group all of these factors in your imagination, by thinking of them as acting in a finer interior field within your system.

In other words, turn your attention upon the psychological field within your own personality. Then concentrate upon that field, with a deep, strong desire to feel and realize absolute harmony and equilibrium among all the elements and factors in that field. When concentrating, be calm, positive and determined; and hold in your mind the idea of interior harmony so deeply that the feeling of this harmony will penetrate every fiber, nerve and cell in your entire body. Thus you will steadily, and surely, create interior harmony throughout your entire system. You will establish psychological equilibrium among all the factors and elements within you; and when this equilibrium has become a permanent state in your deeper life, you will find that order, harmony and perfect health will be realized in your physical life.

Very Important. — Remember this, that so long as there is perfect harmony within you there will be perfect health in every nerve, fiber and cell in your system. The attainment of psychological equilibrium, therefore, is an attainment of the highest importance. But this interior harmony must be perfect.

Chapter 4

Nourishing the Body

First Rule. — When you enter the dining room, array yourself in the garment of joy. Forget your troubles, if you have any, and be happy. Talk happiness; think happiness; feel happiness; radiate happiness. Live in the spirit of mental sunshine, and give no serious thought to anything whatever. Light-heartedness and good cheer should prevail at this hour; and during this hour count it your privilege to eat, drink and be merry. And you can. Realize that when you are in the dining room you are in another world, away from problems, difficulties or weighty themes. You have come to enjoy a feast; so, therefore, make it a feast in every sense of the term.

Second Rule. — Do not merely eat to live; and do not merely live to eat; there is a happy medium. Make your eating not the whole of your life, but a very important part of your life. Enjoy your meals; and enjoy them thoroughly. A meal that is thoroughly enjoyed will be thoroughly digested. Please remember this great fact. And it is a great fact, for a perfect digestion is not only necessary to the best expression of the body, but also to the best expression of the mind and the soul. Everything in your system works better when digestion is good. And as the body is the instrument of mind and soul, it is clearly evident that mind and soul can act as they should only when the body is in perfect condition. The piano must be perfectly tuned if the music is to be perfect in harmony and superior in quality. Think of your body as a musical instrument. Then remember that the perfect harmony of that instrument depends so much on a perfect digestion; and realize that every meal will be thoroughly digested if thoroughly enjoyed.

Third Rule. — In making the proper selection of your food, do not be too particular. See that the food is nourishing, wholesome, clean and correctly prepared. Then make up your mind to enjoy it all to the full. Do not go to the table in a fault-finding attitude. So long as you are in that attitude you cannot digest anything. Your indigestion, therefore, will not be the result of your food, but the result of your disagreeable state of mind. Remember, that a disagreeable state of mind can upset your entire system, and even convert the digestive juices of your system into poisonous elements. So do not blame the food. Most food is harmless. But see that your mind is right before you enter the dining room. Never eat when cross, upset, agitated, nervous, worried or in a state of fear. Throw these things off. First, get your mind right. Turn on a goodly supply of mental sunshine, and be glad. And by all means, never get into the habit of thinking that you cannot eat "this" or digest "that." The fact is you can eat anything that is wholesome and nourishing; and you can digest every bit of it, if you think so, and partake of your meals in the spirit of sunshine and joy.

Fourth Rule. — When you are in the dining room, take your time. Hurried eating means nothing but loss all along the line. Hurried meals are never digested perfectly; so, therefore, they nourish the system but in part, and they lead to many ailments, which means loss of time, money and pleasure. When your meals are properly digested, you can accomplish more in one hour than you can in three when digestion is not good. Sufficient time for your meals, therefore, is a good investment, both, for the present and the future. Take all the time necessary to fully enjoy your meals, and permit mind and body to remain relaxed and care-free for about thirty minutes more. You owe this time to your body. Be good to your physical body. It is your duty and your privilege. If your body is treated well it will serve you long and serve you well; and, in addition, contribute immensely to the joys of existence.

Fifth Rule. — Consider the entire process of digestion, and remember that this process begins the very moment you can taste your food. Therefore, do not ignore this first part of the process. On the contrary, continue to taste your food as long as you can; that is, continue to masticate every mouthful as long as it can be tasted. This is one of the most important secrets to a perfect digestion. It matters not how weak your stomach may be, if you continue to masticate every mouthful as long as it can be tasted, and eat moderately, the entire meal will be well digested. And your stomach will gain in strength every day, until perfect health and vigor is regained. In addition to this, it is a fact that a thoroughly masticated meal will give from ten to one hundred per cent more nourishment to the body than a meal partaken of in the usual manner. And the better you nourish your body the better will be your health, the stronger you will be, both physically and mentally, the longer you will live, and the easier you will find it to stay young as long as you live.

Sixth Rule. — It is highly important that the circulation be full and vigorous throughout the digestive system. A full circulation will not only promote digestion, but will also give a more immediate and a more perfect distribution to the nourishing elements secured from the food. This matter, therefore, should receive our best attention, and we shall find it an excellent practice to concentrate the mind, gently and peacefully, upon the abdominal region, for a few moments preceding every meal. During this concentration we should deeply desire the increase of the circulation throughout that region, and we should try to feel that increase actually taking place. This simple method will add remarkably to the vigor of the digestive organs; and this method alone will cure almost any ailment of the digestive system. It will always give relief; and when combined with the other secrets to good health, will cure every ailment that may be connected with the digestive process in any form or manner. If there seems to be considerable difficulty with digestion this method may also be applied for a few moments immediately after each meal. And when the digestive organs do not act as nature intended, use this method thoroughly, several times every day. Concentrate deeply, with a will, especially upon the lower parts of the abdominal region, and deeply feel the desired action taking place. Make it a point at all times to see that your circulation is full and vigorous all through your body. There is nothing that will do more than a good circulation to keep the body clean, wholesome and well. And you can increase the circulation in any part of your body through right and harmonious use of mind, thought, feeling, concentration and will.

Seventh Rule. — To nourish the body properly it is not necessary to adopt any particular system of diet. Anything that is wholesome and properly prepared may be partaken of freely, if partaken of in joy. Never be a "crank" about your food. A "cranky mind" is an enemy to good digestion; and you will find that people who are following "fads" in foods, are forever "dieting" to keep their digestion in order. Take the common sense way and select freely from all kinds of food, always selecting the wholesome and the clean. Then eat, in the spirit of good cheer, what your system seems to require, and think of it all as good — very good. Eat what you want, but only as much as you need, and enjoy every meal as you would a royal feast. In fact, think of every meal as a royal feast, and so it will be to you.

Eighth Rule. — Think of your food as not merely having physical elements, but also finer elements. All food is charged, so to speak, with finer elements and energies; and, if we recognize these in our own minds, at every meal, we will assimilate them more thoroughly, and thereby add remarkably to the vitality of the system. Train your mind to think of your food as having, stored up in every atom, life-giving energies, in addition to nourishing properties and elements; and you will soon find that every meal will give you far more energy, vitality and working capacity than you ever realized before. In addition, you will find yourself gaining more and more of that finer force that makes the human personality something more than a physical body with a nervous system. And, as we all desire our personalities to attain that "something more" state of being, this part of our theme will be found extremely important.

Chapter 5

Nourishing the Mind

Fundamental Law. — As the mind is, so is also the body. When the mind is in order, the body will be in order, and vice versa. When the mind is in good health, the body will be in good health. When the mind begins to lose hold upon life, the body will gradually weaken until personal existence cannot be maintained any longer. When the mind lays hold upon more and more life, the body will steadily gain in the possession of life, until there is sufficient life and vitality, in every organ in the body, to eliminate every ailment in the present, and prevent all ailments in the future. When the mind is young, the body will be young. And whatever is realized in the mind will be expressed through the body. See that the mind is right, and all else will be right in the human system.

Leading Essential. — To keep the mind right, every part of the mind must be properly nourished. And the real secret in nourishing the mind is to see that every part of the mind is constantly interested in the new, the larger and the higher. In the body, it is nourishment that produces growth; in the mind, it is growth that produces nourishment.

Food for the Mind. — It is new thought that constitutes the proper food for the mind; and the more new thought the mind is given the privilege to create, the better the mind will be nourished. To create new thought the mind must constantly advance towards the new, into the new, and up into the larger and the higher. And such an advancement can only follow a deep, strong and ceaseless interest in the new, the superior, and the most perfect everywhere.

Mental Expansion. — If mental expansion be made perpetual, health will become perpetual, and youth will become perpetual. The body cannot become old so long as the mind continues to grow; and as long as every part of the mind is active and alive, every part of the body will be strong, wholesome and well. When parts of the mind become inactive, groups of cells here and there in many parts of the body will also become inactive; and inactive cells not only become obstacles to the natural functions of the body, but these cells will soon harden and ossify. And it is the hardening of the cells that produces old age. The hardening of the cells also produces many ailments, because nature cannot do its work properly when dead and hardened cells are scattered in groups here and there all through the body. It is impossible, however, for a single cell in the body to harden or ossify so long as every part of the mind is alive. The mind is in vital touch with every cell, fiber and atom in the physical body; and as every cell responds absolutely to the actions of the mind, no cell can be dead so long as every part of the mind is alive.

The Growing Mind. — To keep every part of the mind alive, the whole mind must be well nourished; and the only mind that is well nourished is the growing mind. The mind feeds on change. The mind that does not change will starve; and when the mind starves the body dries up, withers, becomes old and ossified. This condition may take place however well the body may be nourished; for, although it is well to give proper nourishment to the body, it is more important to give proper nourishment to the mind.

Very Important. — We must remember this, and remember it well, that every cell in the body is closely connected, through the nervous system, with the mind; and also that every cell is directly influenced by the mind. In fact, all the cells in the body tend to act as the mind acts, tend to become what the mind becomes, and tend to change or improve as the mind improves. Therefore, if certain parts of the mind should become inactive, a great many of the cells in the body would also fall into inactivity. And an inactive cell soon becomes a dead, hardened or ossified cell, which means the coming of disease, old age or inability in one or many ways. It is absolutely necessary, therefore, if we wish to retain health and youth, that every part of the mind be alive — that the whole mind continue to grow, expand and develop perpetually.

Practical Methods. — In the first place, remember the great law, renew your mind and be well. And to renew the mind we must be interested in the new — deeply and vitally interested in the new along all lines. We must learn to live for the growing, advancing, expanding life; and we must become enthused over every step in progress that the race may take, in any direction, or under any circumstance. Everything that is new must arouse and attract our attention; and we must keep our eyes open to the new, everywhere, with an interest that is thoroughly alive, and thoroughly wide awake in every form and manner. In brief, we must develop an intense passion for the new — the new in all things, and the new in higher and greater things. The entire soul must be aroused with a ceaseless desire to realize the new, and to change perpetually into more perfect states and degrees of the new. And this process must become a positive force in the system — so positive and so strong that every fiber and cell is thrilled with the spirit of a new life.

First Exercise. — The first thing to do is to wake up the mind — every part of the mind. And remember that the moment every part of the mind is thoroughly wide awake, every cell in the body will be thoroughly alive. This means the coming of good health, for when all the cells in the body are thoroughly alive, there can be no disease in that body whatever. A cell that is alive cannot be sick. It is the dead cells and hardened cells that cause all the trouble. But when all the cells are alive, there will be no dead or hardened cells to give the body trouble; and, in consequence, health, order and harmony will prevail throughout the system. To proceed, apply the will upon every part of the mind, with a deep, strong desire to become mentally wide awake in every form and manner. Continue this process for a few moments, and repeat several times every day. The result of this simple exercise alone will, in a very short time, renew the entire body; for the fact is, that an awakened mind will renew itself very quickly; and when the mind is renewed, the body is renewed in a similar manner.

Special Exercise. — Make it your purpose to look for the new everywhere, in all things, and at all times. And awaken within yourself a deeper and a stronger interest in every manifestation of the new. Try to interest every part of your mind in the new along all lines; and try to arouse your whole mind to become wide awake to the force of growth and progress at work in all the world. Whenever you have a moment to spare, think of the new; think of new possibilities and new developments; and engage your attention, with the greatest enthusiasm, in everything new you can observe at the time. The effect will be remarkable, as it will not only awaken many parts of the mind that have heretofore been dormant, but will also train the mind in the art of discerning the new, the larger and the greater in all things. And it is such a mind that will become a growing mind, which is most important because so long as the mind continues to grow, the body will continue to be well.

An Excellent Practice. — Begin the day by resolving to see how many new things you can find during the day. Also begin the day by resolving to think more new things than you ever thought of in any day in the past. This will keep the mind awake to the new all through the day; and the mind that is continually wide awake to the new will continue to be a growing mind. This same practice will make every part of the mind more and more alive; and this means that every cell in the body will become more and more alive — the very purpose we have in view; for it is absolutely impossible for a cell to be sick that is thoroughly alive. And here it is well to repeat that it is impossible for the body to get sick or get old so long as the mind continues to grow. The growing mind is the one great preventative for sickness or age; and the growing mind is the greatest remedy of all, whatever the ailment or difficulty may be. See that your mind continues every day, and every hour, to be a growing mind, and you will always have health and youth, no matter how long you may live.

The Great Law. — Everything must be nourished if it is to continue to live; and everything will continue to live so long as it is properly nourished. But the mind of man has not been properly nourished; accordingly, the mind has weakened from year to year; and what happens to the mind happens to the body also. From this weakness, or lack of abundant life, has come ailments and age, all of which could have been pre-vented through the proper nourishment of the mind. The mind, however, is not nourished by what comes from without, or by what may be received from external sources. It is new thought alone that can nourish the mind; and the only thought that is new to any individual mind is the thought created by that mind itself while in search of the new. The great secret, therefore, in nourishing the mind is to train the whole mind to develop an intense passion for the new — the new in all things, from the most simple to the most sublime. Such a mind will indeed be a growing mind; and so long as the mind continues to grow the body will continue to be well. And, also, if mental expansion be made perpetual, health will become perpetual, and youth will become perpetual.

Chapter 6

The Will to Be Well

Know the Will. — We must understand the will, and its true function, if we would always be well. And the reason is evident. The will is one of the most important factors in the human system, and contains, within itself, powers and possibilities that the majority have never called forth into action at any time. These powers, however, can, when applied, turn the tide of life in our favor, no matter what the difficulties or circumstances may be. And this is especially true in the realization of perfect health.

The Power of Will. — We must always will to act before we can act, whether the action be physical or mental. And the more we express in the action the more powerful and effective will that action be. Whatever we do, therefore, results will depend largely upon how much will we give to the work or purpose in hand. This being true, we should always turn on the full current of the will. We should never act in a halfhearted way, but should invariably act with all the power and will we possess. We should always will to be our best, and will to do our best. The increase, when we come to measure results, will be very great indeed.

Important Fact. — The more will you apply along any line of action, the more energy and power you cause to flow into the same line of action. Continue to will, with force, determination and persistence, upon any purpose or project, and you will gradually draw more and more energy into that purpose, until all the power within you is working with you, and for you, in the realization of that purpose. Then you can certainly get results, the greatest and best results possible.

Will to Be Well. — The same rule holds good in your purpose to gain health, or build up a greater measure of health. Will to be well; and you cause all the energies within you to work for better and better health. Will to be strong; and you aid nature, both directly and indirectly, in building up the strength, the vigor and the virility of your entire system. Turn on the full current of the will, and you aid nature immensely. You turn the tide of life in your own favor. You inspire all the elements and forces within you to leave the side of weakness, and go over to the side of life, power and strength. You turn conditions round about completely, so that the things that were against you will henceforth be for you. You can do all these things, if you use the will — the full current of the will, and always will to be what you want to be.

First Exercise. — Take positive hold of your will, and be determined, henceforth, to apply the full power of the will — and always for more life, for more energy, for greater strength, for better health, and for everything that can add to your greatest welfare and highest good. Take hold of the will in this way, many times every day; and in every instance feel deeply, and be tremendously in earnest.

Second Exercise. — Turn the power of the will upon all the conditions of your health; and train yourself, more and more, to will greater vitality and better health into every part of your system. And whenever you use the will feel deeply. Try to feel that the force of your will comes forth from the great and invincible powers of the soul; and try to feel that whatever you will to realize or attain must come to pass. The power of the soul can never fail; and your will — your true will — is the power of the soul in positive, determined expression.

Third Exercise. — Turn the power of the will upon that part of your body that may need better health. Then will more and more life, power and health into, and through, that part of the body, until you can actually feel every cell thrill with vigor and virility. Think of that part of the body, with depth of feeling, and will to be well. Concentrate all your thought, and the full power of mind and soul, upon that part of the body, and will to be well. And know that the power of your will comes from the limitless power of your own invincible soul. You may therefore have unbounded faith in what you are doing, because you know that the results you desire must positively follow.

The Strong Mind. — Whenever you think, or use your mind in any form or manner, use more and more of the will. Make your entire mental world positive and strong. And always remember to combine deep feeling with every exercise or expression of the will. This is most important, because the deeper the feeling, the stronger the will under every circumstance. And a strong, deep will means a strong mind; which, in turn, means greater power of mind over all physical conditions. The mind is by right the master over the body. Therefore, the stronger the mind becomes the greater becomes your power to master and regulate every part of your body. And this is a power we all want to possess. When the mind can control the body perfectly, then we may always have perfect health, an unlimited amount of vitality, and an abundance of rich, wholesome, energizing life.

Personal Power. — Use the full power of the will upon your entire personality. Make your personality strong, positive, alive. Will to have more personal power. Will to express more personal power in every movement of the body, in every feeling of the mind, and in every action of the soul. Will more life and more energy into every cell in your body, into every nerve, into every fiber, into every force, into every

Healing Yourself

function. Be determined to be personally strong and virile. And use the full power of the will with this important end in view. The result will be that you will gain in every form and manner, especially in vigor and in health. When you apply the full power of the will upon every part of the personality, you arouse, to positive action, all the vital energies within you; and when your personality is thoroughly alive, it is absolutely impossible for any ailment whatever to enter your system.

Do Not Give In. — When conditions in your system seem adverse, do not permit yourself to ever think of giving up, or giving in. Will to pull through. For the fact is, that so long as you hold on, with the full power of will, the forces of life in your system will be on your side working in your favor. The forces in your system will never give up so long as you refuse to give up. And there is no condition in your system that the forces of life, in your system, cannot overcome if you give them sufficient time, continuous encouragement, and the full force of your own determined will. Will to stand by the powers within you, under every circumstance, and those powers will stand by you. They will positively see you through; and you will come out with full victory, and with a greater realization of freedom than you ever knew before.

Most Important. — Train your mind to realize, more and more deeply, that will power is soul power; that the real power of the will comes from the soul; and that the soul is positively invincible. Then proceed, in this realization to will to be well. Continue, under every circumstance, to will to be well, knowing that the limitless power of the soul is back of your will, in your will, and working positively, with full force, through your will.

Special Exercise. — Take several moments, three or four times every day, and give special attention to the making of the will stronger, deeper and more positive. First, simply will to will more; that is, think of your will, knowing what it is, and determine to express more of the power of will in every act of the will. This, in itself, will, even in a few days, strengthen the will remarkably; and you will find that you can give a great deal more power and effective action to everything you purpose or undertake. Second, concentrate the will, with deep feeling and more determined action, upon the various faculties and qualities in your mind, and upon the various functions in your personality. In fact, proceed to train the mind to express more will into everything in your entire system. Third, direct your subconscious mind to give greater force, greater volume, greater positiveness, greater power, and deeper action to every expression of your will. This is most important; and here we should remember, that the subconscious will invariably does whatever it is directed to do, provided we feel deeply when we give the directions, and continue to be tremendously in earnest.

Gaining Ground. — The more you apply the foregoing methods and principles, the stronger and deeper will the will become. And as the will develops in force, positiveness and power, you will find that you will gain ground continually in the building up of mind and body, provided you make it the great rule of your life — to will to be well. And results will increase the more deeply you feel that the limitless power of the soul is back of your will, in your will, and working positively, with full force, through your will.

Chapter 7

Interior Relaxation

The First Principle. — Nature demands recuperation. If all the functions of nature are to perform their duties properly, there must be periods set aside, every day, for complete recuperation. The energies that have been utilized must be replaced; and the cells that have served their purpose must be eliminated, and new ones built up instead. In brief, the entire physical and mental system must be reconstructed and made over new; and all the natural processes of repair, renewal and reconstruction must be given the opportunity to complete their work thoroughly, at least once in every twenty-four hours. And this opportunity, when fully realized, constitutes complete recuperation.

Important Fact. — If the entire human system were given the opportunity to recuperate thoroughly at least once every day, it would be impossible for disease of any kind to enter the sys-tem; and conditions of old age could never gain a foothold in a single organ or cell in the body. And the reason why is this, that complete recuperation would mean, first, complete renewal of all the cells; and second, the thorough recharging of every part of the system with vital energy. Thus the two great essentials to health and youth would be provided, because it is impossible for any kind of disease to enter the human system so long as there is a full supply of vital energy; and it is impossible for old age conditions to gain a foothold anywhere so long as nature is given the privilege to renew every cell in the system the very moment the former cell has fully served its purpose.

The Second Principle. — Complete recuperation of mind and body can take place only when the entire human system is thoroughly relaxed; and relaxation is thorough only when it becomes, what we may well term, interior relaxation. That is, the process of relaxation must originate in the within, or on the subconscious side of life, and must penetrate, in every form and manner, both the interior and the exterior phases of the personality.

Meaning of Relaxation. — In the usual state of conscious activity, the human system continues to give expression to all its forces and elements. The exterior side of the personality is in a positive attitude, and all life and power moves from the within towards the without. In other words, all the energies of the system are going out into, and through, the various organs, to carry out the active functions of mind and body; and in this process a large part of the available energy is utilized, and many of the cells complete their period of usefulness. But when relaxation takes place, the course of action in the system is reversed; that is, all the elements and forces of the system move from the without towards the within. The process of expression discontinues, and the exterior phase of the personality becomes passive instead of positive.

General Exercise. — Whenever you wish to relax, turn attention towards the within, or towards the subconscious, and "let go," fully expecting all the forces of your system to turn about and move, gently and peacefully, toward a state of interior calm. In a few moments you will feel relaxed all the way through, and a serene, restful feeling will gradually come over your entire personality. This exercise can be taken to advantage, for five or ten minutes every two or three hours during the day; and should be taken, with unfailing punctuality before every meal, regardless of time, place or circumstance.

Results. — The value of this exercise will be found in the realization of renewed supply of life and energy, at frequent intervals, which means that power and capacity will continue to be up to the mark all through the day; and this will mean more work and better work invariably. And when this exercise is taken before meals, the system will be recharged with vitality, so that the process of digestion can be carried on perfectly. In fact, if you relax thoroughly, for five minutes, before every meal, you can say farewell, for all time, to all kinds of ailments or annoyances in your digestive functions.

The Third Principle. — The human system is repaired, renewed and recharged by the subconscious side of life. And in order that these necessary processes may take place, there are two essentials that must be provided. First, the exterior phases of every cell must be passive; and, second, consciousness must function principally through the interior phases of every cell at the time. And these two essentials are provided perfectly when we are in a state of interior relaxation. That is, when we relax, the outer side of life becomes passive; positive expression is discontinued; the working forces are withdrawn from the external elements of the personality, and our conscious actions are "let go" so that all our feelings are permitted to "sink in" to the deeper subconscious life, where all is peaceful and serene. And here it is well to remember that the subconscious always works in perfect peace. Subconscious activity is absolutely still at all times, so therefore you may know that when you feel deeply, and feel absolutely still in the within, the subconscious side of your life is doing its work perfectly. And this is the state you should enter when you are to realize interior relaxation.

Relax Before Sleep. — We can enjoy sleep only when we relax thoroughly for some time before going to sleep. In many instances, nature is able to provide perfect relaxation just as we are falling asleep; but nature has been interfered with in so many ways, that many of the natural processes do not perform their functions properly unless assisted by mind or thought. We should provide this assistance, therefore, by making it a practice to enter a state of interior relaxation for at least ten minutes before we are ready to go to sleep. And we shall find that the purpose of sleep will, in this simple practice, be realized to the fullest and the most perfect degree.

Special Exercise. — Take thirty minutes every day, preferably early in the evening, or during the latter part of the afternoon, for the purpose of entering completely into a perfect state of interior relaxation. Begin by turning attention upon the within. Know that the within is always peaceful and still; and know that your own mind and personality will also become peaceful and still the moment you come in conscious touch with the within. Then "let go." Try to feel that all the forces within you are moving towards the serenity and calm of the subconscious side. Breathe peacefully and gently at the time, and as you "let go" of the contents of your lungs with each exhalation, also "let go" of your own feelings — letting them "sink in" to the stillness of the within. Continue by thinking quietly of your external personality as being perfectly passive; and picture in your mind, as clearly as possible, the forces of your system, moving inwardly, gently, serenely, towards the subconscious side. Repeat these various processes, in the deep, quiet faith that perfect and interior relaxation is being realized. Gradually, you will find your conscious feeling in a state where you can actually feel that your interior life is fully relaxed; and this is the real purpose you have in view.

Further Exercise. — Your object should be to become so familiar with the state of interior relaxation, that you can actually see a mental picture of this state whenever you so desire. For the fact is, that whatever you can picture in your mind, that you can realize at any time. In other words, when you can "mentally see" a perfect state of interior relaxation, all you need do is to turn your attention upon that mental picture whenever you wish to enter the relaxed state. The elements and forces within you always proceed at once to do whatever you can perfectly picture in your mind as doing. It is highly important, therefore, to learn to "mentally see" the relaxed state as you know it to be.

Special Information. — When you are not in good health, it is most important that you relax more frequently, not less than three or four times every day. And as you relax, concentrate subjectively upon that part of the body that may lack in health and vigor. When you concentrate subjectively upon any part of the body, you think of the finer life that permeates the physical side; and therefore, if you relax at the same time, you will cause the processes of repair, renewal and recuperation to work more perfectly and more quickly in that part of the body, thereby hastening recovery to a marked degree. In fact, when subjective concentration and interior relaxation are combined upon that part of the body that is ailing, it is possible to secure complete recovery in one-half, or even in one-fourth, the time usually required by nature herself under similar circumstances. We can truthfully say, therefore, that these two great factors — subjective concentration and interior relaxation — when perfectly combined, constitute one of the greatest curative agents known to modern science. And they who will learn to apply these two factors perfectly, in combination, will acquire a secret, the value of which will be nothing less than extraordinary.

Chapter 8

Imagine Yourself Well

The Principle. — The mind always creates what we imagine; and it is the imaging faculty that determines what we are to think. We are as we think; and we think as we imagine. Therefore, if we are to think as we wish to think, and be what we wish to be, we must first learn to use the imaging faculty according to fundamental principle and exact science.

The First Rule. — Continue to imagine, under every circumstance, what you wish to become, gain or realize; but never imagine, for a moment, what you do not want. Train your imagination, in a most positive manner, every day, to comply with this rule; and gradually you will find that all the conditions of mind and body are becoming more and more as you wish them to be.

General Exercise. — Form a mental picture of yourself, in your imagination, as you wish to be in mind and body. See yourself well and strong with the eye of the mind. Imagine that you have become what you wish to be; and try to feel, through and through, what you have imagined. Train your mind to enter as deeply as possible into every correct move you make with the imagination, and be determined to see and feel the perfect picture you have formed of yourself. Make a special effort, to this end, many times every day, and in fact, whenever you have a moment to spare. Think of this perfect picture of yourself, as frequently as possible, as much as possible, and as deeply as possible. And be tremendously in earnest.

Important Fact. — The human system is constantly filled with creative energies; these energies are at work night and day, building and creating; and they always select those things, as their patterns, that we imagine with the deepest of feeling and the greatest of force. Imagine yourself sick, and if you give much force and feeling to that imagination, the creative energies within you will thereby create, in your system, the very ailment you imagine that you have. In like manner, imagine yourself perfectly well, and those same energies will proceed at once to create perfect health in every part of your system. But your imagination must be positive, deeply felt and thoroughly alive through and through. Imagine any condition in yourself, and the creative energies will create that condition, provided the imagination be deep, vivid and intense. This fact proves that the power of imagination is a marvelous power — in truth, the greatest there is in man.

Remember This. — More than ninety per cent of the ailments that appear in the human system come largely from the misuse of the imagination. And it is a positive fact that no sickness could appear in the life of any living entity where the power of imagination was applied in a positive, wholesome and constructive manner during every moment of existence.

The Great Law. — When the imagination of man is right, everything in the life of man will be right. When we imagine only the true, the perfect and the ideal, we shall constantly grow into higher and higher realizations of the true, the perfect and the ideal. Thus we gain freedom from the lesser or the wrong by constantly rising into the greater and the right.

Special Exercise. — Take ten or fifteen minutes of silence, preferably alone. Turn your attention upon the great within of your own mind and soul. Then picture, in the within, the perfect form of health and power that you wish to realize in your external personality. Think of this perfect picture, so deeply, and so vividly, that you can actually see it in the light of your own marvelous imagination. And having formed the picture in the within, proceed to concentrate upon that picture with all the mental power you possess. Focus attention so absolutely upon that picture, in the within, that you know nothing else whatever for the time being. Persevere until your concentration becomes perfect; and repeat the exercise two or three times every day. The result of this exercise will be that you will actually create, in the within, that very form, or new creation, upon which you concentrate with such determination and mental power. And whatever we create in the within will positively express itself in the outer personality.

Remarkable Law. — Concentrate mind, thought and feeling upon any condition in your system, and you create that condition invariably, provided the power of concentration is directed inwardly, and repeated frequently, with all the power you possess.

Interesting Experiment. — Turn your attention upon the great within, and picture, in the within, a counterpart of yourself having all the elements, qualities and appearance of external youth. In brief, imagine the internal existence of a new physical form — young, vigorous, virile — alive with the fire and splendor of youth. Then concentrate upon this internal form of virility and youth, in the same deep and powerful manner, as was indicated in the preceding exercise. Repeat many times every day; and the result will be that you will actually create, in the within, another personality — a personality with youth, life and power. And gradually this young personality, from within, will come forth into the outer physical form, and cause the outer physical form to regain, in every mode and manner, all the elements, conditions and powers of youth. In brief, the newly created personality of youth and virility from within will remove all the conditions of age that may exist in the outer personality, just as darkness is dispelled by the light; and will thereby restore natural youth to the physical body — something to which every physical form is entitled as long as life continues in that form. The possibility of this law is extraordinary — in fact, limitless in its own field; and the truth is, that any man, even though he might have the appearance of ninety, could regain the appearance of thirty-five if he would apply, in a thorough and effective manner, the full power of this remarkable law.

The Unfailing Truth. — Whatever we create in the within, the same will positively express itself in the outer personality. And the creative energies within can create any condition or quality we desire, provided they are properly directed by the marvelous power of imagination.

Curative Power. — The fact is that the creative energies in your system can restore any part of your body to perfect health. The curative power of those energies is positively limitless. But they must be given the proper direction; and this imagination alone can do. Proceed by turning your attention to that part of the body that is ailing. Then imagine that part of the body perfectly well. Proceed farther, by trying to see and feel what you imagine; that is, imagine that you see every fiber perfect and whole; and imagine that you feel perfectly well throughout that part of your system. Proceed still farther by concentrating all the power of mind and soul upon what you now imagine in that part of your body. Focus attention absolutely upon what you now see and feel in that organ or muscle or nerve; and the very thing you imagine, that you will create. You will create perfect health and a superabundance of vital energy at the very point where your concentration is directed. These are the results that you will positively secure; but your feeling must be deep; your concentration must be absolute; your imagination must be perfect; and you must be tremendously in earnest.

Vitally Important. — Never use the power of imagination, at any time, for any other purpose than that of building for the true, the perfect and the ideal in yourself, in your life, in your world. Imagine always the higher, the greater, the wonderful, the sublime. Train your imagination to look towards the heights and create the richness and the glory of the heights for every part of your world, here and now.

Chapter 9

The Real Living of Life

First Rule. — Learn to live more. All power comes from life. To increase power, physical or mental, we must increase life; and we increase life by constantly living more.

Second Rule. — Learn to give a more positive expression of life into every part of body, mind and soul. To live more we must express more life through every channel of consciousness; and this expression must be positive and strong, and at the same time perfectly poised and deeply serene.

Third Rule. — Learn to feel the real, interior action of life, at all times, and in every part of the system. To live more life we must feel more deeply the reality of life itself; that is, our conscious feeling must penetrate into the very spirit of life so that we can actually realize ourselves in the limitless life-current.

Important Fact. — We do not really live until we can feel the limitless life-current pulsating in every fiber and vein. We do not really live until we live in the very spirit of life; and to live in the spirit of life is to feel, through and through, the power of ceaseless, limitless, invincible life.

Remember This. — All ailments, of whatever nature, can be traced to insufficient life. But it is impossible for any ailment to enter the system, under any circumstances, so long as there is an abundance of life. And to maintain an abundance of life, the law is, to constantly live more.

Fourth Rule. — In order to live more, we must place ourselves in perfect harmony with the law of advancement.

The soul was made to advance continuously — to move upward and onward eternally; and therefore we are not true to the soul unless we so live that this advancement of the soul may be promoted, in the fullest and most thorough manner, without any interruption whatever. And to promote this continuous advancement of the soul we must enter, more and more perfectly, into the spirit of life — into the interior force of the great invincible life current. This current is forever moving forward into more life, into a larger life, into a higher life, into a greater and more powerful life; and we may move upward and onward with this current if we learn to live, more and more deeply, in the very spirit of real life.

The Real Cause. — If we should undertake to trace any particular ailment back to its real cause, we would find that cause to be the advancement of life coming to a full stop. For the fact is, that whenever we come to a full stop in our advancement or growth, we lose hold upon the real life current; that is, we step aside from the life current, and, for the time being, are not filled with the life of that current. The result is that we fail to receive our full supply of life; the life force within us is not replenished at the time, and our supply is not sufficient to carry on, in a perfect manner, the natural functions of existence. Accordingly, conditions arise in the system that may lead to physical ailments, mental inefficiency, or adversity and wrong in general. To state it briefly, we cause our supply of life to diminish whenever we come to a stop in our growth or advancement, because whenever we make such a stop, we step aside from the life-current, and, therefore, are not receiving our supply of life at the time. And whenever we diminish our natural supply of life we make it impossible for mind and body to perform their functions perfectly. The consequences will be that ailments, wrongs and troubles of many kinds will follow.

The Great Law. — Continue to advance in the within — in the soul — during every moment of existence. Do not come to a stop at any time, or under any circumstance. The purpose of life is to move upward and onward eternally. Be true to that purpose, and you will ever receive more and more life. Continue to live and move and have your being in the very spirit of the great life current; do not step aside for a moment. Be in that current eternally, and you will always be filled, through and through, with all the life you can realize, appropriate and apply.

Fifth Rule. — If you do not realize at once the existence of the life-current within you, proceed to imagine the interior existence of that current. Make this imagination so clear and so vivid that you can actually see that current moving upward and onward eternally, and with invincible force, through the entire domain of your soul. Then imagine that you are in that current, moving with that current into more and more of the one invincible, limitless life. Proceed more deeply into this realization, and imagine that you actually feel the full force of that life and that current in every fiber and vein. The result will be, that you will enter more and more deeply into the very spirit of limitless life. You will then be in the full force of limitless life; and when you are in that life you will be so full of life that there will be no room, anywhere in your system, for discord, ailments, weakness or wrong. You will have turned on the full light of life and power, and all darkness will have disappeared completely.

Deep Feeling. — Know the truth that there is within you the force and power of limitless life — that a great, invincible life-current is eternally passing through your soul, giving more and more life to every element in your soul. Know this great truth; then proceed to feel, more and more deeply, the very spirit of this wonderful life-current. And the more deeply you feel this current, the more thoroughly you will enter into the full force and power of that current. You will constantly receive more and more life; you will live more and more every moment; and to live more, that is the secret to complete emancipation. Give more life to every atom in your system, and your entire system will become pure, wholesome, vigorous, powerful, virile and absolutely well.

The True Life. — When we enter into the spirit of the full life and the real life within us, then indeed shall we begin to live the true life — the life that is ever becoming larger, richer, more perfect, more beautiful, more ideal. We shall not only gain health and freedom, but shall, as well, gain more and more of all that is worthy and desirable in human existence. But we must first gain pos-session of more life. We must first learn to live more, and forever more. We must first learn to live and move and have our being in the great life-current — the limitless life that is all within us and all about us everywhere. And to learn these things we must place ourselves in perfect harmony with that great law of the soul that is ever prompting all life to move upward and onward forever. We must live constantly in the spirit of this law so that we may enter, every moment, into the deeper life, the larger life, the richer life, the greater life, the more spiritual life. Our living must become real living; and in real living there is peace, there is power, there is purity, there is wholeness, there is freedom; and there is perpetual increase of real life, and of all that is worthy and good in life. The great secret then is this, enter forever and ever into more life. Then all that is good must inevitably follow — and in a constantly increasing measure.

Chapter 10

The Right Use of Body, Mind and Soul

First Principle. — In order that perfect health may be realized and maintained in the human system, it is absolutely necessary that complete and continuous harmony be established among the three great factors in the human entity — body, mind and soul; and one of the first essentials to this end is the right use of these three factors in their respective fields of expression. The body must be used, under all circumstances, according to its true nature and real function; and the same is true with regard to the mind and soul; but it is not possible for any one of these three factors to be used as it should unless all three are used as they should. For this reason our purpose must not be confined to the right use of the body, or of the mind, or of the soul, exclusive of the others; but our purpose must be to find and continue the right use of all three in perfect harmony. There are many things that can be done to the end that this right use of body, mind and soul may be maintained; but the first essential is to inspire every element and force in the system with a strong, continuous desire to bring about this right use at once, and to the most perfect degree. In other words, we should resolve, from this moment on, to use the body, the mind and the soul according to their true nature; and we should make this resolution so strong that every part of body, mind and soul will feel the power of that resolution. The result will be that the entire system will respond more and more to what we have resolved to do, and in consequence we will develop within ourselves a second nature, so to speak, having a tendency to promote the right use of everything that exists within us. The law is, whatever you make up your mind to do that every power within you will help you to do; but your resolution must be strong and positive, and must continue to inspire every element within you all through life.

Second Principle. — Every element and force in the human body should be placed in action, at least to a certain extent, every day; and therefore, the great rule in physical culture is, to exercise daily every muscle in the body. The value of this rule becomes more and more evident the more perfectly we realize the fact that life can find expression only through those physical fibers that are exercised or that are given a certain amount of action every day; and in order to maintain health all through the system, the life force should be expressed continually through every part of the system. When a muscle remains dormant or unused for some time, it is weakened, and, in addition, may harden or ossify, and thereby originate old age conditions. Perfect health, however, demands perpetual youth all through the body; that is, perpetual renewal of all the elements all through the body, and also the full expression of life, vitality and virility through every fiber and cell. One of the first things, therefore, to do in this connection is to adopt a simple system of physical exercise that will insure the placing of every muscle into action at least for a few moments every day. To outline such a system of exercise will not be necessary here, as anyone can, through the use of a number of well-known exercises, ascertain what is necessary to place every muscle in motion every day. But these exercises when applied should never be strenuous, nor should they be carried out in a mechanical manner. The rule should be, when taking physical exercise, to try to combine the mind with the exercise, and expect results mentally, with full faith and enthusiasm. In other words, train the mind to enter into the exercise. You will thereby call into action the finer energies of the body as well as the purely physical energies; and this is exceedingly important, as a good, healthy body demands the full expression of all the forces of the personality, the finer nerve forces and vital forces, as well as the physical forces.

Third Principle. — In the right use of the body it is absolutely necessary that the life force be expressed and exercised in every cell and fiber of the body. No cell can be in good health unless it is absolutely filled every day and continually with the life force; and to this end, we should aim to secure a stronger and more complete expression of the life force throughout the physical personality. To proceed, concentrate your mind for a few moments upon the different parts of the body, and arouse at the time a strong desire for the full expression of the life force in every fiber and cell. In addition, try to picture or imagine the full expression of life in every part of your body, and enter into the exercise with the deepest depth of feeling that you can possibly realize at the time. This mode of concentration should be taken for a few moments several times every day; and if it is made strong, positive, deep and penetrating, the results will invariably be the increase of life and energy all through the physical system. Every cell will be made more active, every organ will perform its functions more perfectly, and there will be a decided increase in vitality, vital energy and working capacity. Besides this, a deeper realization of the life more abundant will be gained for the body; and we know full well, that the more life we feel in the body, the greater becomes the joy of living. This exercise, therefore, will accomplish many things, and should be entered into with earnestness and enthusiasm.

Fourth Principle. — The mind should be wholesome at all times and under all circumstances; and every form of wrong thinking should be eliminated completely. We cannot use the mind rightly unless every state of mind is wholesome, harmonious and constructive; and therefore no adverse mental state must be permitted at any time. To cultivate a wholesome mind the first essential is to train the mind to entertain harmony, purity, mental sunshine, positiveness, kindness, sympathy, loftiness of thought, aspiration, and the tendency to always look for the good and true and the beautiful in everybody and everything. The law is this, that it is practically impossible for ailments of any kind to enter the body so long as the mind is thoroughly wholesome; and, therefore, the cultivation of a whole-some mind becomes one of the great essentials in the attainment of perfect health.

Fifth Principle. — In the right use of the mind, it is necessary that we learn to think with the entire personality; that is, we should not simply think through the brain, but we should think through every nerve and fiber throughout the entire personal form; in fact, every cell in the system should act as a channel for the expression of mental power. To accomplish this, try to think of the entire personality whenever you use the mind in any way, or whenever you entertain a wholesome or constructive state of mind. In other words, whenever you think, or whenever you enjoy, invariably think of the entire personality, so that the enjoyment and the thought may, to a certain extent at least, enter into the personality and find expression through various parts of the personal form. In addition, take special moments every day for the purpose of training the mind to use the whole of the personal form as a channel for thought; and the exercise may be as follows: Take any quality such as health, life, power, personal worth, ability, or any quality desired, and turn your attention upon that quality with the deepest of interest. Then as you feel your mind entering into this quality with genuine interest, try to project the activity of the mind down through the personality; that is, try to extend mental action to every cell in your body. The mere effort to do this will produce results to a certain extent, and as the principle is practiced, you will find that the mind will, more and more, extend its activities to different parts of the personality. Later you will discover that you can actually feel the action of thought in every fiber in your system; and it is then that you are really beginning to build up for yourself a powerful mind. No mind can become powerful so long as it uses the brain only; but when it begins to express itself through the entire brain, through all the nerve centers, through all the nerve fibers and through every physical cell in the system, as well as through every force in the personality, then the channels of expression for the mind will become so numerous and so extensive that all the latent forces and powers of the vast mental world will begin to come forth in greater and greater measure. The reason for this is evident, because when the mind can use the entire personality, the scope of mental action will increase to such an extent that the free and easy expression of every mental force may be promoted thoroughly and completely. This principle, in addition to the remarkable increase of mental power, will also establish greater harmony between mind and body, which is extremely important, because the mind cannot control the body so long as it finds expression only through the brain; but when the mind begins to express itself through the entire personality, then every part of the body will become more responsive to mental action, so that the complete mastery of the body by the mind may be realized; and the mind should exercise complete mastery over the body because in this way alone can the physical instrument be maintained in perfect condition under every circumstance.

Sixth Principle. — The mind should aim to fashion all thought in the image and likeness of the ideal. We do not use the mind properly unless we are always thinking towards the ideal; and the reason for this is found in the fact that we do not think the truth unless we are constantly aiming to enter into the realization of higher and greater truth; and to enter into the realization of higher and greater truth, we must think towards the ideal. The effect of this process upon health is readily discerned, because the mind will, when thinking towards the ideal, create more ideal and more perfect conditions in the mental world; and every condition that is created in the mental world will, sooner or later, find expression in the physical personality. The same practice of thinking towards the ideal will tend to perfect all the expressions of life through the mind or the body; and this is most important because it will tend to develop those finer states of life that are always wholesome and pure and in perfect harmony with the true order of the higher life within. To carry out this principle, we should select a number of the highest and best ideals that we can think of, and establish those ideals before the mental vision as clearly and distinctly as possible. Then we should frequently turn attention upon those ideals, and at every opportunity express a strong and intense desire for the mind to work up towards those ideals, or reach out for the higher realization of the truth and the life and the power that we know those ideals to possess. However, the application of this principle must be continued with faith, determination and enthusiasm. We must develop a passionate love for the ideal, and the entire system must become so filled with intense desires for the ideal that every fiber and atom will respond to the force of those desires. No effort must be half-hearted; but every effort must be whole-hearted. And as we proceed with the whole heart, we shall soon succeed in renewing the mind upon a higher plane of thought and life, and thereby transform the entire personality in the image and likeness of those higher and finer things that we are realizing in our growing consciousness of the ideal.

Seventh Principle. — The first essential in the right use of the soul is to think of the soul as the real you, as the real individuality, as the real self, and as the real and permanent master over everything in the human system. It is the soul alone that has the full light; it is the soul alone that has the full power to lead and to guide; therefore nothing can be right in mind and body unless it is inspired by the soul. It is the soul alone that knows what should be done or what can be done; therefore, the soul must occupy the throne. To apply this principle, we should train ourselves to think of the soul as the real self, and as the ruling power in everything we do; and we should also think of the soul as having the power to do everything right, and the wisdom to know what should be done at any time or under any circumstance. In the application of this principle, we will find that our consciousness will gradually rise more and more into the realization of the soul life; and as this higher realization is gained, we will begin to live in the soul instead of in the body where we previously lived. But our living in the soul will not weaken the body. On the contrary, the more fully we live in the soul the more life and power we will express both in mind and body; therefore, the result will be great gain in every possible manner. The law is this, that when we live in the higher, we become more able to provide everything necessary for the lower; and this is self-evident, because all life and power comes from the higher. When we learn to actually live in the soul we shall be able to gain possession of a far greater measure of life and power; and whatever we gain possession of in consciousness, that we invariably express throughout the personality. In addition to other gains that will be realized in this manner, we will find that the entire personality will be refined and made superior. But we must remember that this refining process in the personality will not make us more susceptible to the ills of life. It is the contrary that is true, for the fact is that the more refined and spiritual the personality becomes, the more immune the personality becomes from all weakness, from all ills, or from any adverse condition whatever. We shall find that the power of the spirit, when expressed in the body, can protect the body; and when this spiritual expression becomes strong, full and positive, the protection will become so complete that no ill can befall the personal form henceforth.

Eighth Principle. — The soul should be lived in every element and in every atom of the body. We should not simply be conscious of the soul, or conscious of the great truth that we are living in the soul; but we should live the life of the soul throughout our entire system; and then make that living so full, so strong and so thorough that we can actually feel the soul life in every part of mind and body. The soul is always pure, wholesome, harmonious and powerful; therefore, the more perfectly the soul is lived in mind and body, the greater will be the purity, the wholeness, the harmony and the power that we will realize in every part of mind and body. Perfect health must follow because when the pure, the strong, the perfect, the wholesome is expressed in every atom, there will not be room for discord, disease, weakness, or any adverse condition whatever. To apply this principle, proceed by training your consciousness to realize as fully as possible the existence of the soul life; in other words, try to become more and more conscious of the soul. Then enter so deeply into this consciousness of the soul that you can actually feel the life and the power of the soul. This feeling will gradually find expression throughout your personality; but you should increase this expression by creating a strong, positive desire for this expression, and by giving this desire added force and determination under every available opportunity. In brief, learn to live in the soul, and learn to give the soul life to every fiber in your being. This will mean the coming forth into the personality of that which is always well, always perfect, always wholesome, and always in peace, power and harmony.

Ninth Principle. — The conscious realization of the existence of body, mind and soul should be present to the fullest possible degree, in every thought, feeling and action; that is, whatever we do, we should always recognize all those three factors as being indispensable factors in every expression of life. The practice of recognizing body, mind and soul in everything we do, and the practice of giving fuller expression to body, mind and soul in everything we do will tend, first, to produce a larger and a more perfect manifestation of the elements, forces and powers that exist within us on all planes; and, second, to produce a more balanced and more harmonious state of relationship among these three great factors; and in health as well as in all desirable attainments, it is highly important that body, mind and soul harmonize, and also that the largest and best from the spiritual, the mental and the physical, find the fullest and most perfect expression possible. We should always make it a point to give soul to everything we do, and should always think of the soul as taking part in every action, whether of mind or body. We should always make it a point to combine mind and body in all life, in all enjoyment and in all functioning of the personality, whether physical or mental or both. Through this practice the three great factors — body, mind and soul — are trained more and more to work together in all the actions of life, and in all attainments and achievements we may have in view. And the greatest results must naturally follow where these three factors work together in harmony, and to the most perfect degree possible. Our aim should be to consider body, mind and soul in everything that we carry forward into expression, whether the plane of expression be physical, mental or spiritual.

Tenth Principle. — The soul is always perfect, and can be used as it should in life only when constantly recognized as perfect. Under all circumstances, therefore, we should think of the soul as being absolutely perfect in every form and manner. The mind grows more perfect as it grows more and more fully into the realization of the perfection of the soul. Therefore, we should encourage and prompt the mind to act more and more fully towards the perfection of the soul, because such action will invariably tend to develop the realization of perfection in every part of the mind. When the mind continues to ascend towards the marvelous, the wonderful and the sublime in the soul, every part of the mind will, accordingly, take on more and more of all that is high and lofty and perfect in the soul. The body, with all its conditions and states of expression, is invariably the direct effect of the present development and conscious realization of the mind. Therefore, when the mind ascends into the realization of the perfect, the complete, the higher and the better, the body will naturally respond, and will give expression to the higher and the better in all its functions and manifestations. In the attainment of health, we understand fully how the application of this principle must work wonders. In the first place, we realize that the soul is well; in the second place, the mind takes on the perfect health of the soul as the mind grows into the consciousness of the perfect health of the soul; and in the third place, the body becomes like the mind, therefore grows in the expression and manifestation of perfect health, as the mind grows in the consciousness of that perfect health that always exists in the soul. The application of this principle should receive our best attention, and should be entered into with unbounded faith and enthusiasm. This will mean a wonderful change for the better, which will finally culminate in complete emancipation.

Chapter 11

The Finer Curative Forces

Finer States of Mind. — Whenever the mind is in action certain forces are expressed, and if the mind is in a higher or finer state of action at the time, the forces expressed will be both finer and more powerful; and we realize that the finer energies of the mind have the power to exercise a far greater influence over the body, and, in fact, over the entire personality. Therefore, whenever we proceed to apply wholesome and constructive states of mind, we should try and make the actions of the mind as high, as fine, and as deep as possible; and one of the first essentials to this end is to become mentally serene — not only serene in a general sense, but become so perfectly still that you can actually feel the stillness of life and soul throughout your system. When the mind is in that state, it invariably gives expression to very fine energies. Those energies invariably have the power to penetrate all conditions of the system, to eliminate every condition that is not in harmony with perfect peace, perfect health and the perfect expression of true being.

There is a current belief that in order to change physical conditions, we must exercise a great deal of mental force; but this is not true; in fact, it is the reverse that is true. It is not a great deal of force that is necessary, but a deep, serene, highly refined state of mind, because such a state gives expression to those purer, more wholesome and more harmonious life currents that have the power to penetrate all through the system, healing, purifying, building up, harmonizing and making things right in every form and manner. And we realize that if these highly refined life currents could continue in expression all through the system, every day, for some time, all adversity would finally be eliminated, no matter what the conditions might be.

When we proceed to cultivate this conscious expression of the finer forces and the finer states of the mind, we build up a constructive process that will steadily take hold of the finer side of life, and will work through the interior currents, or the undercurrents, and gradually re-establish perfect health and perfect harmony throughout the deeper life of the system; and whenever the right is established in the deeper life of the system, the right will invariably manifest all through the external organs or form of the system.

Whenever we gain this finer understanding of life, our first object should be to train ourselves to enter into this higher, more refined and more serene state of the mind, and try to feel that we are actually reposing in that beautiful state — the state of perfect harmony, peace and wholeness, and, in fact, resting there in the full realization of the great truth that we are, in real being, always in perfect harmony and health. If we would continue in this state, we would find that we should not have to do anything else to regain perfect health, because that state of mind alone will gradually and steadily place in action all those higher and finer life currents — those life currents that invariably can and will restore order, harmony, health, wholeness and freedom to every part of mind and body. The Finer Energies of Thought and Feeling. — One of the great laws to be considered in this important study is this, that whenever we actually feel perfectly well, regardless of physical conditions, we will begin to manifest perfect health from that very hour. The reason for this is found in the fact that feeling always goes beneath conditions and manifestations; that is, it goes down to the very root, so to speak, of all expressions of life, so that whenever we feel well in this deep, interior sense, we place in action a health producing life force at the very root, or at the very beginning, of all expressions and manifestations. The result, therefore, must be that all expressions and manifestations will become the way we feel, that is, wholesome, healthful and harmonious.

When we establish health, wholeness and harmony at the very beginning of all the manifestations of life — in the interior state of consciousness, we will naturally manifest health all through the system; and, therefore, we realize the immense importance of cultivating that deep, interior feeling of perfect health, that is, the power to feel well in the within at all times and under all circumstances. In this connection we must remember that the way we feel inwardly, that is the way we become outwardly, provided, of course, that this interior feeling is thorough and continuous along the line of feeling that we have chosen.

We all know that if we could feel young in this interior sense, and continually, instead of simply believing that we would like to be more youthful, the spirit of youth would be expressed all through the system, and we would gradually change the physical personality until it manifested the same condition of youth that we had continued to feel in the within. This is a law that cannot fail, and, therefore, we must not fail to apply it. It is true that the power to enter into this deep interior feeling, and feel the way we wish to feel, may involve much practice and concentrated action; but it is an attainment that we all can reach. And knowing that we invariably become in the without as we feel in the within, we should proceed toward this attainment with the greatest enthusiasm possible, and with the application of all the truth and information we have been able to gain on the subject.

To establish this deep feeling, we shall gain largely by realizing continually the great fact that we all are in the within perfectly well; that is, we should dwell on the great truth that the soul is always well; then we should proceed to enter into the feeling of that health and that wholeness that constitutes a permanent part of the soul life. When we know this truth, we know that our effort to feel perfectly well in the within is based upon a scientific principle, and that we are simply trying to feel what is absolutely and eternally true — that is, that we always are well in the within, and therefore we always should feel well in the within.

The Subconscious Forces. — There is no field of consciousness in the human mind that is so vast, and that contains such a large number of the finer life currents as the subconscious field; and, therefore, we realize that every effort that we may make to awaken the larger subconscious life will invariably result in the expression of a larger measure of life, especially the finer and higher states of life. In dealing with the subconscious we are dealing with a large subject, too large for detailed analysis in this connection; but in order to secure the best results in the simplest manner, we should realize that the subconscious mind will invariably respond to our conscious directions, and that whatever direction we may make to the subconscious, with a view of awakening the higher and the finer life currents from within, will be followed by response from within, at least to some measure; and as we learn to apply the law through which the conscious mind directs the subconscious for greater action, we will find that the finer life currents from within will express themselves more and more until the outer personality becomes literally charged with life and power from within — life and power of a very high and fine order. Every effort we make, therefore, in this connection will result in great gain both for the realization of perfect health and for the realization of greater personal power.

Spiritual Exaltation. — Among the many forces of life that may be found in the higher and finer states of consciousness, there are none that are finer or more powerful than those forces that are awakened and expressed when the mind enters what we may call spiritual exaltation; that is, when the mind is placed in an exalted state of consciousness. There are many experiences in the past as well as in the present, illustrating the fact that marvelous cures can be produced by what we term the exaltation of spirit. At certain times the mind is lifted and wonderfully exalted beyond material things, beyond anything in the objective — lifted up into another world, so to speak, where power is immense, where the light of truth is as brilliant as the shining sun, and where the consciousness of the perfect, the true and the absolute becomes an actual realization.

We know that faith invariably has a tendency to exalt the mind; and there are many lines of thought, such as worship in all its phases, that have the same tendency to lift the mind into the spirit. Besides this, there are many other tendencies that may come in daily life that tend to exalt the mind; and we shall find it profitable to employ any or all means that may have this tendency, although we can produce this remarkable exaltation in ourselves by turning our attention to the highest and purest state of spiritual being that can imagine — then with all the power of life and mind and thought and soul, desire to realize the high spiritual state upon which attention has been directed.

When we proceed in this attitude, we will gradually turn all the energies of life upward, and those energies will begin to work toward the higher, rising continually in the scale of consciousness and lifting the entire mind upward into higher and finer states of being, until the state of glorious exaltation is realized. In many instances this exalted state is reached in a few moments of such consecrated effort; but under any circumstance, we can, through such consecrated effort, steadily and surely lift the mind more and more until the exalted state is realized absolutely; and when we do enter the exalted state, every adverse condition of the body disappears instantaneously. The reason why is this, that when consciousness is exalted, it enters into a world of pure spirit and marvelous power — a power that is perfect, whole, clean, healthful and thoroughly good in every way — a power that has the power to fill the entire being of man through and through and give expression to the pure, the wholesome, the harmonious and the perfect in every part of mind or personality.

In this connection we should also remember the great law that whatever we become conscious of, that we invariably manifest in mind and body; and, therefore, since we become conscious of this marvelous power when we enter spiritual exaltation, we invariably do, according to the law, give expression to that power, and that power acts as a consuming fire, purifying the entire system and making every part of the system absolutely pure and whole. In brief, the power that we become conscious of through spiritual exaltation will express itself all through mind and body, pouring through the system like a powerful life current, or like a powerful refining current, removing all adversity and discord before it, and restoring absolute harmony and perfection to every part of the human entity.

Remarkable Possibilities. — If people who have distressing ailments and who have tried so many things without results, would proceed at once to train their minds to enter more and more into this state of exaltation, they would not continue very long in their present adverse condition. To proceed, they should turn attention upon the highest and finest state of being that can be realized and imagined, and then with the whole of life, that is, a yearning that is irresistible, and a desire that thrills every atom, try to realize this wonderful state of spiritual exaltation. If they would continue in this way faithfully, day after day, and week after week, if necessary, they would finally lift the mind out of the bondage in which they have been living, or would gradually rise more and more into the higher and finer, until some glorious day they would find themselves in the exalted state; and when this experience was realized, a marvelous change would come speedily.

Here we must remember that it is impossible for any ailment to continue in the body after the mind has been exalted in the spirit, because whenever that exaltation is realized, the entire system is literally flooded with new life, with new and highly refined forces, with new and wholesome states of being, with new and harmonious states of consciousness, with new and powerful states of mind; and in brief, complete renewal of the entire system is brought about, because the higher and finer powers from above have come down into the physical being, changing everything and bringing about a new order absolutely. The possibilities, therefore, that are within easy reach of everybody, in connection with what we term spiritual exaltation, are remarkable, indeed; and among all great means of healing there is no method that is more remarkable or more powerful than that of spiritual exaltation. It invariably means the absolute changing of everything, the lifting of life into the higher and the finer and the perfect, and the restoration of that perfect state of being that we know to be our inheritance from life — that perfect state of being that invariably finds expression all through the system when the power of the spirit is given full freedom in mind and body.

The Spiritualizing Process. — What we may term the spiritualizing process constitutes one of the most direct and one of the most effective means of cure that is known; and it consists, first, in realizing the power and the presence of the spirit in the system; and, second, in taking hold of the power consciously, and directing it wherever healing is desired. To illustrate, there may be a condition in your system that you wish to change, and your object will be to spiritualize that part of the body; or you will want that part of the body to undergo spiritualization, and you wish to apply the spiritualization process to that organ or function or part, whatever it may be. You proceed in this manner. You first realize the fact that you have conscious possession of certain spiritual forces — forces that are serene, harmonious, highly refined — pure white energies with healing on their wings. You realize that you have full conscious possession of those forces in your own being. You realize that you can direct them as you may desire, and cause those forces to act in any part of the body as you will. Thus you turn your attention to that part of the body that needs attention, and while concentrating there positively and with deep, calm feeling, you think that you are directing those spiritual forces all the way through that part of the body, causing those forces to move to and fro in that part of the body, literally penetrating every fiber and nerve, and entering into every atom, spiritualizing every element through and through in that part of the system. Briefly, that part of the body is being spiritualized by the moving to and fro of those fine, powerful life currents — currents that are purely spiritual and that invariably work for purity, harmony, health, wholeness and perfection of being.

Through this method you are not only establishing a spiritual process in that part of the body, but you are also giving expression to the higher and finer life currents that invariably find expression wherever the power of the spirit is directed. The result will be that you can almost see those finer spiritual forces with the eye of the spirit, gently but positively moving all through the atoms, elements, veins and fibers of your system, penetrating them all in this beautiful manner, giving powerful expression to this gentle, peaceful, harmonizing process. We repeat, you can almost see this wonderful, spiritual process taking place; and as you continue you will begin to feel that physical conditions are gradually losing their hold or dwindling away, or changing, or modifying, according to the powerful expressions of this deep, fine and health-producing force of the spirit. The undercurrents and the inner life, including the chemical actions of the body, are being acted upon, and are being influenced to change so as to harmonize perfectly with the true order of things. A greater power is in their presence, and therefore the lesser powers of the body will obey perfectly, and proceed at once to resume a state of order, harmony and health.

We realize that it is a very fine art to take hold of these wonderful spiritual life currents, direct them through consciousness, through the finer and more serene control of the will, and thus cause those higher forces to pass through and spiritualize any part of the body. And we should repeat frequently, until those finer forces, those pure white spiritual energies, gain complete mastery of the situation. For here we must remember that those spiritual forces always work for the good and the right and the true; and when they do secure mastery of the situation in any part of the body, the good and the right and the true will prevail in that part of the body. Emancipation will have been secured; health, life and power will have been restored, and all will be well again.

To train the mind to apply this process, we must develop a deep, serene state of mind, and try to enter more and more deeply into that perfect faith and perfect realization of the spirit wherein we absolutely know that we are in conscious touch with the powers of the spirit. Then we realize that we can direct those finer life currents and express them anywhere, just as readily as we can move the hand physically, or direct any part of the body; and wherever we may direct those highly refined spiritual forces, there those forces will proceed to act in a strong, positive and yet serene manner, always refining, always harmonizing, always healing, always restoring perfect order. They will spiritualize and make perfect; and wherever conditions are made perfect or spiritualized in any part of the human system, all ailments and all discord must instantaneously disappear. Results, however, will depend very largely upon our realization of the great truth that whenever we apply the spiritual process we are giving expression to higher power. We must be able to say to the body, "The greater is at hand." Then all physical conditions must obey absolutely and resume that higher, finer and more perfect state of being that is invariably produced by the presence and the power of the greater. We must also remember that there are no obstacles in the physical world to that power. That power can overcome any and every obstacle; and it always works for health, for peace, for harmony, and for the life more abundant.

Chapter 12

Living in the Absolute

The Absolute State of Being. — When we speak of the absolute we have reference to that state of being that is changeless because it contains everything that life can hold; that is, everything that really is in life. The absolute is limitless and perfect in the extreme sense of those terms; and when we speak of the absolute, we refer to that state of perfection that has reached the climax, or where all perfecting processes have completed their work. However, we cannot conceive of any process as ever coming to an end, and yet there is one thing that we realize no matter how we may approach the subject, and that is, that everything that is to be perfected must first contain the possibility of perfection within itself.

We say that the soul will continue for all time to rise in the scale, ever becoming more perfect, meaning that the soul will continue to give expression to a larger and a larger measure of its own inherent life or divinity, its own inherent qualities and powers, all of which must be absolute — containing within themselves all that any quality can contain; in brief, we say that the soul in its growth and development continues to give expression to more and more of that which is inherent in the soul. But if the soul can continue to give expression to more and more of its inherent qualities, or its real spiritual life, and continue thus for an endless period of time, we must come to the conclusion that the soul already has within itself everything that can be expressed through an endless period of advancement and ascension.

The soul must necessarily have within itself absolute perfection if it can continue for all time to express more and more perfection; and we know that if the soul did not have within itself absolute perfection, it would in its development come to an end sometime. However, if the soul never comes to an end in its process of development, but continues to rise in the scale for eternity, it must necessarily possess within itself at the present time the absolute state of being; and here let us remember that the absolute is without conditions, without limitations, and is not circumscribed in any way, but contains everything in the perfect, limitless state of real being.

The Unconditioned. — When we consider the absolute, we realize that we shall have to think quietly and deeply, because it is something that cannot be discerned unless we enter into the very spirit of Divine Wisdom; but we cannot enter into that spirit unless we are absolutely serene and the whole of life consecrated to the very highest we can think or know. When we enter into this deeper and more serene state of contemplation, we begin to understand what it means to live in the absolute.

As we approach that state, let us imagine an absolute state of being where the mind would be conscious of a perfection that could not be made more perfect, where the mind would be conscious of a life that was so beautiful that it could not be made more beautiful and where the mind was conscious of power and wisdom of all the qualities of the Divine — all that Divine Being could imply. In approaching such a state of consciousness, the first great truth that we would discover would be that there are no conditions in the absolute state, and there is nothing in that state that is undeveloped; in truth, in the absolute state all things are as they can be in the most extreme or highest form of being; but this is something that cannot be described in words. We can realize this only as we develop spiritual consciousness.

In contrast to this higher consciousness we find when we look upon our physical bodies, that the manifested side of life is full of changing conditions; and when we look upon the mind we find that there are degrees of manifestation and understanding; in brief, there are certain states that are constantly improving or in a process of perpetual growth. This is true of the entire personality, and is a part of the great plan; but in the absolute state there are no changes, no conditions, no growth, no advancement, because everything in the absolute state has reached the All in All.

Contains Everything. — When we consider this wonderful theme very closely, we find that, al-though the absolute state contains within itself everything that we can conceive of as existing in perfect being, still we must make a distinction between being perfect in the absolute, and manifesting perfection in the outer life; and in this connection there are three views that we can take of the subject. The first view would be simply to consider the external side of life in a process of growth, and try, in the best manner we know, to improve upon that process continually through life. We would do this, however, without any regard to what we might possess in the within; but in trying to grow or express ourselves without drawing upon the within, we would not accomplish very much. The reason for this is evident, because if we cannot secure the greater supply, we will necessarily continue in the same state of development all along until the greater supply is secured, which could only follow after we had placed ourselves in contact with the absolute life within.

We might take a second view, which would be to give no attention to external growth whatever, but simply live in the belief that we were perfect now, and, therefore, need give no further thought to external changes. In taking this view, our object would be to enter as deeply as possible into the consciousness of divine life, or realize the absolute state; and seemingly this would be the proper course to pursue; but there is another side to this great theme. The truth is that the mere act of becoming conscious of perfect being is not all there is in life. We must also consider manifestation. The fact that we are growing and constantly manifesting more and more in life proves that there is a purpose in such manifestation; and we know that the principle of that manifestation is this, that we do not really live, or cannot really live, without giving expression to more and more life. The giving of expression to more life involves the giving of expression to everything that pertains to life or that comes from life — all the powers, qualities and talents that exist in the human entity. Here we must also remember that it is not possible to manifest perfect being by simply working for the consciousness of perfect being. There are other essentials as we shall understand as we proceed.

The Higher Understanding. — Realizing then the great truth that growth, manifestation and expression are necessary factors in real living, we come to a third view of this subject; and that is, that our object in trying to live in the absolute should be for the purpose of manifesting a greater and a greater measure of the life of absolute being. Our purpose must not be to hide ourselves in absolute consciousness, or try to withdraw from manifested life, or in any way enter into that state of abstraction where we become more or less unconscious of things in the external. This must not be our object, although we know that it is possible at certain times to enter so completely into the abstract that we become in a measure oblivious to conditions. We find, however, that this state of obliviousness to conditions generally means that we have become insensible to them, and not that we have necessarily overcome them. However, while we are in that state we feel absolutely free from conditions; and a great many advanced minds have taken the view that real freedom can come only as we confine consciousness more and more to this abstract state where we become oblivious to the sensibilities of external life. But this is not the truth.

We know that, although we may live for a time in abstract consciousness, and in a measure realize freedom from pain and illness, still growth and manifestation will be taking place as usual in our external life. The body will continue its changes and the mind will continue to seek new forms of expression; natural processes will go on in the personality as before, and we shall soon find that the personality will require further attention. The fact is, we may isolate ourselves from personal conditions for a time, and it may be a delightful experience; and during that time, the personality may continue to run like a clock that has been wound up; but sooner or later the clock will run down, and the personality shall have to receive attention. In other words, the ego will be drawn out suddenly into manifested life to take care of its instrument. In the meantime, there may have been considerable loss sustained in the process of growth and development; and after all we shall find that there has been no real gain.

Dwelling in the Abstract. — There are many illustrations in history of this practice of the ego hiding itself, so to speak, in the abstract, and neglecting the personality; but in every instance, the personality either weakened or met with dissolution, so that there was no gain and much loss on the manifested side. True, there are advanced minds who argue that the personality is of no value in any case, and it matters not what happens to it so long as the soul finds absolute truth. But, whatever our view may be of that subject, we must come to the conclusion that the fact that we are here in this sphere of existence, in the possession of a personality, proves that our being here is for a purpose; and also that we have received this personality in order that we may use it as an instrument in fulfilling our purpose in this realm of existence. There may be times when it is well to enter the abstract for a short period, and thereby withdraw consciousness from the world of sense, but in most instances this is neither necessary nor desirable. It is not the highest light on this great subject; and it is the highest light that we all seek.

The Great Problem. — Considering the more rational view of this subject, that is, that the personality is necessary as an instrument of the soul, serving a great purpose, and that we should enter more and more into the consciousness of the absolute in order that we may further manifestation and growth in the personality, we are face to face with the great problem of adjusting ourselves to these two great phases of the truth. When we consider the external side, we find it undeveloped, and when we consider the spiritual side or the real I AM, we find that it is absolutely perfect, in need of neither growth nor further development. But we shall find the solution of this problem as we realize that growth in the personality depends more and more upon the deepening of consciousness in the absolute; and also that real living will increase or perfect itself only as we cause the perfect being in the I AM to manifest itself more and more in the outer life. You may enter into consciousness of the absolute, and you may discern that absolute being is changeless, perfect, beyond further growth, and yet the moment you become conscious of the absolute state you will realize that this state inherently demands continuous manifestation. In other words, the deeper you enter the absolute state, the greater becomes your desire to manifest more and more of the absolute in and through your external being.

Wonderful Truth. — The statement has been made that even though the Infinite is perfect, still the Infinite cannot be satisfied unless divine expression through the great family of human souls is made constant; and whatever we may think of this statement, it is most delightful to believe. It leads to the conclusion that we are just as necessary to the Infinite as the Infinite is to us. Infinite life, therefore, although inherently perfect, beyond all limitations, is not complete in its consciousness of life unless that life is manifested more and more through the countless souls of the cosmos. The more we think of this, the more reasonable it becomes, the more desirable it be-comes and the more beautiful it becomes; and we find in the realization of this truth the very secret of secrets concerning the nearness between God and man.

The truth is that if we are just as necessary to God as God is to us, we have therein the real principle and the real need of divine unity. We all must admit that it is inconceivable to think of the family of human souls as being one with God if neither were necessary to the other; but the fact that they are all necessary to each other gives an eternal reason for endless unity between the Infinite and every soul in existence. The same idea is applicable to the individual I AM and the manifested life of the personality. Our conclusion here must be that although the individual I AM is perfect in being, living in the absolute, still manifestation through the personality is absolutely necessary to the conscious existence of the I AM.

The I AM cannot live consciously without giving expression to life; and the giving of expression to life demands an instrument through which that expression can take place. If there were no manifestation the I AM would simply exist in a state of unconscious abstraction, and we can conceive of no reason why the I AM should exist at all if its existence simply meant eternal sleep in the absolute. We must have a reason for things; things must explain their existence or state of being in a satisfactory manner; and if anything exists at all there must be some cause for that existence. However, we can find no cause for an existence that would mean nothing more than isolation in an abstract state, or eternal sleep. We must accept, therefore, the other view, or rather the higher understanding of this great theme.

Absolute Consciousness. — When we take this other or higher view of absolute consciousness, and proceed to penetrate deeper and deeper into the marvelous state of absolute being, becoming conscious of more and more of the absolute in order that we may manifest the greater life of the absolute, thus expanding the mind, perfecting the personality and enlarging the life of the soul, we find not only a reasonable cause for all existence and all experience, but we discover before us a wonderful path — a path of endless existence and ascension too marvelous to even imagine. Beginning with this higher view of life, that is, that we grow and develop in the manifested life as we gain a deeper and a deeper consciousness of perfect being, we meet the great law that whatever we become conscious of, that we invariably express. Our purpose, therefore, must be to become conscious of a larger and a larger measure of the limitless life and the perfect life that already exists inherently in absolute being. And the more we become conscious of, the more we will manifest in the without, thereby making existence upon all planes richer, more wonderful and more ideal at every step of the endless way.

Health and Emancipation. — The problem in this connection is how to apply this principle to the attainment of health and emancipation. We know that in absolute being there can be no sickness or weakness or discord of any kind. There can be no such conditions, or any condition whatever in absolute consciousness; and the more deeply we penetrate absolute consciousness, the further we get away from all forms of conditions or limitations. The question then is, how we may, through the gaining of absolute consciousness, secure emancipation from adverse conditions. In this connection we must consider the great fact that whenever we become unconscious of weakness or sickness or discord those conditions disappear entirely from the personality. We will suppose that you have a pain in your body, and that you wish to become unconscious of that pain. But here let us remember that there is a difference between becoming unconscious of a pain and insensible to a pain, because we become insensible to a pain only when our nerves are deadened. Here, then, we find a marked difference. However, when we become unconscious of a pain, we do so by withdrawing consciousness from the field of action of that pain; and the fact is that those forces in your system that were producing the pain cannot act in that manner unless you continue to be conscious of the pain. You must be conscious of the pain in order that those forces can produce that pain, and when you cease to be conscious of that pain the forces in that part of the system can produce pain no longer. This may seem strange, but it is a strictly scientific fact. It is absolutely true to natural law, because mind and body are so closely related that the mind must give its consent to a process before that process can begin or continue anywhere in the physical system.

We will suppose again that there is discord in your system, and that it began through the violation of some law; you at once become conscious of that discord, and immediately your consciousness admits the existence of discord in that place — the existence of certain activities that can produce pain. Your consciousness continues to give its consent to those activities continuing in that mode of action that will sooner or later produce pain; and when the pain comes, consciousness immediately admits the existence of that pain, thereby giving those activities permission to continue in the producing of more pain. However, the very moment consciousness would refuse to grant further permission to those activities, and withdraw its presence from that part of the body, those activities would cease, and they would no longer produce pain. The fact is that whenever you withdraw consciousness from any field of activity in your physical system, those activities will subside or cease altogether; and therefore what those activities produced previously will not be produced any more; that is, the pain will cease to be, and nature will resume normal conditions. This is a law that we can reason out and prove for ourselves very readily, and we will soon be able to understand how no form of action can continue anywhere in the system unless we are conscious of it — unless consciousness is there permitting those conditions to continue.

The Great Secret. — The problem is to withdraw consciousness from any state of activity that we do not care to encourage; and there is where we find the consciousness of the absolute life to be indispensable. We know that we cannot cease the consciousness of the lesser until we gain consciousness of the greater; in other words, we cannot withdraw consciousness from a state of discord unless we can direct consciousness upon the opposite state — a state of harmony.

And we can withdraw consciousness from anyplace only when we are able to direct consciousness to that which is the very reverse. In the personal life, however, we find a bundle of conditions, the very reverse of the absolute state. Therefore, if we wish to withdraw consciousness from those conditions, we must consecrate consciousness to the absolute state; that is, we must continue to approach the absolute so as to become more and more conscious of the absolute.

Understanding the Absolute. — To understand what it means to be in the absolute state, or even to imagine the existence of such a state, we shall find it necessary to give much thought to the very highest states of consciousness; and, although we may not always be able to form a perfect conception of the absolute state of perfect being, still we can form mental conceptions that are so similar to that state that they will give us, for the time being, an indication to how and where we should turn attention. And here we should remember that although we may become conscious of perfect being, that does not mean that we have become conscious of all there is in perfect being. Such a consciousness would require an eternity; but we can become conscious of perfect being; we can draw so near to the absolute state that we can form a clear conception of the life of the absolute. However, we can never become conscious of all that is in the absolute, because again, that would require an eternity. It is true that all who are spiritually awakened are conscious more or less of the absolute, and there are times when they can draw so near to perfect being that they can really feel that they are in reality the I AM. And here you should remember that whenever you can feel that you and the I AM are one and the same, then you are in absolute consciousness. However, you may continue to penetrate more and more deeply into that state for eternity, and the more deeply you penetrate into that state the larger the I AM becomes in your conscious understanding.

Art of Overcoming. — Resuming our consideration of the possibility of withdrawing consciousness from conditions by entering more and more deeply into absolute consciousness, we shall find that this practice will prove of exceptional value in daily life. The illustration given with regard to pain will hold elsewhere; and, in fact, there are a number of illustrations that could be mentioned. We will suppose further that there is a chronic ailment in your system; and if you know that the forces of nature are perpetuating that ailment simply because your own consciousness gives consent, you realize that you can overcome that condition and find emancipation by ceasing to give conscious consent to the perpetuation of that ailment. Here we find the chief secret of those who deny the existence of disease. They continue their denial until consciousness becomes more or less oblivious, both to the disease and to that part of the body. But it is not necessary to deny the existence of disease, although the method is more or less effective as it helps consciousness to get away from that form of confused activity, the fact being that when consciousness withdraws from any place in the system, it will no longer give cause to the discord or the disease that may be in action in that place; that is, the forces of nature can no longer proceed as before to reproduce that particular ailment. However, it is not necessary to deny the existence of disease in order to withdraw consciousness from the field of discordant activity. We shall find that the other method is far more effective; that is, the method of withdrawing consciousness from the world of conditions by consecrating consciousness upon the absolute. You realize, therefore, that if there is an ailment in your system you may secure emancipation from that ailment and overcome it and become unconscious of those activities by becoming more fully conscious of the absolute, which is unconditioned, and wherein all things are absolutely perfect, containing the All in All.

Image the True. — We shall find it an excellent practice to try to imagine the reality of the absolute state, and try to imagine that it is a state wherein there are no conditions — a state that involves the complete, the perfect, the All that is in Divine Being; and when we imagine such a state and try to direct consciousness upon that state, or try to combine our own present consciousness with the consciousness of that state, we shall find that in every instance our present consciousness will enter so deeply into the unconditioned state of the absolute that we become unconscious of conditions in the without. Thus consciousness will withdraw from the world of discord and confusion, and will no longer take part in the producing of ailment or pain; and here let us remember that when our own consciousness no longer takes part in the producing of ailment or pain, it is impossible for ailments or pain to continue another moment in mind or body. This indeed is a great truth, a most wonderful truth, and the more deeply conscious we become of the vastness and possibility of this truth, the sooner we shall realize complete emancipation, absolute health and all those higher and more beautiful states of being that we know we can find in the consciousness of the ideal. Our purpose, therefore, must be to enter more and more perfectly into the consciousness of the ideal, which is, in truth, the consciousness of absolute being — in absolute being every ideal is real; and when we have entered that state where we know and feel that every ideal is real, then indeed are we living in the spirit of the absolute — in the pure, white light of eternal truth.

Just Be Glad

Just Be Glad

ALL things respond to the call of rejoicing; all things gather where life is a song. This is the message of the new order, the new life and the new time. It is the golden text of the great gospel of human sunshine. It is the central truth of that sublime philosophy of existence, which declares that the greatest good is happiness, and that heaven is here and now. To live in the spirit of this wonderful message; to be a living example of this great gospel, to work out in everyday life the principle of this inspiring philosophy, the first and most important thing to do, is to lay aside our sorrows and glooms, and just be glad.

Wherever you are, or whatever has happened, just be glad. Be glad because you are here. You are here in a beautiful world; and all that is beautiful may be found in this world. It is a world wherein all that is rich in life may be enjoyed beyond measure; a world wherein happiness may overflow eternally in every human heart; a world wherein all the dreams of life may be realized, and all the visions of the soul made true. Then why should we not be glad; first of all, that we are here; that we are in this world; that we may stay here for a long time if we so desire, and enjoy every minute to the full.

The real truth is that this world is nothing less than a limitless sea of happiness, the vastness and glory of which we are just beginning to know. And life itself is a song, while time is one eternal symphony. To be in tune with life, therefore, and to be in harmony with the endless music of time, we must of necessity be glad. But after we have learned to be glad, under every circumstance, it is no longer a necessity; it is a privilege, and has become a part of our active, living, thinking self.

Just be glad, and you always will be glad. You will have better reason to be glad. You will have more and more things to make you glad. For great is the power of sunshine, especially human sunshine. It can change anything, transform anything, remake anything, and cause anything to become as fair and beautiful as itself.

Just be glad and your fate will change; a new life will begin and a new future will dawn for you. All things that are good and desirable will begin to come into your world in greater measure, and you will be enriched far beyond your expectations, both from the without and from the within. And the cause of the change is this, that all things respond to the call of rejoicing; all things gather where life is a song.

When you are tempted to feel discouraged or disappointed, be glad instead. Know that you can, say that you will, and stand uncompromisingly upon your resolve. Be strong and be glad. For when strength and rejoicing combine in your soul, every trace of gloom or despair must disappear; because such conditions can exist only where weakness is the rule and mastery the exception.

Combine strength with rejoicing and you will exercise a magic power and you will possess a secret that will serve you royally no matter what your difficulties or obstacles may be. All joy is light; and it is the light that dispels the darkness.

When things are not to your liking, be glad nevertheless, for the glad heart can cause all things to be as we wish them to be. When things do not give you pleasure, proceed instead to create pleasure in your own heart and soul. And you can if you will always be glad. Besides, things will soon change for the better if you continue in the spirit of rejoicing. It is the law that all good things will sooner or later come and be, where the greatest happiness is to be found. Therefore, be happiness in yourself, regardless of times, seasons or circumstances.

Just Be Glad

When things do not please you, resolve to please yourself by being glad, and you can add immeasurably to your happiness in this simple manner. Then you must remember that the fountain of joy within your own soul is infinitely greater than all external sources of joy combined. But as far as we can, we should add the joys from without to the joys from within, and in all things be glad.

Rejoice in your strength, rejoice in your talents and powers, rejoice in the wonders of your own nature. For there is far more in you than you ever dreamed. So whatever may come, you are greater than it all, richer than it all. And knowing this, why should you not be glad.

When evil befalls you, consider the fact that the good that is yet in your possession is many times as great as all the evil you could ever know. Consider this stupendous fact and be glad. Then remember, with rejoicing, that neither evil nor wrong can exist very long in the radiant sunshine of a glad triumphant soul.

If you have lost anything, have no regrets. Be glad and begin again. Be glad that you can begin again. Be glad to know that the future is always richer and better than the past if we only try to make it so. Then forget the loss, and rejoice in the fact that you have the power to secure something far better in return. You know that you have this power; then you can never be otherwise than glad.

Whatever comes or not, sing again and again the song of "the soul victorious"; and mean it with your whole heart. Enter into this song with all the power of mind and spirit, for it is always that which we know and sincerely believe that contains the greater worth and power.

Just Be Glad

When you resolve to be glad at all times and under every circumstance, resolve also to give your whole heart and soul to the spirit of your rejoicing. Give power to your gladness, and give life to your song. Open the way for all the sunshine of your soul; and see that every sunbeam from within be one of power as well as one of joy.

It is the full joy of the soul that makes the heart young and the mind great. For as it is in nature, so it is also in man. It is the full glory of the noonday sun that quickens the earth, that makes the fields green, that causes the flowers to bloom. Where the sun is strong all growth is luxurious and all nature bountiful. It is the same when the sunshine of the soul is full, strong and constant in the daily life of man. So therefore rejoice with great joy. Rejoice always and give life and power to your joy.

There is magic in the sunshine of the soul; there is a charmed power in the radiant splendor of a beaming countenance. Such a countenance can dispel anything that may threaten to give disappointment or dismay. So remember to be glad and mean it. It is the greatest remedy in the world, and the greatest protector in the world. It can harm nothing for it turns all wrong into right. It is the sunshine from within that causes all darkness to cease to be. It therefore brings good to everybody, and he who is always glad is always adding to the welfare of every member of the race.

When fate seems unkind, do not be unkind to yourself by becoming disheartened or dismayed. Instead, rejoice in the great fact that you are greater and stronger than any fate; that you have the power to master your whole life, and determine your destiny according to your own invincible will. Then resolve that you will begin at once to prove that strength, and cause all the elements of fate to come with you, and work with you, in building for that greater future which you have so often longed for in your visions and dreams.

Therefore, whatever your fate may be, just be glad. You can change it all. And as you proceed to exercise this divine right, the darkness of today will become the sunshine of tomorrow, and the disappointments of the present will become the pastures green of the future.

When calamities or catastrophies have overtaken your life, do not think that fate or Providence has ordered it so. Do not think that it has to be. Instead, forget the sorrow and the loss, and congratulate yourself over the fact that you now have the privilege to build for greater things than you ever knew before. Do not weep over loss; but rejoice to think that now you are called upon to prove the greater wisdom and power within you. You have been taken out into a new world. Before you lie vast fields of undeveloped and unexplored opportunities fields that you would not have known had not this seeming misfortune come upon you. So count it all joy. All things are working together for a greater good. Now it is for you to come forward in joy and accept the greater good. A richer life and a greater future are in store.

Therefore, rejoice and be glad, and give strength to your rejoicing. Let your soul repeat again and again that sweet reassuring refrain just be glad. In that refrain there is comfort and peace; it lifts the burdens, removes the clouds, dispels the gloom; it takes away the sadness and the loss, and all is well again. And naturally so, for all things respond to the call of rejoicing; all things gather where life is a song.

There is more to live for than you ever imagined. Thus far most of us have only touched the merest surface of human existence; we are only on the verge of the splendor of life as it is; we are standing on the outside, so to speak, of the real mansion of mind and soul; and one reason is we live too much in the limitations of our disappointments, our lost opportunities, our blasted hopes, our vanquished dreams. We remain in that small world, deploring fate, when, if we would only permit mind and soul to take wings and go out upon the vastness of real existence, we would find, not only freedom, but a life infinitely richer than we had ever dreamed.

But if mind and soul are to take wings in this fashion, we must learn to be glad. The heart that lives in disappointments is heavy. It will sink into the lowlands, and remain among the marshes and the bogs. But the glad heart ascends to the mountain tops. Therefore it is when we have such a heart that we can go out in search of new worlds, new opportunities, new possibilities, new joys. And the glad heart always finds that for which it goes in search. The reason is simple; for all things respond to the call of rejoicing; all things gather where life is a song. The great soul is always in search of ways and means for adding to the welfare of others. But no way is better, greater or more far-reaching than this, just be glad.

Life becomes worth the living only when the living of life makes living more worthwhile for an ever increasing number. It is only the joys we share that give happiness; it is only the thoughts we express that enrich our own minds; it is only the strength we use in actual helpfulness that makes our own souls strong. Therefore, to add to the pleasures of others, is to add to our own pleasure; to add to the wealth and comfort of others is to add in like manner to our own. This the great soul knows; and every soul is great that has learned to be glad regardless of what may come or go in the world.

Just Be Glad

To be glad at all times is to be of greater service to mankind than any other thing that we can do. If we have not the power or ability to apply ourselves more tangibly in behalf of others, we can instead be glad. We can always give sunshine. And we shall find that just being glad is frequently sufficient, even when needs seem great and circumstances extreme. In most instances it is all the world wants; but it does want human sunshine so much, that those who can give it at all times need not do anything else to reap immortal fame.

Surround us with an abundance of human sunshine, and the day's work will easily be done; we shall, with far less effort, overcome our obstacles; our troubles will largely be removed, and our burdens entirely laid aside. Give us the privilege to work to the music of rejoicing and our work will become a pleasure; every duty will become a privilege, and all we do will be well done. This is the way the world thinks and feels. So therefore be glad. Give an abundance of human sunshine everywhere and always, and you will please the world immensely.

Then turn to the home. Can we picture anything more beautiful than a home where every soul therein is a sunbeam; where every countenance is ever lit up with the light of rejoicing; where every word spoken rings with the music of love; and where every thought, uttered or unexpressed, is inspired by the spirit of joy.

It is in such a home that the beautiful, the great and the wonderful in human nature will grow; it is in such a home that our highest ideals will be realized and the divine within find full and resplendent expression. But it is not necessary to describe the pleasures and privileges of such a home; only to say that if you want such a home, just be glad.

Then consider again the worker, and where the workers must gather; what a power for good human sunshine would be in such a place. Consider how all things change when the glad soul arrives, and how all work lightens when the spirit of joy is abroad. And every man has the power to dispense the spirit of joy wherever he may work or live. Every man can ease the ways of others in this remarkable manner; and the secret is simple just be glad.

The work you do, be it with mind or muscle, invariably conveys the spirit of your own soul. Therefore work in the spirit of joy and your work will be the product of joy a rare product the best of its kind.

It is the man who blends rejoicing with his work who does the best work; it is the man who deeply and sincerely enjoys his work who gives the greatest worth to his work; and the more worth we give to our work the more of the rich and the worthy our work will bring to us.

We realize therefore that it is profitable in every way to learn to be glad. But it is not only profitable to ourselves; also to all others that we may reach through word or deed. Then the profit that comes from the art of being glad is never the result of selfishness. The glad heart is never selfish. The sunbeam does not dance and sing to please its own restricted desire; it does what it does because it is what it is a happy, carefree sunbeam. It is the same with the glad heart, it sings because it has become the spirit of song; and all are charmed with the song.

No selfish heart can really be glad. No soul that acts solely for personal gain can enter the spirit of joy; and no man who seeks only his own pleasure and comfort can ever take part in the music of rejoicing. And yet, the glad heart receives far more of everything of worth in life than does the one who forgets gladness in pursuit of gain for self alone. And again the answer is simple. For all things respond to the call of rejoicing; all things gather where life is a song.

Be glad for the things you have, and you will find you have far more than you thought. Then you will not miss, in the least, the things you have not. Besides, the happier you are over what has come to you, the more and the more will come to you in the future. This is indeed a great secret, and if universally applied would cause want to disappear from the face of the whole earth.

Be glad, for nothing is as serious as it seems to be. Then remember that sunshine can banish any gloom; and you can create in yourself all the sunshine you need; so just be glad. When trouble and misfortunes surround you, just be glad. The glad heart and the cheerful soul always make things better. It is the happy heart that has the most courage; it is the joyous soul that has the greatest power; and it is the presence of sunshine that keeps darkness and gloom away.

When things go wrong, do not become disheartened; it is much easier to set them right when your soul is full of sunshine; so just be glad. It is the best way out. When all seems lost, remember that it requires strength to regain everything; and it is the glad heart that remains strong. When the heart saddens, weakness will overtake you, and it will not be possible to regain your position. So therefore be glad regardless of what may transpire. It is one of the royal paths to everything that life holds dear.

But sadness does not merely bring weakness, it also brings illness, and age, and it shortens the length of our days. In gladness, however, there is health and youth, strength and longevity. The glad heart will not grow old, nor can illness ever enter where the spirit of joy is supreme.

Just Be Glad

When in pain, be glad; and you can. Be glad that you are greater than pain. Be glad that pain has come to prevent you from going wrong. Be glad that you can prevent all pain in the future. And be glad that it is wholly impossible for pain to come any more after gladness has become the rule of your life.

For your own advancement, be glad. The spirit of joy is the spirit that makes the heart kind, the soul strong and the mind brilliant. It is this spirit that makes for greatness, for nobleness, for excellence, for worth. We repeat it, therefore, just be glad.

Would you be a pleasure and a delight to others, then be glad always. And would you add to the measure of your own joy, then give all the joy you can to the largest possible number. This you can do by living more and more in the spirit of that joy that is in itself the essence of real joy. And it is better to become the living incarnation of this spirit than to possess all the wealth in the world. It is better to have attained to perpetual gladness than to have become the crowned monarch of an entire solar system. The reason is simple. The glad heart is the sunshine of all life, a benediction to every man, a perpetual blessing to everything in creation. Inspire every atom in your own being to thrill with the spirit of joy; not the joy of sentiment, but the joy of strength, of triumph, of victory the joy that inwardly feels its power sublime as the soul ascends in masterful mien to the splendor of empyrean heights. It is such a joy that makes life a power, a blessing, an inspiration. And it is such a joy that comes perpetually to him who causes his soul to repeat again and again, that sweet reassuring refrain just be glad.

Sing ever the song of triumph, of victory, of freedom the song that declares the supremacy of the spirit over all that may be temporal or wrong. Sing the song of the soul rising

Just Be Glad

above adversity or loss, proclaiming its freedom over all that is or is to be. When the soul continues to sing in this triumphant manner, all the elements of life follow the music of that which is always well; and in such a spirit everything must be always well.

Be glad, and smile with the smile that is sincere, the smile that shines just as sweetly and as naturally as the sunbeam. It is such a smile that is a smile indeed; it is such a smile that comes from the soul from the soul that is ever singing just be glad. And how soon such a smile can change the world.

Meet adversity with such a smile; charm away tribulation with such a smile bursting forth into song; and let the music of the soul restore peace, love and harmony where these might have been absent. Then be stronger than adversity; rise superior to tribulation, and know that you are infinitely greater than all that is unfortunate or wrong.

In the midst of adversity combine strength with rejoicing, and fate must change. Before that music of the soul that is so high and so strong that it stirs the depth of every soul, all the world pays homage on a bended knee. And wisely, because such a power can change anything, transform anything, elevate anything, emancipate anything.

Go forth therefore into life with strength in your soul and music in your soul, and the future shall steadily and surely shape itself to comply with your dearest wishes and your highest aspirations. Array yourself in the strength of truth, conviction, courage, faith, resolution, victory and triumph; and add to these another raiment — the music of gladness — and yours will be a life filled with glory, power and light.

Just Be Glad

The spirit of gladness when combined with the spirit of strength, will enlarge the mind, expand the soul, and enrich all thought and life; it is the moving mystery from within that makes everything good in human nature grow; that makes man noble and great; that makes human existence a world of immeasurable richness and sublime worth. It is the same spirit that makes life "a thing of beauty and a joy forever;" that makes the lovely and the true become the tangible and heal; that causes all things we have loved so much come forth into our world m abundance. Therefore be glad when you feel strong, and be strong when you feel glad; and always know that you can.

Whatever your present position may be there is a way from where you now stand that leads to better things and greater things for you than you ever knew. So whatever happens, just be glad. Live the spirit of gladness; think in the spirit of joy; thus you will be able to see the royal path, for the mind that is illumined with gladness is never in the dark, never under the clouds of doubt or dismay.

When overtaken with calamity or tribulation, come forth undaunted and undismayed. Inspire the soul to reach for the high realms of victory and joy; and hold fast to that lofty position even though the whole world seem to disappear beneath your feet. With such a victory for your strong inspiration, your own soul will prove more than sufficient for all that life may demand of you.

Then remember that mankind stands ready to welcome and exalt every soul whose strength is greater than any circumstance, whose joy is greater than any tribulation, and whose faith is greater than all doubts and failures in the world.

Just Be Glad

When your plans cannot be carried through at present, do not feel downcast or discouraged. Just be glad. Give gladness to your mind and you give clearness to your mind; and a clear mind can see how to evolve better plans.

When your dreams do not come true and your ideals do not become real, refuse to be sad or disconsolate. Instead, rejoice with great joy to know that you are greater than your dreams, and wholly sufficient unto yourself regardless of what may transpire in the real or the ideal. Thus you will give expression to that greater power within you which surely can make your ideals real and make all your dreams come true.

Prove that your cherished dreams are not necessary to your happiness, and all of those dreams will come true. Prove that you do not need the things you want, and you will get them, provided of course that you give all that is in you to the life you live. Prove that you already are sufficient in yourself, and have sufficient in the richness of your own world, and more and more will gather for you, both in the within and in the without. It is much gathering more; much in the within gathering more everywhere; it is your own strength inspiring all things to come with strength; it is the spirit of the great life aroused in yourself causing all things of greatness and worth to come and gather in the entire world of your own life. And it is in this spirit that we live and move and have our being, when the soul continues to sing that sweet reassuring refrain just be glad.

Whatever may be, therefore, or come to pass, continue in the spirit of this refrain. For to live in the music of such a refrain is to enjoy life infinitely more than it was ever enjoyed before. And that in itself is much indeed. Besides, be glad whatever happens, and something better will happen. When the good happens, let the soul sing with rejoicing; then greater good will happen, and there will be cause for greater rejoicing. When that which is not good happens, let the soul sing in the same triumphant spirit, and the power of that spirit will cause all ills to vanish as darkness before the glory of the morn.

Remove the cause of sadness by giving all the elements of life to the spirit of joy. Smile away the darkness and the gloom; sing away the discord and the pain; banish tribulation with rejoicing; then you may in truth be joyous and be glad; and every hour of your long and triumphant life will add new evidence to that great inspiring statement all things respond to the call of rejoicing; all things gather where life is a song.

Whether we believe that life was made for happiness or that happiness was made for life, matters not. The fact remains that he alone can live the most and enjoy the best who takes for his motto just be glad. Whatever comes, or whatever may fail to come, this one thing he will always remember just be glad. Though every mind in the world may give darkness, his will continue to give light; and though all may be lost, so there seems nothing more to give, he will not forget to give happiness. The one great thing to do under every circumstance and in the midst of every event is this just be glad. Wherever you may be, add sunshine. Whatever your position may be, be also a human sunbeam. What a difference when the sunbeam comes in; then why should the sunbeam remain without?

There is a sunbeam in every heart. Why hide it at any time? Does not the world need your smiles? Is not everybody made happier and better when in the presence of a radiant countenance? Do. we ever forget the face that shines as the sun? And does not such a memory continue to give us strength and inspiration all through the turnings and complexities of life? We are not here to give sadness, but joy. We were not made to hide our souls in a dark thunder cloud, but to let the spirit shine in all its splendor and beauty. We are made to make life an endless song, and the sweet refrain of that beautiful song is just be glad.

When things go wrong, just be glad. It is sunshine that brings forth the flowers from the cold and soggy earth. It is lightheartedness that puts to flight the burdens of life. It is the smile of human sweetness that dispels the chilly night of isolation and brings friendship and love to the bosom of the yearning soul. Then why be sad when gladness can do so much? Why be sad for a single moment when the smile of a single moment has the power even to change the course of human destiny. We all remember how soon a smile of God can change the world. Why not always live in that magical smile and just be glad? Then we should remember that all things respond to the song of rejoicing; all things gather where life is a song.

Do you think that life is too difficult for smiles, and that you have too much to pass through to ever have happiness? Then remember that the glad heart knows no difficulty. The sunbeam even smiles at darkness, and converts the blackness of the storm into a brilliant rainbow. Just be glad, and your tears shall also become a bow of promise; yes, and more, for in that promise you shall discern the unmistakable signs of a brighter day upon the coming morn.

Do not think that happiness must keep its distance so long as you have so much to pass through. The more you have to pass through, the more you need happiness. It is the shining countenance that never turns back; it is the glad heart that finds strength to go on; it is the mind with the most sunshine that can see the most clearly where to go and how to act that the goal in view may be gained.

Just Be Glad

Just be glad, and half the burden is gone. Just be glad, and your work becomes mostly pleasure. Just be glad, and you take the keenest delight in meeting even the greatest of obstacles and the most difficult of problems.

When you meet reverses, just be glad; for do we not again remember how soon a smile of God can change the world? It is not gloom that dispels darkness; it is not disconsolance that makes the mind brilliant and the soul strong. But if we would turn the tide of ill fortune we need all our brilliancy and all our strength. To master fate, to conquer destiny, to make life our own, we must be all there is in us to be.

Then we must remember that it is sunshine that makes the flowers grow, and that transforms the acorn into a great and massive oak. Everything in nature, and in man, the crowning glory of nature, responds with pleasure to the magic touch of the smiling sunbeam. For again we must remember that all things respond to the call of rejoicing; all things gather where life is a song.

Promise yourself that whatever may come you will always remember just be glad. When good things come into life, gladness will make them better. When things come that should not have come, gladness will so brighten your mind that you can see clearly how to turn everything to good account. Whatever happens or not, just be glad, and it will be much better than it possibly could have been otherwise. Therefore, gladness is not a mere sentiment. It pays. It is not a luxury for the favored few alone. It is a necessity that all should secure in abundance.

If it is your belief that there is nothing in your life for which you can justly be glad, stop and count your blessings. You will surprise yourself; and you will then and there

Just Be Glad

resolve never to depreciate yourself again. Henceforth, you will find it easier to be glad; and you will also find that the more things you are glad for, the more things you will have to be glad for. Gladness is a magnet and it draws more and more of everything that can increase gladness. Just be glad always and under every circumstance, and nothing shall be withheld from you that can add to your welfare and happiness.

Should you find it easy to be glad when things go right, and difficult to be glad when things go wrong, you are not creating your own sunshine; and it is only the sunshine that we create ourselves, in our own world, that makes things grow in our own world. Be glad because you want to be glad, regardless of events, and you will have found that fountain of joy within that is ever ready to overflow. Be glad at all times because it is best to be glad at all times; and be glad in the presence of everything because gladness makes it better for everything.

Just be glad, and the world will be kind to you. The sunbeam has no occasion for regrets. It is always welcome; it is always loved. Just be glad, and you will have friends without number; and it is he who has many friends, friends that are good and true, who finds everything that is rich and beautiful in human existence. Just be glad, and you will be sought for, far and wide. The world is not looking for gloom and depression; it is looking for sunshine and joy.

Just be glad, even though the whole world be against you, and all the elements of nature be in a conspiracy to place you in the hands of destruction. Even at such a time, just be glad. Thus you prove your strength. And he who can prove that he is stronger than any adversary, will win the respect yes, and the friendship, of every adversary. What was against you will be for you. And this was your secret you refused to be downcast, you refused to weaken, you refused to be less than your greatest self even when everything seemed lost, you were strong enough to be true to all that you knew to be true, and you tuned your life to the music of that sweetest of all refrains just be glad. Because you were glad, even when there was nothing to make you glad, you proved that you deserved everything that has the power to make you glad. And that which we truly deserve must come to remain as our own.

Just be glad. Whether there is anything to be glad for or not, just be glad. It is the royal path to happiness.

It is the royal path to all that is worthy and beautiful in life. Above all things, possess gladness, and you will soon possess those things that produce gladness. Be your own sunbeam, and you will attract a million sunbeams. Be your own source of your own joy, and you will attract everything and everybody that can add to your joy. To him that hath shall be given. And he already hath who has found the riches of his own nature. To find those riches is the first step. All else must follow. All other things will be added. And to find those riches, use well every talent you possess. Then whatever comes, just be glad. For all things respond to the call of rejoicing; all things gather where life is a song.

Leave it to God

Leave it to God

When we place our lives and our affairs under the direction of Infinite Wisdom, everything will be taken care of perfectly. This we all can understand; and we know, as an inner conviction, that nothing could be more evident. Indeed, it could not be otherwise. It is something we know with a positive assurance. It is something we may depend upon absolutely. Our spiritual discernment declares it; and experience proves it unmistakably. It is the outstanding promise of the high teachings of the ages; and, we go far to do this marvelous thing, when we think and say, with the whole of heart and soul, that "we leave it to God."

There can be neither misstep nor error at such a time; and no ill can come nigh our dwelling. Infinite Wisdom can guide and protect to the utmost. The best will come to pass; and all things will work out in the most harmonious and most successful manner. Our problems will be solved, and we will accomplish what we have in view. We will find what we seek, and our desires will be realized. Our needs will be provided for, promptly and adequately; and whatever our activities and aspirations may be, the outcome will be all that we could possibly wish for. It must be so; for God is not limited in any way. God does not postpone His goodness.

When we place our lives and our affairs under the direction of Infinite Wisdom, everything will change for the better; troubles and ills will decrease, and then vanish completely; obstacles will be removed, and the way cleared for the achievements and the demonstrations that we have in mind. Adversity will be transformed, and that which was against us will be for us. The crooked will be made straight; and all our activities will be brought into adjustment with divine law. All of this and vastly more of like nature, we may expect when we leave it to God; when we place our lives and

Leave it to God

our affairs under the care and guidance of the Spirit. We all have sought ways and methods through which we might find freedom and peace, health and abundance, harmony and strength, light and understanding; ways and methods through which we might meet life in the best way, and realize the greatest measure of the good that life has to give. And, among the many ways and methods that have been found, there is one that excels tem all: leave it to God. All other methods have their service to perform, at the various steps and stages of our development; and they lead up to this greater method. We praise them all therefore; but as soon as we possibly can, we should turn to this one method that is always supreme; we should learn the secret of this remarkable statement: "leave it to God."

When we leave it to God, we are directed by a power that is absolutely good, and at always works for the good. We are opening our lives to the One who knows all things, and can do all things. Anything that is good and great and wonderful may be expected, therefore, at such a time. Surely, all our affairs will be taken care of, in the most perfect and most successful manner, when Higher Power comes into life, into thought, into consciousness. There will, indeed, be a great transformation when the Supreme takes charge; when Divine Wisdom becomes our guide and inspiration; when the Great Light shines through. The clouds will pass; illness and weakness will disappear; we shall lack no good thing; and life will become richer and fairer than we ever visioned before.

To leave it to God is a marvelous thing, when we do so in the right spirit, and with understanding: when we know what this remarkable statement actually means; and when we can see clearly what takes place as we turn our lives and our affairs over into the keeping of the Supreme. We do not leave it all with God in the usual sense of that term. We do not cast our burdens upon the Lord with the thought that now

Leave it to God

there is nothing for us to do. We do not step aside with the hope that "God will attend to this." No, we do not step aside; nor do we entertain the belief, for a moment, that there is nothing more for us to do. There will be more for us to do than ever before; and, instead of stepping aside, we will go deeper and deeper into the work, the power and the glory of it all. No it is not a matter of enlisting a higher power to do everything for us. That is not the idea. The true idea here infinitely greater than that.

When we leave it to God, we move towards God, and with all the purpose and eagerness we possess; withal the soul and devotion that we can awaken. We take our affairs to God, where they can be acted upon by divine wisdom and higher power. We take ourselves to God, where we may come under the guidance of the Spirit and the inspiration of the Almighty. We respond to the principle that God works with those who work with God; and that the Spirit enters the lives of those who enter the Life of the Spirit. "Come unto me, saith the Lord, and I will come unto thee."

When we say with inner purpose and conviction, that we will leave it to God, we actually go to God in our thought; and we place our lives and our affairs in the wisdom that knows all things and in the power that can do all things. We take our problems into that wisdom that can see through everything instantly, and give the perfect answer at once. We take our own lives into that Life and love that can transform every life completely; and that can enlarge, enrich and perfect every life even to the utmost degree.

To leave it to God, is to go to God, and to leave everything with Him; and especially to leave ourselves with Him. It is to go into that state of nearness to the Spirit where we can respond absolutely to the highest. And how wonderfully well everything must work out when we fully respond to the

Leave it to God

highest. All things will work together for good at such a time; and the greatest and best will come to pass — on all levels of life. We will find more, secure more and realize more, by far, than we possibly could through any personal or merely human method. Indeed, we will, both in experience and accomplishment, go beyond anything we ever hoped for or visioned before.

To leave it to God, is to go so far into the light of the Spirit that we may open our minds to that light. Then, our thoughts will be divinely created. We will think the good, the true, the high and the perfect, in clearness and purity; and, as we think, so we become in mind, character, consciousness and personality; so we become in our physical condition; so everything works out in our affairs. Our lives and our affairs, at such a time, will be directed and inspired by divine thinking; and the outcome must be the best conceivable.

When we leave it to God — which means going into the presence of God — we will be taken up into a larger and a brighter world; into a higher and a more perfect world. We will therefore, see more, know more, understand more, enjoy more and receive more. We will also achieve more, whatever our work may be, for we are working under the power and the wisdom of the Supreme.

And we will be so near to the light of the light of that wisdom, that we may see clearly where we should go, how we should act and what we should do. We will step into the right place; and we will do what is best for all concerned. The greatest good must come, whatever the situation may be; and everything will work out perfectly at the right time.

We can be positively assured that this is how it will be, and there need be no doubt, fear or anxiety over anything that may threaten to disturb or destroy. For, what are we

Leave it to God

actually doing when we leave it to God? We are placing ourselves in that position where the One who knows everything may direct our thoughts and activities; where the One who can do everything may work for us, and for the purpose we have in view. Anything, therefore, even the greatest and the most perfect conceivable, may be expected at such a time. Indeed, we should expect the utmost, in every way, as we go forth to use this marvelous method.

We can see clearly, as we examine this method, that it may be used upon every occasion that calls for added strength and wisdom; and in connection with every important event or circumstance that we may meet in life. The Spirit can add wisdom and power to it all. The light of the Spirit can clear it all. The love of the most High can bring harmony and peace. We may know, therefore, that everything will be taken care of when we leave it to God: and it will be taken care of in such a manner that greater joy and greater good will come to everyone. The Spirit does not bring the less of anything, but always the more. The Spirit does not bring pain or illness, loss or sorrow. The Spirit brings wholeness and life, freedom and power, harmony and abundance. It is not the will of God that anyone should suffer, or be deprived of anything that is good and desirable in life. "It is the will of the Father to give us the Kingdom." And the kingdom means the aggregation of every conceivable good in creation — and in limitless measure.

Such thoughts, and all similar thoughts, must lead invariably to the conclusion that we have here a method that is indispensable and invariably to the conclusion that we have here a method that is indispensable and invaluable. And that is true, whether we are in the midst of practical affairs, or interested in higher attainment. Many illustrations may be given as to how and where this method may be

Leave it to God

employed; and a few, among those that are especially helpful in our daily activities, may be mentioned in brief.

When you are undecided as to when a certain thing is to be done, what plan you are to accept, or what part you are to play, remember, there is One who knows. Do not be fearful lest you make a serious mistake. Do not "rack my brain" for the answer. Leave it to God. Ay so in deep sincerity, and in the feeling that you are doing this marvelous thing. Take those things up into the Light. You will soon know; or something will occur that will guide you perfectly in your decision.

If there is delay, refuse to be impatient. Know it is for the best. It must be so, for the Highest has taken charge. Or, if everything develops quickly, accept that as the way it all should go. Proceed calmly in the faith that the entire situation is in the hands of the wisdom that know.

When we meet what seems to be enmity or opposition, we will not become alarmed. We will not go out to battle, nor try to overpower this thing or the other. We will leave it to God. We will not be disheartened or discouraged when the world seems to be against us; when every friend seems to be gone; or, when adversity seems to have the upper hand. We will know that the Great Love can change all of this. We will open our lives to that Love. Then everything and everyone will be for us.

When there is something that others may wish you to do — something that you would rather not do, or that you think would be unwise refuse to be concerned or disturbed. Do not say that you hope the matter will be dismissed, or that you are going to object. Say, instead, that you will leave it to God. And, whether it be small matter, or something of vital significance, this wonderful step will clear it all. Something will happen that will change the situation to the greatest good for everyone. Or, you may suddenly feel the urge to do this thing — and be deeply grateful that you were given the privilege. And, if it be something monumental, or extremely difficult, you will be given the power and the understanding. We are released from the unwise when we go up to God; and we receive all necessary help for that which should be done.

When we meet losses or reverses, and when all doors seem to be closed against us, we will not fall down into gloom and despair. We will remember that God can open all doors for us — even those doors that open everywhere into infinity. We may regain our loss when we leave it to God. We may enter pastures green, and realize more than we ever visioned before. The doors of infinity open to realms that are vast, and to richness that is limitless. And, we all understand that the Spirit leads in that direction.

When we seem to have lost our way, and do not know where to turn; when situations are confusing, and darkness enfolds our world completely, we will into be dismayed nor fearful in the least. We will remember that God knows the way; and we may, even in the blackest of darkness, be led by the Spirit. There is a Light that is stronger than all the darkness in the universe. That Light can clear the way, and lead us directly into freedom and peace. It is, indeed, remarkable how soon darkness disappears, how soon the clouds pass, how soon confusions are stilled, how soon conditions adjust themselves and adversities change into blessings, when we can say, in perfect faith and sincerity of soul. Leave it to God."

When you are tempted to be disturbed, disappointed or fearful over someone; or, if someone near you seems to be in danger, do not become alarmed. Meet it all in calmness and faith, and leave it to God. The Spirit can guide and protect —

even to the utmost. The Spirit can lift and transform — even the one that seems farthest down. The Spirit can give life and strength and intelligence — even where these seem largely absent. The Spirit can heal and renew the body, quicken the mind, and set the soul on fire. We need never be concerned nor alarmed, therefore, over anyone at any time. We may expect everyone to be guided, protected and saved — and come forth in the most remarkable manner — when we leave it to God. But we must say, again and again, that we leave it to God; and actually feel, as we make this statement, that we are placing it all in the spirit of the Supreme.

We need not be anxious, fearful or concerned, about anyone or anything, when we leave it to God. And, indeed, how could we be fearful or anxious when we know that Infinite Wisdom and Goodness is in charge of our lives and affairs. We will, instead, develop a marvelous faith — a faith that comes from that supreme assurance that now all will be will; now, everything and everyone will be cared for and protected to the utmost. Surely, faith must grow and increase, to an amazing degree, when we realize that our lives are in the keeping of the One who knows everything and can do everything. And, to have such a faith is enormous gain. As our faith is, so shall it be. A great faith, therefore, can bring results beyond anything ever known before — even results that may seem to be the work of miracle power.

When you feel concerned over the life of someone who seems to be on the verge of passing on, declare, in high faith, that you leave it to God. The Spirit can heal and restore anyone at any time. That man will not pass on — when the Spirit takes charge. He will, instead, come forth into perfect health and full strength.

He will "take up his bed and walk." There is a general belief among many that God is eager to take away, to

Leave it to God

himself, those whom we hold dear. But, we must teach our minds, positively, that God does not take anyone or anything away from us. God does not deprive anyone of anything that has worth and reality. The only things that we lose, when we go to God, are our ills and illusions. Indeed, if we would be safe and secure, and retain our friends and possessions, the one perfect way is to leave it to God. The wrong will be taken away, but the good will remain — and be multiplied, again and again, without end.

When we have obligations to meet, and the means are not at hand, we will not be fearful for a moment. We will meet the situation in calmness and faith — in the full faith that every need will be met if we look to the Spirit; or, that we will be led by the Spirit to that very place where we may find what we seek. We will leave it to God. We will place it all under the direction of Infinite Wisdom. We will know that Infinite God can take care of everything — promptly and completely. We may rest assured in that sublime thought; for it will be so. There is enough and to spare of everything in the vast kingdom of the Great Good; and that kingdom is here and everywhere — closer to us all than life itself. We become conscious of it, and partake of its treasure, as we live a life of increasing nearness to God.

Here we should consider well the great truth that God is not limited in any way; neither in the capacity to give, nor in the desire to give. Indeed, it is the ceaseless desire of the Spirit to give in fullness to everyone, everywhere, every moment in eternity. God need not be urged nor implored. "Behold, I stand at the door and knock." The gifts of life are present — waiting to come forth and overwhelm us all with abundance. But we are to open the door; and this we accomplish through increasing nearness to God. And, it is most vital to note, that the more we look to God, and leave it all to God, the closer we draw, in thought and consciousness, towards the presence of the most High.

When the road seems hard, and you meet difficulties and obstacles of every nature, know that the Supreme is greater than all of that. Know that such things cannot remain, and are not true, where God reigns. The Spirit can make every pathway peaceful and pleasant. The Spirit can remove every difficulty, and make nought of every obstacle. We will leave it to God. That will change everything. And when your demonstrations are not made, and you do not succeed with your purpose, take it into the Wisdom that knows, and the Power that can. You will positively have your demonstration when Higher Power takes charge. You will accomplish what you have in view, however remarkable it may be. You will find that you see — even the mysteries of the kingdom and the deep things of God.

Herewith it is most important to note, that we actually unite our minds with greater wisdom and Higher Power when we use this method; and this is enormous gain whatever the purpose, the problem or the aspiration may be. We can accomplish more, see more and know more, by far, when we unite our minds with the wisdom and the power of the Spirit. We can be guided rightly, and inspired wonderfully, at such a time. It is inevitable, therefore, that every situation will be met, and everything taken care of, when we leave it to God.

When we have higher aspirations, and do not see our way to their realization; or, when we feel inadequate for this larger attainment, we will not wait, nor abandon our lofty vision. We will proceed in the faith that the most High can give us the wisdom and the power to realize anything. We may, in lifted consciousness, be taught of God. We may during moments supreme, be clothed with marvelous power. We may, as we draw very near to the Infinite, open our lives to the transforming power of Spirit; and all things will be changed. We may become channels through which the light, the perfection and the glory of the Presence may shine forth. Then it shall be on earth as it is in heaven; that is, it shall be in our own outer and personal life as it now is in the spiritual domain.

Our highest aspirations will be realized; for all things become possible when we leave it to God. We will use this same marvelous method when we are tempted to become concerned over the problems and the tribulations of the world. We will have no fear. We will change our fears into faith. We will say to ourselves and to everyone: "Let not your heart be troubled." We will know that the Supreme is greater than all else in creation — and works eternally for the highest good to everyone. We will go where that highest good is in action. We will open our vision and see the Presence of the Power — and "see the salvation of the Lord." We will, before that lofty vision, calm our thought and raise our consciousness. We will, thereby, be lifted up, and become a power and an inspiration wherever we go. And, when we are lifted, many will be lifted. When a few come out of the darkness, many will rise into the light. Thus we, who decide to leave it to God, and actually go to God to demonstrate this truth, will lead the way to peace and order everywhere. We will prove, that great is the power, the influence and the inspiration of those who abandon their fears, and draw nigh unto God.

When we say that we leave it to God, we are not making that statement in a negative, dependent or resigned attitude. It will be the very reverse; for, we are entering a state that will mean greater strength for mind and body, greater spiritual power and understanding. It could not be otherwise, for we are drawing nearer to the Supreme; we are taking a much higher position in thought and consciousness; "we are

Leave it to God

raised up;" and so, we receive more, become more and realize more than ever before. There is no weak, dependent or resigned feeling in such lofty and powerful consciousness. To the contrary, we feel and know that we are working with God; and, therefore, we can go forth and achieve the impossible.

When we make this great statement, we make it with the strength and the aspiration of the spirit; with the whole of heart and soul — lifted into the Presence; with a deep feeling that we are actually entering the Presence; and, with a deep knowing that this amazing thing is true. We do not make this statement in the belief that there is nothing now for us to do; but, with understanding that now we may do more than ever before; that now we may work in and with the One that is almighty. And, furthermore, we make this statement in the understanding that now we may use, to the full, all the gifts and the powers that we have received from the Great Source.

We have, according to modern discovery, marvelous powers — even miracle powers — in the depths of mind and soul; and they are there to be used. We can use them, however, only as we deepen our thought, raise our consciousness, and go farther into the spirit; or, as we go to God, and place our lives in the Life of the Supreme. There is much that we may do, therefore, considering the gifts and the powers that we have to work with; and, we should aim to do our utmost in every way. But the question is, if we are to live and work out here in the smallness of the personal, or take our lives, our affairs, our activities and aspirations into the Great Wisdom and the Limitless Power. Surely, there can be only one answer.

We will take our gifts, our talents and our powers into the Spirit. Vastly more will be accomplished and realized through such a course. Everything becomes possible as we

Leave it to God

move in that direction, step by step, as we make it the rule of life to leave everything to God — with God.

It is the highest way and the greatest way, whatever the need, the problem or the situation may be; and its effectiveness becomes more and more apparent as we use this method at every step of the way. Its possibilities are innumerable and unlimited; and we discern the principle when we note what can, and what cannot take place, where the Spirit is at work. We can see at once that there can be no evil or trouble, pain or loss, hurt or harm, where the Spirit is at work. There can be no fear or failure, darkness or confusion, adversity or opposition, in that place. There will, instead, be harmony and peace, wholeness and strength, wisdom and power, victory and abundance, understanding and love. All is well, in every way, and to the greatest conceivable degree, where the Spirit is at work. And, when we leave it to God, we take our lives and our affairs into that place where the Spirit is at work.

We can see, with absolute clearness, that the best, the most desirable and the most perfect must come to pass when Higher Power takes charge; when Divine Wisdom is the guiding light; and when the Great Love rules the way. It must be so. These laws are exact; and these things are true, whether it be in simple matters or in monumental situations. Everything works out in the right way, and in the most wonderful way, when we leave it to God. And when we go far enough, with this method and principle, we meet miracle power — where anything can be met, achieved, demonstrated and transformed.

There is never any limit to what the wisdom and the power of the most High can do — and seeks to do. We may feel weak, small or incapacitated out here; but the Spirit within can do all things. God lives and works in us all, and

Leave it to God

God can. Our circumstances, conditions and obstacles may seem to be too much for our present strength; but God can. We need not think, therefore, that this day will be lost, or that our greater plans will have to be abandoned. We may leave it all to God — in the full assurance that everything will be accomplished. And, also, as we do take our lives and our affairs into the Spirit, we will be clothed with new strength. We will arise and go forth in victory and triumph.

When we say that we leave it to God, it is supremely important that we have, at the time, the greatest and the highest thought of God conceivable. The more perfect and more brilliant our vision of God, at such a time, the greater will the realization — whatever our purpose or prayer may be. We should think of God as absolutely good: doing the good and creating the good everywhere every moment. We should think of God as manifesting the good, every moment, in every place throughout the whole of creation. We should think of the goodness of God as limitless and overwhelming; and we should think of the wisdom, the power and the love of God in the most marvelous fashion. We should think of God as a glorified Presence — closer to us all than life itself. And we should know that, as we come near enough, in thought, to this Presence, we will be healed instantly; our ills and troubles will disappear completely; our losses will be regained; and we will enter into realizations, of the great and the good, beyond anything ever known before.

It is such thoughts about God — and the greatest and most inspiring thoughts about the Supreme that we can possibly vision and create — that we should entertain when we make this statement; when we say we will leave it to God. For the truth is, that the greater our thought of God at such a time, the more faith we will have; the higher our consciousness will rise, and the nearer we will draw towards the One Source. Our thoughts, therefore, should take wings

Leave it to God

at such a time, so that we might see vastly more of Supreme Goodness and Love; so that we might look farther into the Soul of Infinity, and magnify the Lord more and more — even to the utmost. And so, we shall prove that there is no limit to what may be done — and what we may receive, attain, discern, and understand — when we leave it to God.

The blessings that come, as we always leave it to God, are numerous and remarkable; but the greatest of them all is this: we will think more about God, and we will think far more of God. We will look more to God for everything, and we will live closer to God. We will become conscious, in increasing measure, of the Supreme Presence; and this is not only great gain, but enormous gain. For, indeed, in such a consciousness, anything that is good and great can happen.

Truly, can we imagine anything amazing, stupendous or miraculous that could not happen when we are actually conscious of the Supreme Presence.

When we look more to God, and think more about the Infinite, we will enlarge and perfect our vision — our vision of the One who is Goodness and Life and Love. Then, we are on a path where something astounding will come to pass. The way we vision, that is how we will think; and, as our thoughts are, so we become — so everything works out in our lives and in our experience. Better thoughts will produce the better — on all levels of life. And, when we develop our vision of God so far that we think only the good. This will mean that we think only the good; and according to the law, that like thoughts produce like effects, only the good will happen to us. What an amazing prospect. But it is not, necessarily, a faraway event. The truth is, that everyone who looks more to God, and goes more to God, is on the way to the realization of that very experience.

Leave it to God

When we draw nearer to the Most High, the possibilities of living, knowing and attaining become remarkable. For, imagine, drawing nearer to the One who knows all things, and who has the power to do all things; drawing nearer to the One who is perfection — glorified perfection; drawing nearer to the One who can answer every prayer instantly — no matter how astounding or colossal the request may be; drawing nearer to the One who does answer the prayers of everyone who comes close enough to the presence of His goodness and love.

We conclude, therefore, that we have here a method that can do amazing things. Its powers and possibilities are, indeed, without limit or end — both in daily living and in higher attainments. It is a method that can help us in every way, every hour, in our personal problems and activities, and at the same time, take us back to the Source. And we all know that anything, that is good and great, can happen, or come to us, on that ascending pathway. It is a method that can bring us peace, wholeness, freedom and light, and, at the same time, lead us farther into the kingdom of Spirit. It is a method that can give us guidance and inspiration, for every desire and need, and also lift our minds towards the Supreme. It is a method that will encourage and teach our thoughts to keep the eye single upon the most High; and such thinking will, eventually, lead us into oneness with God — the deepest desire and the highest aspiration of the soul. It is a method through which anything can be realized — from the simplest to the greatest conceivable; and this we all can understand; fro we are using something that moves towards Infinity. And so, whatever we may meet, seek, or purpose in life, it is the utmost of wisdom to think and say: "We leave it to God."

On the Heights

On the Heights

Walking With God.

My God, my Father, I AM Thine;
Thy heavenly riches all are mine;
Thy spirit reigns within my heart,
From Thee my soul cannot depart.

Wher'er I go, I walk with Thee,
Upon my path, Thou leadest me;
In all my ways Thou art my guide.
For Thou art ever at my side.

I live in Thee, and think Thy thought,
In every deed Thy power is sought,
I consecrate my life to Thee,
And all is ever well with me.

On The Heights

WHEN we transcend the world of things and begin to live on the borderland of the splendor and immensity of the cosmic world, we discover that the vision of the soul was true. Those lofty realms that we have dreamed of so often and so long are dreams no more; we find those realms to be real, the prophetic visions of our sublime moments are fulfilled, and our joy is great beyond measure.

The soul no longer dwells in the limitations of personal form, but is awakened to the glory and magnificence of its own divine existence.

The mind is illumined by the light of the great eternal sun, and the body becomes the consecrated temple of the spirit. The ills of life take flight, the imperfect passes away, and we find ourselves in a new heaven and a new earth.

Beautiful beyond description is the new life we have now begun to live; every moment is an eternity of bliss, and to live — simply to live — that is sufficient. We can ask for nothing more; we have received everything that the heart can wish for; we are in that higher world where every prayer is answered, where every desire is granted, where every need is abundantly supplied; we are ON THE HEIGHTS, where God is closer than breathing, nearer than hands and feet.

It is the world beautiful, the world into which the Christ ascended when his face did shine as the sun and his garment became white as the light. "And where I AM there ye shall be also." The gates are ajar; we may enter today and dwell therein while still in personal form. It is the sublime world of the life eternal, and when we enter that life, it is then we begin to live.

On the Heights

To enter this beautiful world is to find the joy everlasting, the peace that passeth understanding, the harmony that is endless symphonies divine; and as the soul is touched by these symphonies of heaven, we mount upon the wings of the spirit and soar to empyrean heights.

The veil of mystery is taken away, we meet Him face to face, and the great secret is revealed. "Eye hath not seen, nor ear heard, neither hath it entered into the heart of man what God has prepared for them that love Him;" but now we are ON THE HEIGHTS, far beyond the life of mere man, and we have seen what eternity has in store. The supreme significance of life is revealed, and when we think that this is life — our own eternal life — our hearts are filled with unbounded thanksgiving.

Henceforth we have something to live for; existence itself has become an endless inspiration; everything is animated with a great divine purpose; nothing is in vain; all is beautiful and all is good. We have entered into the realization of the great truth that "God's in his heaven, all's right with the world," and again our hearts are filled with unbounded thanksgiving.

The world into which we have ascended is God's own world; it is the real world, the true world, the world of the spirit where all things are created in the likeness of God. Therefore, in that world, all is right and all is well. It is the world of spiritual existence, where the eye is too pure to see anything but that which is good, where the mind is too luminous to know anything but that which is truth, where the body is too wholesome to feel anything but that which is health and purity. It is the world of complete emancipation the great inheritance that eternity holds in store for man.

On the Heights

But this inheritance is not simply for the eternities that are to be; it is for all eternities — the eternity that now is and the eternities that are to be. It is the kingdom of heaven that is now at hand, the kingdom that shall evermore be at hand, and we may enter its many mansions when we begin to live ON THE HEIGHTS.

On the Heights

WHEN we ascend to the heights and begin to live in the luminous splendor of the cosmic, our spiritual vision is opened to the great truth that "there is another and a better world." This better world is the home of the soul, the kingdom of the spirit, the celestial city on high.

It is not a faraway place but a realm of the spirit here and now. Its jasper walls, its golden streets and its crystal spires — all may be found on the shining shores of the great within.

That better world is not simply for some future state of being; it is the home of the soul today, and when the soul is awakened to the splendor and beauty of its own sublime existence, we shall find that this spiritual kingdom is our home now.

Though we may manifest ourselves in the world of things, we are living in the world of the spirit, and to know that we are living in the spirit — that indeed is life.

To live ON THE HEIGHTS is to be in harmony with all the world.

In this transcendent realm we are in spiritual touch with the divine side of every living creature. We see all things as they are in the true reality of being, and in the light of this reality all is beautiful and all is well. There are no imperfections ON THE HEIGHTS; nothing to censure, nothing to condemn; love is the law of life, and to love all things at all times is a joy that cannot be measured.

In this higher world, to live is to love, and since life is boundless, love is boundless; therefore to love is to love everybody. The love that is boundless goes to all things, encircles all things and loves all things. We feel its exquisite tenderness the very moment we are on the verge of the heights, and with the prophets of other days, we declare from the very depth of the heart, it is good to be here. We are treading upon holy ground and we know that the kingdom is at hand.

When we enter the kingdom we learn the beautiful secret of love; we then understand those loving words of the Christ, "Come unto me and I will give you rest;" for the soul abides forever in the arms of Infinite Love, and this is the rest that is in store. Well may the prophet proclaim in language divine, "There is another and a better world."

This better world is the secret places of the Most High; that inner state of divine being where we enter into oneness with the Infinite, and meet Him face to face. It is the true house of prayer, the temple of God, the sacred tabernacle of the soul. To enter therein is to walk with God — to feel that He protects us and keeps us, and to know that He is with us always, even unto the end of the world.

To dwell in the secret places of the Most High is to live under the guidance of the Almighty; therefore no ill can befall us; we cannot go wrong; we are led by the spirit and the spirit invariably leads towards the heights. What we may desire to know we shall be given the wisdom to know; what we may desire to do we shall be given the power to do, because God is with us, and with God all things are possible.

To be led by the spirit is to be led into greater and greater good always; the spirit leads away from the ills of life into the greater joys of life; the ways of the spirit are ways of pleasantness and all her paths are peace; and the ways of the spirit shall be our ways when we begin to live ON THE HEIGHTS.

On the Heights

THE supreme goal of human life is cosmic consciousness; to live in the cosmic world — the sublime world of the spirit — this is the dearest desire of every awakened soul. It is in cosmic consciousness that the fullness of life, and the divine sweetness of life is realized; and it is in the cosmic that the soul finds the great climax of every joy in the world.

It is cosmic consciousness that reveals everything that is lofty and beautiful, everything that is pure and perfect, everything that is created in the likeness of the Most High. It is in the cosmic that our yoke becomes easy and our burden light; it is in the cosmic that we find the love that abideth forever, the power that cannot be measured, the truth that gives freedom to body, mind and soul, the wisdom that is luminous as the light of the eternal sun; and we shall enter the splendor of the cosmic when we begin to live ON THE HEIGHTS.

When we enter the cosmic we find the real sweetness of existence; the ills and imperfections of life have vanished; the mind can know no evil, the body can feel no pain. We are far beyond the clouds of doubt and fear, because we are in that world where everything is true and everything is good. We are under the clear sky of Infinite Light, on the verge of the great beyond, on the borderland of the limitless, on the shores of the great eternal sea; we have found the heaven of perfect bliss, and every moment is an eternity of ecstasy divine.

When we have been within the pearly gates of the cosmic world, even but for a moment, life is not the same anymore; life is no longer mere existence but a sacred something that we hold too precious to even mention in spoken words. It is beyond words, and beyond thought, too great, too marvelous, too wondrously beautiful for mind to fathom or tongue describe. The soul alone can know such a life, and after we have tasted the fruits of the cosmic, the meat that we know not of, nothing less than such a life can satisfy.

The personal man may feel contented to exist in the valley of mere things, but not so with the awakened soul. The soul that is awakened must live on the mountain tops of the spirit; the joy of the soul is ON THE HEIGHTS, and we give the soul its greatest ecstasy when we mount upon the wings of spirit and soar to empyrean heights.

On the Heights

TO LIVE ON THE HEIGHTS is to enter into the realization and the conscious possession of the best that life can give, not only on the spiritual plane, but on all planes; and the higher we ascend towards the greater heights the more we shall receive of everything that is rich and beautiful in human existence made divine.

The life sublime is therefore the life of the greatest good to the entire being of man — body, mind and soul.

It means health, wholeness and purity for the body, wisdom, power and illumination for the mind, and the glories of the cosmic realm for the soul.

When we live ON THE HEIGHTS the body is filled with the wholeness of the spirit, the mind is inspired with power from on high, while the soul is basking eternally in the sunshine of Infinite Love. Every impulse of life is music from enchanted realms, and every thought is an angel, radiant with loveliness and joy. And this is life — the most beautiful gift of God.

To ascend to the heights is to reach that coveted goal where the ideal is made real, where every dream comes true and where every vision of the soul is transformed into that tangible something we have wished for so long. The supreme heights do not simply present us with the mental picture of that which we long to receive; when we reach the heights we receive the substance of things hoped for and the evidence of things not seen. We receive upon earth what we hoped to find in heaven.

In the cosmic world the ideal is real and the real is ideal. Therefore, to ascend to the heights is to find that our ideals are not mere pictures, but realities — substantial things of a higher order — the product of workmanship divine. And these sublime realities are so constituted that they can be made tangible parts of daily personal life. This is the Word becoming flesh, the life of the soul unfolded into the beauty and the charm of exalted personal expression.

To heal the body and emancipate the mind, the secret is to ascend to the heights. In those lofty realms no ill can come to man, neither can the turmoil of the world affect him anymore. Whatever his outer conditions may be, he remains untouched, unmoved and undisturbed. He is living in that beautiful calm "where dwells the soul serene," and all is silent and still. And out of that silence comes the symphony of life, the tender tones of heaven-born music taking him away to those enchanted realms where life itself is an endless song.

To feel the touch of the silence of the soul is to fully understand those inspired words, "Let not your heart be troubled"; there is a place prepared for us where troubles can never enter, where pains are forever barred. This sacred place is the heaven within, and it is the will of the Most High that we should enter now while still in personal form.

When we live ON THE HEIGHTS we realize that we live and move and have our being in a great divine sea. We feel that we are fully surrounded by the essence of pure spirit, and we can touch God everywhere. We are in a world that is luminous with spiritual light, and we can see clearly the meaning of everything. Nothing is mysterious anymore; our minds are full of light; and we know the truth, and this truth has made us free.

We also realize that we are in a world of higher power, and we can feel that power working with us whenever we wish it so to be. This power is limitless, and here we find the secret why those who live ON THE HEIGHTS can never fail.

On the Heights

They are carried on and on to victory whatever conditions may be. Obstacles that seem insurmountable vanish in a night, enemies are changed into the most worthy of friends, and on the very eve when all seems lost, the elements are transformed, the tide turns, fate is conquered, and the battle is won.

There is nothing to fear when we live ON THE HEIGHTS, because we may call upon the power of the Supreme, and this power cannot fail.

It will take us safely through the most difficult and the most adverse of conditions, and transform the saddest states of existence into a world of comfort and joy.

When we are ON THE HEIGHTS we can feel this power; we can feel that it is moving, changing and transforming everything, causing all things to go with us to the goal we have in view. And though it may seem to be a power not our own, nevertheless, it is our own, because all that the Father hath is mine.

The secret of all great and lofty souls is found in this higher power; they have ascended to the heights, they are living on the mountain tops of the spirit, and God is with them. They have found that supreme world where my Father worketh and I work, and whatever they may undertake to do the same shall be done. Nothing can stand in their way; what works against them is mysteriously changed, and proceeds with heart and soul to work for them. Their plans for greater things are worked out in a wonderful manner; their lofty aims are realized and their dearest desires fulfilled. Their secret is simple; they are living ON THE HEIGHTS, and the limitless power of the Infinite is with them.

On the Heights

WHEN we live ON THE HEIGHTS we wait eternally upon the Lord, and they that wait upon the Lord shall renew their strength. Neither weariness nor weakness are possible because in the cosmic world we are one with God and to be one with God is to be filled, through and through, with the limitless power of God.

To wait upon the Lord is to give ourselves completely to the Most High; it is to live for the Infinite and when we live for the Infinite, the Infinite will live in us. The power of the Almighty will be given as freely as we can possibly receive, and therefore our strength will ever be renewed.

The limitations of the person will pass away, and whatever we may be called upon to do, we shall receive strength and power in abundance from above. All things will become possible because God is with us, and God is with us because we are with God.

When we choose to go with God, then He will go with us, and we always choose to go with Him when we ascend to the heights. To live in the realms of the life sublime is to live as God lives, and to live as God lives is to be one with God — to live and move and have our being in Him — to feel that His presence is closer than breathing, nearer than hands and feet.

To live ON THE HEIGHTS is to enter into that divine relationship where we know that My Father and I are one. It is in this state that we behold the face of the Infinite, where we awaken to the great truth that His countenance is beautiful — altogether lovely — the fairest of ten thousand to the soul.

And we are created in His image and likeness, heirs to His Kingdom, destined to live an eternity with Him —

On the Heights

destined to manifest the same loveliness, the same perfection, the same divinity, the same supreme joy. Beautiful thought, thought of sweetness and peace! The mere thinking of this thought will inspire the soul to feel the divinity of its own exalted existence and ascend to those heights where the light of His glory is shining forever.

When those gentle moments creep o'er us — those moments that awaken the tender sweetness of life, we long to be with God, we long to feel His presence, and nothing else can satisfy; the soul is calling for its own, waiting and yearning to be taken in the arms of Infinite Love; and those moments are sacred indeed. The soul is awakened; it is on the verge of another and a better world; we are upon holy ground and should lift our hearts in worship as we never worshiped before; we are about to be born again, to be born of the spirit, to be taken in the arms of love to His secret places on high.

Whenever the soul begins to yearn for the Infinite, the divinity within us is awakened, and we are ready to ascend to the heights, we are ready for a better world, and it is our privilege to enter that better world, even now, while still in personal form. The joys of heaven are for the present — the endless present, and the soul that lives ON THE HEIGHTS may inherit those joys today.

The secret path that leads to the heights may be found in the stillness of the soul. To meet the Infinite we must enter the silent within, and when we enter into His presence we are lifted at once to the heights. To be with Hun is to be ON THE HEIGHTS, and the beautiful within is the gates ajar to His Kingdom.

The sacred stillness of the beautiful within no tongue can ever describe; it is one of those secret places of which we are not permitted to speak, because it is beyond the power of speech. To know the within we must enter the within, and faith is the open door — the faith that is born of the spirit — the faith we feel when we are touched by the spirit.

The true spiritual faith knows; it knows because it is animated by the spirit, inspired by the spirit, illumined by the spirit; it knows the way, it knows the truth, it knows the life; therefore if we follow this faith we shall find what we seek; we shall enter the beautiful within and ascend to the glories of the spiritual heights.

To follow the ascending light of the true spiritual faith is to keep the eye single upon the great eternal light, and so long as we see that light and that light alone we shall pass upward and onward eternally towards the greatest heights of God's transcendent worlds. We shall turn neither to the left nor to the right, because our minds will be filled with the one light, and that light alone will guide us.

Thus we shall follow the straight and narrow path — the path that leads into life — the limitless life of the beautiful cosmic world.

To enter into the realization of that life is to live from above, to have eternal being in the lofty realms of the spirit, to be safely fixed on high; and to be fixed on high is the secret of that unbounded spiritual strength that gives the ascended soul its great invincible power. The soul that has gained this power has entered into possession of supreme spiritual mastery; such a soul may truthfully and eternally declare, "None of these things move me anymore. God is my strength and my power, and His Will alone shall remain."

On the Heights

THERE is nothing in the world that will not change, and change most beautifully when we begin to live ON THE HEIGHTS. That which is not good disappears completely, while that which is good becomes infinitely better. And the secret of this change is found in the realization of one of the most inspiring truths that the human mind can ever know.

When we ascend to the heights we meet the smile of God, and "how soon a smile of God can change the world." The elements of life are illumined with the radiance of His glory, and the tenderness of His loving smile inspires everything to be good, beautiful and kind. We are transported, body, mind and soul, into a new world, and how good it is to be there.

We can see the smile of God in everything; all things become mirrors, reflecting the joyousness and the sweetness of the smile from on high. Darkness changes into light, pain changes into pleasure, tribulation changes into peace, adversity changes into love, and life becomes an endless song. Wherever we go we radiate the smile of God, and all things reciprocate by smiling in return.

A great change has come over us, and everybody can see it. We are no longer mere humans, nor do we dwell in the valley anymore; we are living ON THE HEIGHTS and we belong to a higher, finer world. There is something in our nature, our countenance and our speech that inspires others to be happy; we bring sunshine wherever we go, and to be with us is a joy that cannot be measured.

To serve us in every conceivable manner is counted a rare privilege by everybody; we are giving so much to the world, and the world gains pleasure from giving us much in return. Nothing is too good for us, we are everywhere in demand and a royal welcome is everywhere in store. Our

On the Heights

friends are as legions and the thoughts of love that we daily receive are as numberless as the sands of the shore.

We have found the great secret; we have been ON THE HEIGHTS; we have seen the smile of God, and how soon that smile has changed our world. Where we saw neither hope nor opportunity we can now see both in abundance. We have more opportunities than we can take advantage of and our hopes are becoming realizations, richer by far than we ever expected. We are living a charmed life and everything we touch turns to happiness.

The world about us everywhere reflects the glory of our own joy; we can see so clearly the good and the beautiful in everything, and all things seem to make a special effort to present to us their most beautiful side only. Even the clouds turn about so we may see nothing but the silver lining, and pain cries aloud declaring it only means to be pleasure whenever we appear on the scene.

The secret of it all is simply this, we carry with us the smile of God, and how soon that smile can change the world. When we see that smile we learn how we are made for happiness, because God is supreme happiness, and we are created in His image and likeness. So great is the joy of the Infinite that to simply touch the hem of His garment is to feel a million thrills of sublime ecstasy.

On the Heights

TO LOVE everybody with the dearest, the purest and the highest love of the soul becomes a part of life itself when we live in the smile of God. This smile inspires real, heartfelt love for everything because it comes from Him who is love. All things were created in the spirit of love and by the power of love, therefore to love everything becomes one of the exquisite delights of the soul when we live in Him whose very life is love.

The smile of God is the smile of gentleness, tenderness and kindness; and when we carry this smile with us, we shall always be kind. Every thought we think will be a benediction, every word we speak will give peace and harmony to life, and everything we do will add to the comfort and happiness of man. To give our very best to the world will be our dearest desire, and our gifts will be precious indeed, because whatever we give, we give also the smile of God.

The more we smile with the smile of God, and the more we live and give in the spirit of this smile, the more abundantly will life be enriched with the treasures of sublime existence.

We gain happiness from every source in the world — the visible world and the cosmic world, because the smile of God not only is happiness but it awakens everything that can produce happiness.

When we live in that smile every movement is a pleasure, every thought is a dancing sunbeam of joy, and every impulse is a revelation of some fair enchanted realm. It is then that work becomes play because all our duties are set to the music of the spheres. The elements of life glide merrily and merrily on as if charmed by the magic touch of some strange enraptured power. And it is true; all things within us and about us are charmed; we are living in a charmed world — charmed with the smile of God.

The forces of adversity, with all their displeasing conditions, can enter our world no more; we are living ON THE HEIGHTS in the smile of God, and where God is smiling, there we shall find neither sorrow nor trouble nor pain. When we ascend to the heights we find healing for the body, emancipation for the mind and inspiration for the soul. We are in God's own beautiful world, and how good it is to be there.

Whatever our conditions may be in personal life, there are better things in store. When things are wrong we simply ascend to the heights and all is well again. ON THE HEIGHTS we meet the smile of God, and how soon that smile can change the world. That which is imperfect passes away as darkness before the glory of the rising sun, and the real beauty of life is revealed in all its loveliness divine.

When we ascend to the heights we find that the richness and splendor of life is not simply beautiful in the highest terms of sense, but that it is gorgeous — indescribably gorgeous, and that the sublimity of its grandeur far transcends our most exalted dreams of the celestial city on high.

"Eye hath not seen nor ear heard, neither hath it entered into the heart of man what God has prepared for them that love Him." The understanding of the personal man cannot discern these things, but the awakened soul ascends to the heights, and beholds what sublime existence has in store.

And it is then that the soul learns to know that God is love, that His goodness abideth forever, and that His kindness is as limitless as the Infinite sea. Everything is

On the Heights

given to man. Nothing is withheld. All that the Father hath is mine. It is His will and His good pleasure to give us the Kingdom, but to receive the Kingdom we must go to Him. We must go and live in God's world, and God's world is ON THE HEIGHTS.

> In the silence of the spirit,
> In the higher realms above,
> In the deeper life within me,
> In the world of perfect love,
> I have found my Father's kingdom
> And his righteousness divine;
> I have sought and found my heaven,
> And all else is ever mine.
> From this higher life within me,
> I shall nevermore depart,
> Living ever in the spirit,
> Seeking Truth with all my heart;
> Drawing nearer, ever nearer.
> To the Source of life sublime.
> Ever rising higher, higher.
> Through the endlessness of time.

On the Heights

Steps To The Heights

WHEN we proceed to ascend to the mountain tops of the spirit, we find a number of steps leading to those sublime heights, and if we follow those steps as they appear in succession upon the rising pathway of life, we shall surely reach our lofty goal. But we must observe that the steps are many, that they are all necessary parts of the path, and that each step must be taken as it appears before us whether it appears in the same manner today as yesterday, or not. All of those steps are met many times on the upward path; sometimes they appear in one order, sometimes in another, because there must be no monotony in the ascending life, and all the elements of the soul must be unfolded in actual expression.

1. Give your best to the world, and give in greater and greater abundance, regardless of what the world may give to you. This giving will awaken the soul, because everything that is to be given must come from the soul, and the more the soul is called upon to come forth with its precious treasures, the more will the soul live in the unfoldment of the richness of its divine life. The soul that gives much becomes much; it gives expression to much, and through this expression unfolds every element of divine being. The beauty of the spiritual life comes forth, the soul is awakened, and it is only the awakened soul that can ascend to the heights.

But this giving must come from the heart; it must be the giving of love, for love gives because it loves to give, and for no other reason whatever.

2. Live in the world of the good, the true and the beautiful, and think on these things. Whatever is lovely, beautiful, perfect, lofty and sublime, let the mind dwell with these things, and let the mind choose such alone for its

On the Heights

ceaseless companions. The mind becomes like its constant companions, and it is only the mind that is true and good and beautiful that can ascend to the heights. The mind that would ascend to the heights must "think beautiful thoughts and send them adrift on eternity's boundless sea", and must surround itself completely with a mighty host of angels — good thoughts, created in the image and likeness of Infinite thought. The ascending soul thinks God's thoughts after Him, and it is upon the wings of such thoughts that the soul is carried to the shining glory of the cosmic realm.

3. Know that you are a spiritual being, and that you live and move and have your being in an infinite sea of pure celestial spirit. Know that you are surrounded, here and now, by the radiant elements of the cosmic world, and in that sublime realization, live, think and act eternally. To give constant recognition to the spirit in which you live is to place the elements of your life in closer and closer touch with the spirit. Thus your body, mind and soul will be spiritualized more and more, the material elements of your being will be removed from your senses and your visions, and your eyes will be opened to the splendor of "another and a better world."

4. Live in the constant recognition of the great truth that God is with you, that He is nearer than your very life, because He is the very Life of your life. Keep this thought before the mind always and draw so near to His nearness that you can feel the glory of His divine presence. This will awaken your own spiritual nature which means that you will begin to live with God and walk with God; and those who are walking with God are on the heights because God is always on the heights.

5. Keep the eye single upon the light of the great eternal sun, and open your mind to the endless influx of that light.

Thus you become full of the light, you will actually live in a sea of light, and to live in the light is to be on the heights. When the mind is illumined with light from above, all the elements of mind and soul will turn towards that light as the flower turns her smiling face towards the light of the sun; and when the soul turns towards the Infinite light, it will begin to ascend, drawing nearer and nearer to that light. In like manner, all the elements of human life will begin to look up, and that which is looking up will rise. Body, mind and soul will begin to ascend, and, in harmony, will shortly reach the lofty goal.

6. Live in the spiritual understanding of the truth. Open the mind to the truth as it is in all things, and know that every creature in the universe manifests truth in its own individual measure. Recognize the truth as the source of all orderly expression, and live perpetually in that consciousness that discerns the reality of absolute truth — the truth as it is in the Mind of God. Thus will your own mind find its true state of being, its true relation to God, to man, to all that is; the mind will be true to itself, it will be truth in itself, it will know that it is, within the reality of itself, the divine perfection of truth. This truth will make the mind free, and when the mind is free the soul ascends to the heights. To know the truth is to live on the heights where all things are created in the beautiful likeness of the Infinite.

7. Dwell eternally in the highest spiritual touch with the divinity that is in every living creature. Live only with the divine, think only of the divine, look only for the divine, and know that the divine is everywhere.

On the heights everything is divinity in expression, and only those can ascend to the heights that recognize the divine that lives in every form of expression. To consciously recognize the divine in all things, and live in spiritual touch with the divine everywhere, the mind must live in that attitude where boundless love is wedded to that realization that knows the spiritual nature of all things.

Think of all things as they are in the perfection of divine spirit, and in that thought love all things with the infinite tenderness of boundless love.

8. Merge yourself with the universal. Come out from the cramped world of limitation and enter the freedom of the limitless. There are no limitations on the heights; we must therefore eliminate every thought of limitation before we can ascend to the heights. The mountain tops of the spirit are in the sublime world of the boundless, where the soul is free to stretch forth its wings and soar wherever it will. There is nothing in the way; everything is free to be all that it is, and in being all, it unfolds the universal, the limitless, the endless, thus living what it is — the likeness of God.

9. Live by that faith that is ever on the verge of the great beyond — the infinite sea of unbounded life; the faith that knows that the unseen is real, that the seeming void is solid rock, that the great beyond is a more marvelous universe inseparably united with that which seems real now.

This faith knows that all is real, that God is everywhere, that the soul may press on into the vastness of limitless worlds and still be ever in the presence of the Most High. This faith removes the veil that seems to separate the world of sense from the universal sea of spirit; it reveals to the mind the great truth that all worlds, visible and invisible, are one world, and in this one world may be found the many mansions of the soul. This faith takes the soul out of the material into the spiritual and when the soul awakens to the spiritual it begins to ascend to the heights.

10. Dwell constantly in a high spiritual touch with the master minds of the ages. Feel that you are one with these in the spirit and that by virtue of that oneness, the secret of their sublime existence is also being revealed to you. Nourish the mind constantly with the inspired thoughts of these great souls, thus preparing the mind to realize and express in real life, the same oneness that already exists in spirit. Live, in spirit, with the Christ, and the true spiritual followers of the Christ, in whatever times or places these may be found.

Let these be the constant companions of the soul, for they constitute the great white throng that is living on the heights. Whether they be in the form or not, if they are in the spirit they are on the heights, and to live in spiritual touch with such exalted souls is to ascend to the heights.

11. Pray without ceasing, and pray with all the power of heart and soul, that you may ascend into God's own beautiful world. Ceaselessly desire the highest, and inspire every thought with the soul of this desire.

The action of every desire, whether of the body, mind or soul, should be animated with a strong ascending life. The whole of life should be made a prayer — a beautiful prayer of faith — a prayer for the spiritual life on high. And whatsoever we desire, pray for, or ask for, we should ask it in the name of the Christ; not simply in the verbal expression of that name, but in the spiritual understanding of that name. To enter the spiritual understanding of the name of the Christ when we pray is to enter into that spiritual world where everything that we may pray for is already at hand for us to receive. Whatsoever ye pray or ask for, believe that ye have received it and ye shall have it. It has already been given; it is already at hand in the kingdom waiting for us to come and take possession; and I AM the door; we may enter the kingdom and receive our own providing we enter in the name of the Christ, in the pure spiritual conception of the divine significance of that name.

12. Thy will be done. To place the whole of life in the power of Infinite Will, is to go with this will, and the Will of God always wills to go to the highest. The Infinite Will is ever ascending, therefore when we choose to accept this Will as our will, we shall also ascend. When we will to do what God wills, we shall go and live in His own beautiful world, because that is His Will. It is His Will that all should enter His Kingdom now, and His Kingdom is ON THE HEIGHTS.

> My life is filled with wisdom,
> With power and with love;
> The light of truth is shining
> With splendor from above.
> My path is strewn with roses,
> My sky is bright and clear
> My heart is filled with virtue,
> And boundless good is near.
>
> My life is filled with glory.
> With happiness and peace;
> I'm free from pain and darkness,
> From sorrow and disease.
> I live the life of spirit.
> The life of love divine;
> The sweetness of existence
> Is now forever mine.

On the Heights

The Soul's Prayer

Infinite Father, Eternal Spirit, Omnipresent Divinity, the highest love of my heart and soul is for thee.

Thou art all that is beautiful, all that is good, all that is true, all that is divine.

From eternity to eternity my life is in thee, and thy house of the many mansions, my everlasting home.

I behold thy shining countenance, radiant with loveliness and infinite joy. I feel thy omnipresence, and know that thou art closer than breathing, nearer than hands and feet.

Thy infinite love is in my heart, going forth to all the world, an angel of peace, kindness and sympathy.

Thy goodness fills me and surrounds me. In thee everything is good. I live in thee and all is good in me.

Thou art perfect being, and I AM thy image and likeness. Thou art eternal, without beginning and without end, and as thou art, the same am I also.

I have always lived in thee, and in thee I shall live eternally; beautiful, endless existence divine.

Infinite Father, God of all that is beautiful and true, I AM one with thee. We are united forever in all that is, for thou livest in me and I in thee.

Thou art perfection, and I AM thy image and likeness. Thou art divine wholeness, and as thou art, I AM, for in all things I AM thy likeness divine.

On the Heights

I AM perfect and whole in body; I AM pure and clean in mind; I AM strong and beautiful in soul, for I AM thy image and likeness.

I AM walking with thee; wherever I go thou art always with me; therefore my ways are ways of pleasantness and all my paths are peace.

The shining glory of thy kingdom is ever before me; in the light of thy radiant countenance do I dwell forever. Every moment of my existence is an eternity of bliss, and I rejoice everlastingly while my heart is singing with countless angel throngs.

Thy beautiful children, the numberless souls of thy omnipresent kingdom, are all with me; they are my eternal companions, their faces beaming with infinite joy, their garments shining with the glory and splendor of thy luminous presence.

Wherever my body may be, wherever my mind may roam, I AM always in thee, living in thy beautiful heaven, abiding forever in thy arms of tenderness and love.

Thy spirit ever leads me through the endless pathways of life's delightful journey, and all that is good is ever coming to me. Thou art my safety, my guide and my protection, and all is well.

I shall be taught of thee all that I needs must know at every step of the perfect way. The light of thy wisdom shall ever shine upon me, and I shall think thy thoughts after thee.

Infinite Father, Supreme Creator of all the world, thou art my life and my power; thou art my wisdom and my understanding; thou art my tenderness and my love; thou art my peace and my joy; thou art my purity and my wholeness; thou art my virtue and my supply. From thee do I ever receive all that eternal life can give, the boundlessness of thy infinite kingdom.

In thee there is wisdom and light; in thee there is power and love; in thee there is glory and joy; in thee there is wholeness and strength; in thee there is virtue and peace; in thee there is freedom and life; in thee there is goodness and truth; in thee there is all that was, is or evermore shall be, and in thee I live and move and have my being.

Thou livest in me, and I in thee; and all that is in thee is in me, for I AM thy image and likeness.

My heart is filled with tenderness and love for all the world; every soul in existence is dear to me, for we are all thy children, forever living in thee, filled and surrounded with thy tender love and care. And before me all is beautiful and all is well.

Infinite Father, to know thee is to dwell eternally in the secret places of the Most High, in the highest heavens, upon those supreme heights where thy infinite glory is shining forever.

And thou hast revealed thyself to me; I have learned to know thee face to face; I AM even now in thy beautiful presence, and before me lies the endless pathway of the life eternal; upward and onward forever, ever ascending into greater and greater glory, ever drawing nearer and nearer to the omnipresent throne of God.

Infinite Father, I AM forever with thee, and how good it is to be here; before me all is beautiful, my very pathway

On the Heights

glittering with celestial brilliancy in the heavenly light of the eternal sun.

This is life, and I thank thee; with all my heart and soul I thank thee forever and ever, for thou art goodness eternal, kindness and love divine.

Thus shall I ever live; filled and surrounded with God; walking hand in hand with the great white throng; abiding in the kingdom; living in the great eternal light; giving to all the world the boundlessness of the gifts of love from on high; dwelling eternally upon the sublime heights of divine existence, the shining mountain tops of the spirit, and ever ascending to the greater glories prepared for me in my Father's House.

> Onward, souls eternal,
> Rise and walk with God;
> Come and tread the pathway
> That the saints have trod;
> Ever upward, onward,
> Soar to heights sublime.
> Live on spirit's mountain
> All the days of time.
> Onward, souls eternal,
> Rise in spirit's might.
> Rise to realms supernal.
> Realms of endless light;
> Live the life of spirit,
> Perfect life divine.
> Live where God's great glory
> Evermore shall shine.
> Onward, souls eternal
> Sons of God to be;
> Rise to endless glory,
> Power and majesty.

Perfect Health

Perfect Health

Table of Contents

Chapter 1 -	156
Chapter 2 -	161
Chapter 3 -	168
Chapter 4 -	174
Chapter 5 -	179
Chapter 6 -	185
Chapter 7 -	191
Chapter 8 -	197
Chapter 9 -	200

Chapter 1

THE principle upon which the higher form of healing is based is found in the statement that man is created in the image and likeness of God. The spiritual man is the real man, and the spiritual man is as God is — eternally perfect and whole through and through. To know this truth is to know the truth that makes man free, and this truth can be known by every mind that will enter into the conscious realization of the spirit of truth. The intellectual understanding does not produce the knowing of truth; to know the truth, the spiritual understanding becomes necessary. The intellectual understanding looks upon truth from without and thus learns to comprehend the outer form of truth; the spiritual understanding enters into the very spirit of truth and thus gains the power, not only to know the truth itself, but also to know everything that exists within the wonderful world of truth.

There is a world of eternal truth where everything is as wonderful, as beautiful and as perfect as the truth itself; and there is a world of mere appearance where everything is passing, and where nothing is real. To live in the world of appearance is to pass through what seems to be real; to live in the world of truth is to dwell forever in that which is real. In the world of appearance we find pain, sickness, evil and death; and we must of necessity pass through those things so long as we continue to pass through the world of appearance. To continue to pass through the world of darkness is to continue to pass through the darkness itself. But in the world of truth, we find neither sickness nor pain, sorrow nor death; those things cannot exist in the world of truth; therefore, we shall be absolutely free from those things so long as we live in the world of truth. And to know the truth, that is, to enter into the consciousness of the spirit of truth, is to enter the world of truth.

Perfect Health

To live in the world of truth is to live in the conscious possession of everything that exists in that world; and in that world everything is a perfect and as beautiful as when it first appeared from the creative hand divine. To live in the world of truth is to be free from those things that are not of the truth, and only those things are of the truth that are perfect as God is perfect. Therefore, in the world of truth there can be no sickness, because sickness is not perfect as God is perfect. Sickness can never enter the world of truth, but to enter the world of truth is to eliminate from the human system every trace of sickness that we ever thought we knew. Enter into the truth — into the very spirit of truth, and you are healed absolutely. You are every whit whole. Your emancipation is perfect and complete.

There are many ways to temporary health and limited degrees of freedom; but to enter the truth — the spirit of truth — the world of truth, is to gain that health that is as perfect and as endless as the truth itself, and that freedom that is as universal and as limitless as the truth itself. Therefore, we can find no better way to freedom, no higher path to health. To those who can understand all other paths are useless, all other methods vain. To follow other paths is to find but fragments; to enter the truth is to find the whole. The truth contains everything that is good for man; it is needless to seek elsewhere; but that which is not good for man cannot be found in the truth.

To enter into the truth the simple secret is to seek the spirit of truth. So long as we seek the mere mental form of truth, consciousness will dwell on the outside of truth; and no matter how much truth we may see, we shall continue to live in the world of untruth. But when we seek the spirit of truth — that divine something that exists within all truth, we enter consciously into the truth, and will therefore be filled and surrounded by the life of truth. We shall, accordingly, live the truth, and to live the truth is to give to life everything that is contained in the truth. Everything that pertains to the true being of man is thus expressed in every element throughout the entire being of man; and as perfect health is eternal in the true being of man, perfect health will likewise become eternal in every part of man. So long as we live the truth, that is, live consciously in the world of truth, not a fiber in the physical body can ever be sick, and not a single adverse mental condition can exist within us for a moment.

We are conscious in every atom in the body, and what enters into consciousness will therefore enter into every atom in the body. When we are in the spirit of truth we are conscious of absolute health; absolute health will thus enter into our consciousness — into every part of our consciousness, which means that absolute health will enter into every atom in the body, because consciousness extends to every atom in the body. To be conscious of absolute health is to possess and express absolute health in every part of consciousness, and accordingly, in every part of the body, for every part of the body exists within the field of consciousness. In like manner, to live the truth is to live the truth in every atom in the body, and thus give, to every atom in the body, the elements of true being, one of which is absolute health. We conclude, therefore, that so long as we are in the truth and are conscious of true being, it is not necessary to give thought to the body. And what is more, to think of the body as being distinct from true being is to hinder the mind from gaining complete consciousness of true being.

To think of true being as being one part of man and the physical body as being the other part, is to recognize two distinct entities in man, one of which is perfect and the other of which is imperfect; but no house that is divided against itself can stand; therefore, so long as we think of the physical body as being a separate and imperfect entity, we are not in the truth, and ills in abundance will appear in the personal life. In the truth there is no thought of imperfection and no thought of separation. In the truth, the being of man is one, and that one is perfect. The physical body is not looked upon as a thing apart, or as a something that can get sick; but is looked upon as a reflection of divine being, and is therefore thought of as having the same perfection as divine being.

The real man is well, always was and always will be, because the real man is created in the image of God. But the body is not separated from the real man; the body is a reflection of the real and is therefore similar to the real man in all things. If the body seems to be imperfect the cause is found in the mind which is the mirror. When the reflection differs from that which is reflected, the mirror does not reflect properly; and the remedy lies, not in trying to modify the reflection, but in trying to remove the defects from the mirror. Do something to make the mirror reflect properly and the reflection will be the exact likeness of that reality that is being reflected. And here we find the secret to the highest healing — the complete emancipation of man.

The true being of man is perfect, and the mind is the mirror reflecting the perfection of true being. This reflection appears in the form of the visible personality, but it may not always appear in the exact likeness of true being. When the personality does not manifest the qualities of true being, we try to change the personality; we try to modify personal conditions by acting upon those conditions themselves, regardless of the cause of those conditions; in brief, we try to "doctor" the effect while permitting the cause to remain undisturbed. The result is a number of confused systems of healing, all of which aim to give relief or emancipation, but none of which can remove the cause. The only good they can possibly do is to stay the actions of the effects temporarily so that man may have occasional periods of peace. Beyond this they cannot go; therefore, man will not find real emancipation until he learns how to remove the cause; and the cause is to be found in the mirror. Remove the defects from the mirror and the reflection will be the exact likeness of the reality standing before the mirror. When the mind properly reflects the real man, the personal man will express the perfection of true being; the personal in man will manifest the real in man, and the real in man is created in the image of God.

Chapter 2

WE have three factors to consider: viz., the real man, the mirror and the reflection, otherwise termed the visible personality. The real man is always well, and lives perpetually in complete emancipation; therefore, the personal man, being a direct reflection of the real man, should also have perpetual health and emancipation. But this is not always so, and the reason why is that the mind — the mirror — does not properly reflect the real man. If the mind was so constructed that it would reflect perfectly the true being of man, the personal man would always be as perfect, as wholesome and as divine as the real man, and neither sickness nor weakness nor any evil whatever could possibly exist in the personal life of man any more. His life would be from above, and from above only, and his emancipation would be complete.

When the mind knows the truth, and actually lives in the consciousness of the spirit of truth, it becomes a perfect mirror and, in consequence, will perfectly reflect the true being of man. The defects in the mirror are composed simply of beliefs that are untrue; these beliefs turn aside some of the rays of light from the divine spirit within, and the reflection is distorted. Thus we have imperfect conditions in the personality. When all false beliefs are removed from the mind, there are no defects any more in the mirror, and the reflection will be perfect. To remove false beliefs from the mind, the simple secret is to enter the truth — the spirit of truth. To know the truth is to make the mental mirror clean and thus cause every ray of divine light to be reflected fully and perfectly. The life, the health, the purity, the power and the wisdom of the within will thus appear in personal form in the without.

Perfect Health

We know the truth when our minds reflect the truth; that is what it means to know the truth; but our minds will not properly reflect the truth unless the mental mirror is clean. Perfection means full expression, and the personal man will be a full expression of the true being of man when the mental mirror is so clean that all of true being is reflected. However, when there are "spots" on the mirror, the reflection will not be complete; some of the rays of the spirit within will be lacking, and it is this lack that constitutes the original cause of every ill that appears in personal existence. When every atom in the personality is full with life and wholeness from within, there can be neither disease nor weakness in any part of the physical body; and this fullness invariably appears in the personality when the mind reflects the whole of true being. When the mirror reflects perfectly, the reflection will manifest everything that exists in that which is being reflected. Nothing will be lacking, and that which appears will be just as perfect, just as beautiful and just as true as that which is. The seeming will be the exact likeness of the real, but these two will be one. The reflection does not exist apart from the real; therefore we must never think of the reflection as real. We must never think of the body as real; it is simply a reflection of the real; and when the mental mirror reflects properly, the physical reflection will be just as beautiful and just as wholesome as the spiritual reality.

When the true being of man is perfectly reflected in personal existence, the Word becomes flesh, and the tangible elements of the body become external pictures of the divine idea within — the spiritual idea of absolute truth. Accordingly, materiality, grossness and physical ills must disappear, because those conditions are simply the result of confused reflections. When the mind reflects the wholeness of the spirit, the body becomes as pure, as clean, as refined and as beautiful as the spirit; and likewise, as strong as the spirit. The life, the power and the divinity that is within will manifest in the without, and as the spiritual man is so will the visible man be also.

To try to heal the body is therefore not only unnecessary, but is actually an obstacle in the way of healing. Emancipation comes to the body only when the fullness of the spirit of truth finds expression in the body, but before the body can receive the expression of truth the mind must know the spirit of truth. The reflection becomes true to the real when the mirror becomes true to its own function. When the mental mirror reflects the perfection of true being the body will express, in every atom, the perfection of true being. But so long as we are trying to heal the body by simply dealing with effects as we find them in the body, we will not give our attention to those causes that exist beyond the body. So long as we devote all our efforts towards trying to remove defects from the reflection, we will do nothing to remove defects from the mirror. It is the defects in the mirror that cause the defects in the reflection; it is untrue states in the mind that produce untrue conditions in the body; therefore, no attention need be given to the healing of the body; such efforts will profit nothing. Do not think of the body, because it is only a reflection and not a reality; give your attention to the mind; make the mental mirror clean; remove the false and the foreign from its surface so that it may become perfectly clear in every part. And you do this by immersing the mental mirror in the crystal waters of the spirit of truth. In brief, enter the spirit of truth, and your mind will become as pure as the spirit of truth. Thus you may clearly see and perfectly know the truth; all your thoughts will reflect the truth, and your visible being will be the expression of truth. Outer being will become a true reflection of true being, and you will realize in personal existence what you have learned to know in spiritual existence.

What we think of as disease is simply a broken reflection, and not a reality in itself. But this broken reflection cannot be reset; it must be removed completely and give place to a true reflection; and the true reflection appears when the mirror is made clean. The reason why the mental mirror is not always clean is found in the fact that the mind can be impressed from without. Everything that enters through the senses will impress the mind, and if consciousness is not selective, many impressions will be formed that are not in accord with absolute truth. Such impressions will become "foreign material" as it were, upon the glass of the mirror, and will hinder true reflection. But we must not close the mind to the world of sense; we are here to manifest the real, and to do so the within must act upon the without; we must be conscious of the without and susceptible to all that is taking place in the external world. However, we should look upon life, not from the viewpoint of the valley, but from the view-point of the mountain top.

When we look upon life through the limitations of the personal vision, we do not see things as they are, and accordingly those impressions that come from without are not true; but when we look upon life through the vision of the spirit and from the heights of absolute truth, we see all things as they are; the mind is thus impressed with the truth, both from within and from without. No "foreign material" is permitted to gather upon the mirror because all the impressions that enter the mind are rays from the omnipresent light of universal truth; and rays of light will not produce "spots" upon any mirror. When we see all things as they are, the mind receives nothing but truth from any source. We can open the mind fully to the world of physical sense as well as the world of spiritual sense; only rays from the light of truth will come upon the mental mirror; and that mirror will reflect only the truth through every part of body, mind and soul.

Perfect Health

To reduce physical substance to its last analysis is to discover that the physical body is not solid. It appears to be solid, because those elements of which it is composed vibrate at a rate that produces a sensation that we interpret as tangible; and that sensation serves a true purpose in our present sphere of existence, but the sensation of a thing and the thing itself are not the same. When we think of the body as solid we not only school ourselves to believe that the physical can only with difficulty be changed or modified by the mind, but we also form the habit of viewing the body as "material" And whenever we think of anything as "material" we cause "materiality" to gather over the glass of the mental mirror. Thus we hinder the true reflection of perfect being, and bring upon ourselves conditions that are incomplete, misdirected, adverse, imperfect and untrue. But when we think of the body, not as solid matter, but as spirit made visible, every thought that we form of the body will be a spiritual thought, and such thoughts invariably convey the health, the wholeness, the power and the life of the spirit.

When we realize that all physical conditions are reflections of mental states, and realize that we can create all our mental states in the exact likeness of absolute truth, we elevate the mind to the lofty position of absolute supremacy over the body. We take our place as complete masters of our own personalities and everything that personal existence may contain; and when we place ourselves in the position of mastership we begin to exercise mastership. He who realizes that he is master of his life, will gain the power to master his life. When we know that all physical conditions are reflections from the mental mirror within, we are no longer in bondage to conditions; we know that we can reflect what we like, and therefore produce any physical condition that we like. Simply to know this great truth is to take the mind out of bondage into freedom, and when the mind is free from adverse conditions the body will be free from those conditions also. The mind that is free from adverse conditions will not reflect such conditions; and your mind becomes absolutely free from all conditions the moment you realize or inwardly know that you can reflect any condition that you may desire.

When you know that you can walk you are not in bondage to the thought that you cannot walk, because there can be no such thought in your mind. Likewise, when you know that you can fill your body with the power of absolute health, you are no longer in bondage to disease. When you know that you have the power to do what you wish to do, it is not possible for you to think that you do not have that power. You cannot feel the absence of something when you feel the presence of that something. When you know that you are true being, it is not possible for you to think that there is anything wrong or untrue in your being; and so long as you do not think that there is anything wrong in your being, no wrong can possibly exist in your being. To think the whole truth is to reflect the whole truth, and when the whole truth is reflected in your life there will not be any room for false' conditions in your life. You will be perfect and whole through and through.

When you realize that your true being is perfect and whole in all things, and that your visible personality is simply a reflection of what you think of your true being, your attitude towards both the without and the within is in perfect accord with absolute truth. You have placed yourself in perfect harmony with the true order of things, physically, mentally, and spiritually, and you may henceforth give full expression to the true in every part of your being. You realize that your personality is completely in your own hands, because he who controls the source of light may determine the measure of light that is to be given. All obstacles to a complete mastery of the outer life has been removed through your realization of the great truth that you can bring forth any measure desired of the inner life. And you find that your greatest purpose is to gain a more and more perfect realization of true being so that you can reflect in the personal man all that has existence in the wholeness, the perfection and the divinity of the real man.

Chapter 3

WHEN we learn that imperfect conditions in the body are produced by broken, distorted or interrupted reflections from within, and that "foreign material" on the mental mirror is the cause of such reflections, we may conclude that the cause of every disease is in the mind, or that it is the mind that is sick instead of the body; but such thoughts or conclusions must never be permitted. The mirror is not defective simple because there is "foreign material" upon its surface; the mirror itself is perfect if it was made right in the first place; likewise, the mind in itself is perfect regardless of the fact that it may contain impressions that are not true. Every mind is formed in the likeness of Divine Mind; every human mind is created right in the beginning and no power can cause that which is right to become wrong; therefore, the human mind is always right, always perfect, always well. Never think of your mind as being sick; the mind can never become sick; sickness can never enter that which is originally and permanently perfect. And never think of your mind as being the cause of disease, or as containing the cause of disease. Perfection can neither be the cause of imperfection nor contain such a cause; and the human mind is, in itself, perfect, being created in the image of Divine Mind.

The real man is well, and the real man is all there in the human entity; therefore, you can never truthfully say that you are sick; the real mind can never be sick, nor can the unreal mind be sick because the unreal does not exist; the same is true of the body; that which is real in the body is a perfect reflection of the real man within, and that which does not reflect the real is unreal, or without existence whatever. The soul cannot be sick because it is created in the image of God; the mind cannot be sick because it is an expression of the mind of God — an individualized ray of light proceeding eternally from the Supreme Light; and the body cannot be sick because it reflects in the visible a portion of the divinity of being that exists in the invisible. There is nothing in you that can be sick; all that is real in you is as God is, and God is never sick. All that is real in any sphere of existence is perfect in that sphere, and that which is perfect cannot be sick. We cannot separate existence from reality, nor can we separate reality from perfection; and to be perfect in any part of the scale of life is to be true to life in that scale. But nothing that is true to life in any scale can be sick while in that scale. To be true to life is to be well, and all that is real in life is true to life.

What we think of disease need not concern us in the least; we cannot produce light by trying to analyze darkness; nor can we produce harmony by trying to understand the nature of discord. All study of imperfection is useless; in fact, more than useless, because the further we delve into the darkness of the false the further we depart from the light of truth. The laws of growth are not discovered through a study of emptiness, nor can we produce health, which is the fullness of life, by acting upon disease, which is the absence of life. To try to modify the effect will not change the cause, nor will a study of effect lead to an understanding of cause. From the view-point of absolute truth we know that disease is unreal and that it does not belong to the real nature of man. What the unreality of disease may consist of is of no importance whatever; first, because we do not care to know disease; and second, because the more we study disease or think of disease, the less we shall know of health. Besides, we can never know that which is not real; we can form mental pictures of the unreal but that is all; that which is not a thing in itself the mind can never know, and every attempt to understand that which is "not a thing" leads to the formation of confused mental pictures. Such pictures invariably "cloud" the mental mirror so that the real man is not properly reflected. In consequence, to try to understand disease is to produce more disease, and to try to analyze the nature of that which is not real is to prevent the full expression of that which is real.

To understand the fullness — the greater and greater fullness of that which is real, is the purpose of the mind. The more we grow into the consciousness of the real the clearer becomes the mental mirror, and the more perfectly the health, the power and the life of the real man is reflected in the personal man. To know the truth is to secure perfect freedom, but we do not actually know the truth so long as we also attempt to know the untruth. We are fully conscious of the real only when we are fully conscious of the unreal, and we begin to understand absolute truth only when we cease to recognize anything but that which is absolute truth or the direct product of absolute truth. The eye must be single upon The Truth, and wherever we direct attention we should attempt to see The Truth as the soul, the life, the foundation, the substance, the being, the reality of everything. Your mind will never be impressed by that which seems imperfect in anything when your sole purpose is to see the true and the perfect in everything. You thus cause the mental mirror to remain perfectly clear and clean, and only the true in the spirit within is reflected and expressed in the form without.

That man is created in the image of God is the basic principle; and since God is absolute health, man must be absolute health also. When man realizes that he is always well in his true being, and that his true being is all of his being, he becomes conscious of absolute health. Whatever we become conscious of we give to every atom in our being, because we are conscious in every atom; and therefore, to be conscious of absolute health is to realize, possess and live absolute health in every atom. To gain and retain the consciousness of absolute health it is necessary to grow in the consciousness of absolute health; and this growth in consciousness is promoted, first, by thinking the truth about true being; second, by thinking only of true being, and third, by thinking that true being is all of being. When these three essentials are fully complied with, every thought will be formed in the likeness of the truth, will contain the truth, will be the truth, and as the mind moves into that which we think of the most, we shall accordingly move more and more into the truth, and into the consciousness of everything that is in the truth. Perfect health is in the truth and therefore, we will, in this manner, grow more and more in perfect health, gaining higher degrees of health as well as greater degrees of physical, mental and spiritual strength. That it is necessary to grow in health in order to retain health, is evidenced by the fact that consciousness cannot remain at a standstill. When we do not rise into the greater we fall back into the lesser, and we will continue to lose ground steadily. But when we continue unceasingly to grow into the greater we not only retain all that we have gained thus far, but we also add to this an ever-growing measure.

To grow into any quality or superior state of being, it is necessary to grow in the consciousness of the truth of that state of quality. We grow into health as we become conscious, more and more, of the truth about health — the absolute truth about perfect health. The truth is the soul of real being, and it is only as we enter into the truth of real being that we become conscious of that which is contained in real being. The same is true of any state or quality; we must know the truth that is in that state, and in that knowing grow perpetually. The truth that is in health is the truth that real being now does possess, and ever will possess, perfect health. Know the truth that you are in perfect health; that you will always remain in perfect health, because the real man is forever well as God is forever well, and the real of you is all of you; then grow in that truth; become more and more conscious of the very spirit of that truth, and the limitless life of the health within you will express itself more and more in the person without. In brief, you will actually live in an ever-growing measure of health, and to live in health is to possess health', through and through, in every atom that is alive, which means every atom in your own domain, because every atom is alive.

To live in the consciousness of any quality is to give the fullness of that quality to every part of being, physical, mental and spiritual; and we always live in the consciousness of health when we inwardly know that real being actually is health. Real being and perfect health cannot be separated; the two are absolutely and eternally one; and you are real being; therefore, you, yourself, are perfect health; the fact that you are alive proves that you are well; in real being, to be alive is to be well; health and life are one in the truth, and the whole of you is in the truth; the whole of you is composed of absolute truth, and the whole of you will eternally abide in the very spirit of absolute truth.

Realize what you are in the divinity of your being. This is the secret. Realize that you are well through and through, because you are well through and through, and you will be conscious only of perfect health. To gain and develop this realization, consciousness must ascend into the true state of being; and consciousness will ascend into the true — will enter into the very life of the true, as we train all the actions of mind to move towards the true. Keep the eye single upon the wholeness of divine being; know that you are in the wholeness of divine being because you are divine being, and desire to enter more and more deeply into that wholeness; then give conscious recognition to absolute wholeness in every thought, feeling and state of mind. You thus inspire everything in your being to ascend in the truth of real being, and, in consequence, every mental action will choose absolute truth as its goal. But such a goal is not for the future alone to reach; the very moment we begin to move towards absolute truth we begin to realize truth; and with the realization of truth comes the possession of all those superior qualities that exist within the world of truth. Among those we find perfect health, the life more abundant, the peace that passeth understanding, the joy everlasting and the power that cannot be measured.

Chapter 4

TO enter completely into the realization of your divine being, have faith in everything that is real and true. Have faith, not simply in that which seems greater than you, but have faith in that divine greatness that actually is you. To have faith is to enter into that in which we express faith, and it is the entering into the true, the perfect and the divine that produces complete emancipation. Faith, therefore, becomes an indispensable factor in the realization of truth. To affirm truth, or to train the mind to habitually think in the exact language of truth is not sufficient; we do not actually think the truth unless we think in the spirit of truth, and it is only through the attitude of faith that the mind can enter the spirit. Without faith, thinking is purely intellectual; but the intellectual understanding of truth does not produce the knowing of truth; we know the truth only when we enter into the spirit of truth, and it is only faith that has the power to enter into the spirit. When the intellect is inspired by faith, all understanding becomes spiritual; the mind no longer looks at the outer form of truth, but enters completely into the real life of truth, and it is when we are actually IN the truth that we know the truth.

To have faith, aim to enter into the inner life of everything of which you are conscious, or to which you give your thought. When you see anything or think of anything, do not simply recognize the outer form; know that there is an inner life, a spiritual life, within the form, and give that inner life your fullest recognition. Whatever you desire, enter mentally into the spirit of the action of that desire; try to feel the power of that limitless force that is within the soul of your desire, and realize that this supreme power can, and will, cause your desire to come true. Whatever you will to do, use the spirit of the will and not simply the external form of the will; recognize an inner power in the will, and will to will with this inner power. The inner power of the will is divine will, and to consciously use divine will is to CONNECT your will with the will of God. You will, in consequence, realize your purpose, because the will of God not only can do all things, but will do all things that we desire to have done. When you combine your will with Infinite will, you invariably gain what you have in view; your will becomes strong enough to accomplish anything; and whenever you enter into the spirit of your own will, you find yourself in possession of the power of divine will. Faith is the secret. To enter into the spirit of anything is to exercise faith, and the more we try to enter into the spirit of everything the more we develop the power of faith. Remove the idea that faith means belief; faith is not to believe something but to do something; faith is not a passive conviction, but a positive action; faith does not rest serenely in the acceptance of some thought, but actually enters into the greater power and the greater life that is found in the vast spiritual domains of that thought.

When you proceed to heal yourself, enter mentally into the spirit of your true being; and when you realize that you are in a more spiritual state of being, proceed to enter into the spirit that is within that spiritual state. You thus gain conscious realization of the spirit within the spirit; your life is deepened, your mind is heightened, and your consciousness of the divine perfection of your true being is perpetually enlarged. It is growth in the spirit that produces complete emancipation, and to continue in this growth we must realize that every spiritual state has within itself a higher spiritual state. However deeply we may enter into the spirit, there is always a deeper spiritual state within the state we have realized; and however high we may ascend in the spiritual scale there is always a higher spiritual world before us. There are spiritual states within spiritual states without end, and there are spiritual worlds above spiritual worlds without end; therefore, to enter into the spirit of anything is not to enter into some final state that exists within the form; to enter into the spirit is to enter the realization of the real and begin an endless path in the realization of the greater and the greater that is contained within the limitless world of the real. The spirit of everything is the real of everything, and the more deeply we enter the real of anything the more perfectly we realize the spiritual life of that truth that is the very soul of everything. To realize that spiritual life is to gain complete emancipation, because to be in the spirit is to be IN the truth, and when we are in the truth we are in those things only that are perfect and good as pure truth is perfect and good.

To enter into the spirit of your true being is to begin to live in the real life of your true being; you live no longer in the confused world of mental pictures, but you live in the calm, illumined world of truth; and in the world of truth there is neither sickness, weakness, evil or wrong; to be in the world of truth is to be free; and we enter the world of truth when we know the truth that is, when we consciously enter into the spirit of truth. When we are in the spirit of truth the mind will not be impressed by that which is untruth; the eye does not come in contact with darkness when it is in the light; in consequence, the mental mirror will be perfectly clear and clean, and will reflect in the person the full glory of that light that is in the spirit. The wholeness of the real man within will thus appear in the visible man without, and we shall find the same purity, health and strength in the body that we find in the perfection of divine spirit. The reflected ray contains the same elements as the original light from which it proceeds, providing the mirror reflects properly; and the mental mirror will reflect properly when its surface is covered with nothing but the brilliancy of divine truth. We conclude, therefore, that so long as you mentally live in the spirit of truth your mind will reflect only that which is in the truth; and as all physical conditions are but reflections from the mind, you will possess only wholesome physical conditions, because there are no unwholesome conditions in the truth.

When the mind is in the truth it reflects only what is in the truth; the body will thus be filled, through and through, with perfect health; the personal man will express the strength, the life and the purity of the real man, and all that is beautiful and ideal in the within will manifest itself more and more in the without. When there is anything that you wish to gain or realize, be it in your own personality or in your environment, enter into the spirit of it; try to place yourself in mental touch with the inner life of the thing desired, and while you are giving recognition to that inner life, desire and pray for what you want with all the power of spirit and soul. Enter into the spirit of health when you pray for health; enter into the spirit of your being when you affirm that you are well, and you will not only gain what you desire, but you will also increase your faith, thus preparing yourself for the gain and the realization of greater things in the near future. To place the mind in contact with the inner life or the spirit of the thing desired will awaken the greater power of the mind — the real, soul power of the mind; and as that power is the coming forth of Supreme power in you, your life is placed in a position where nothing can be impossible. This is how all things become possible through faith. To have faith is to enter the spirit of things, and to enter the spirit is to enter the power of the spirit — the power of the Supreme — that power that can do anything no matter what the circumstances may be. All things become possible to him who has faith because faith CONNECTS the life of man with the life and power of the Most High.

To apply the principle of faith in the realization of perfect health, enter into the spirit of perfect health whenever you think of health. Aim to live in the soul of health, or what may be termed the real, interior life of health. This attitude will bring forth more and more of the power of health until your entire personality is entirely full of this power. You will thus not only realize the fullness of perfect health, but also the vital strength of health; and you will put to flight that erroneous idea that an increase of spiritual power means a decrease of physical power. Real spirituality produces strength, vigor and power on all planes — physical, mental and spiritual. Real spirituality, however, is not based upon emotionalism or negative goodness, but upon the consciousness of absolute truth. To be conscious of absolute truth is to express the life, the health and the power of absolute truth in every part of body, mind and soul; and the power of truth is not limited; therefore, the more we grow in the consciousness of truth the stronger we shall become throughout our entire being. The belief that the soul can, under certain conditions, be stronger than the body has no foundation in truth. When the soul seems to be strong and the body weak, the soul is not properly expressed in the body, and the fault lies in the mental mirror., When you feel a great deal of spiritual strength, you will reflect and express that strength in the body, providing you have a clear understanding of the true nature of that strength. But when the understanding is not clear the mental mirror will not reflect properly, and the strength of the spirit will not come forth to give strength to the body. The remedy is to know the truth — to enter into the spirit of truth, and to know that to be IN the truth is to be filled, through and through, with the limitless power of truth.

Chapter 5

SPRITUALIZE your personality at all times, especially when you undertake to remove some ailment. Spiritualize your entire personality by realizing, through your mental vision, that every atom in your being is pure spirit — as pure and as clear as crystal, and as highly refined as the most sublimated essence of the soul. Spiritualize any part of your body, in the same manner, if that part is ailing, and imperfect conditions will begin at once to disappear. Realize the spiritual perfection and the divine wholeness of every part of your personality; spiritually see the divine counterpart of any part wherein you wish to realize perfect health, and know that the divine counterpart is the all of that part. Know that the physical is simply a reflection of your consciousness of the divine, and that this reflection will become stronger and more perfect as your consciousness of the divine becomes more perfect. When your consciousness of the divine is true, the reflection will be true, and the physical part will be perfect and whole as the divine is always perfect and whole. Deepen the spiritualizing process in any part of the body, and the power of the spirit becomes supreme in that part. In consequence, adverse forces, diseased conditions and all wrongs, whatever their nature, will be removed in the same manner as darkness is removed by the light.

The body cannot be spiritualized through fasting, or through any form of self-denial; we cannot spiritualize the body by taking certain physical things away from the body, but by giving the body more and more of the spirit. And we give to the body of the spirit as we become more fully conscious of the spirit. Never deny the body anything that will add to the comfort, the beauty and the richness of physical existence. Take nothing away that is good in the without, but add more and more of that which is good in the within. Thus we increase the power of the spirit from within, and cause the personality to become a more perfect instrument through which the spirit may find expression.

When the interior life forces in any part of the body are changed, those physical conditions that may exist in that part are also changed; and any group of these forces will change the moment they are animated and permeated by the forces of the spirit. The power of the spirit lies deeper than and within the physical life; therefore, when the spiritual is unfolded, the physical will immediately begin to change to correspond with the nature of the spiritual. This is inevitable, because the spiritual is infinitely stronger than the physical. Any change from within will invariably produce a like change in the without; the realization of perfect health in the spirit must be followed by perfect health in the body, and the consciousness of greater spiritual strength will always bring greater physical strength. Any change from within will always be a change, for the better; the spirit is absolutely good, therefore any change in the expression of the spirit will mean the expression of greater good. You cannot cause the spirit to express less; to act upon the spirit is to cause it to express more. When the spirit seems to express less, the reason is that we have clouded the mental mirror with "impressions of untruth," "mental pictures of imperfections" and other "foreign material" so that the light of the spirit is not properly reflected in the body. When we seem to be buried in materiality, sickness, adversity and distress, the reason is not that the spirit is dormant; the spirit never decreases in life, power and activity no matter what the person may do; but the perverted actions of the person will so confuse the mind that the life of the spirit will, for the time being, be hidden from conscious view. It is at such times that the soul seems to be lost, and that we seem to have lost all the light and all the truth we ever possessed; but the soul is never lost; it is the person that has strayed from the divine presence of the soul; let the person return to its own and we shall find the soul upon the divine throne of being as before, and we shall find again all the light and all the truth that we ever knew before. All that we have gathered of the good and the true is held in trust for us by the hand divine; and if we should lose our hold upon the true for a time we will not lose what was once our own; when we return to the fold we shall get everything back that we ever possessed. There is neither decrease nor loss in the spirit; in the life of the spirit it is always greater gain and continued increase; the limitless is the goal, and upward and onward forever is the path to that goal.

The higher consciousness ascends in the realization of the absolute, which is purely spiritual, the stronger becomes the spiritualizing process in the human system; and the stronger this process becomes, the greater becomes the supremacy of the spirit in human life. The entire human system is thus placed in the hands of the spirit, and wherever the spirit rules, in that place there is always health. Where the action of the spirit is strong, disease cannot possibly exist, and the action of the spirit invariably increases in every physical part where we clearly discern the spiritual counterpart. To more clearly discern this spiritual counterpart, train the mind to think of the spirit that is in everything whenever you think of anything. Let no action of mind cease with the mere recognition of the outer form; cause every mental action, every feeling and every thought to recognize the spirit, the soul and the greater life that is within the form. Gradually, but surely, consciousness will begin to act in the spiritual realm as well as in the physical realm; and whenever consciousness becomes active in the spiritual realm, the action of the spirit will increase in the field of that consciousness. Accordingly, whenever the consciousness of the spiritual is gained in any part of the body, the power of the spirit will rule in that part, and perfect

Perfect Health

health will be the result. The spiritual is always well; therefore, the physical becomes absolutely well the moment the spirit begins to reign.

All thought must be formed in the exact likeness of absolute truth. Whatever you think of, ask yourself what the absolute truth concerning that subject or object would naturally be. This will give the mind the tendency to face the brilliant light of supreme truth at all times, and every thought will be inspired by that light and formed in that light. The absolute truth is not a phase of truth or the truth about certain parts of being; it is the truth in the fullness of truth; it is complete in itself and lacks nothing that pertains to truth. Therefore, when all thought is formed in the likeness of absolute truth every thought will be complete in its own domain, and will express completeness wherever it may have the tendency to act. The expression of completeness means health, and it is thought that determines the nature of every expression that takes place in the human personality.

Perfect health is never the result of a certain part of truth or of right thinking in any one of its phases. Perfect health can come only from absolute truth and from thinking that gives expression to absolute truth. To aim to think the truth in some of its phases while other phases are neglected is to confuse the mind and thus cloud the mental mirror so that the perfection of the real man is not properly reflected. The knowing of truth has nothing to do with phases of truth or parts of divine reality. To know the truth is to live in the allness of the spirit of truth and to realize that the perfection of being means the perfection of the whole of being. Perfect health is an inseparable part of absolute truth, and is gained only as the mind enters into the very life of absolute truth; that is, as the mind gains that position in spiritual consciousness where all things are discerned as reflections from the divine perfection of supreme reality. When this position is gained, all things are seen as they are — not as imperfections but as images of the divine, and to know that everything is as God is, is to know the absolute truth. It is this truth that gives freedom, because when the mind knows only the divinity of things it is not impressed with "thoughts of imperfection" The mental mirror is clear and clean, and the life, the health and the power of the divine man is perfectly reflected and expressed in the personal man — through and through every part of the personal man. To place the mind completely in the consciousness of truth, it is necessary to realize distinctly what you are in the supreme state of your being. To know the truth, you must know the truth about yourself; and to enter the world of truth you must enter that real world in which you, yourself, have your true being.

This world is the sphere of the "I AM"; in other words, that state of being wherein you become actually conscious of the great truth that "I AM" is identical with you. When you can clearly think of yourself as "I AM," and can actually feel that "I AM" is neither mind nor body, soul nor spirit, but is above all of these in the most supreme state of individualized being, you are beginning to enter within the sacred domains of absolute truth. Affirm as frequently as possible the statement, I AM THE REAL I AM, and try to realize, whenever you make that statement, that "I AM" is the reigning power in your being; that "I AM" is God individualized in your being; that "I AM" is the only begotten Son, the Christ enthroned in your being; and that "I AM" actually is the "real you" of your being. You thus not only recognize the supreme position of "I AM," but you also recognize yourself as being "I AM"; you lift your consciousness of yourself out of "material thought" into the pure light of spiritual thought; you find your real self and you discover that you — the real you, the whole of you, reigns on high, where all life is forever in purity, health, power, freedom, truth; you become conscious of yourself in the world of supreme spiritual consciousness, and your eyes are opened in "another and a better world," to the great truth that you are, here and now, not only the likeness of God, but the individualized spirit of God. You find that the only difference between the "I AM" that is you and the "I AM That I AM," is that the former is individualized while the latter is infinite.

Chapter 6

DEFEND absolutely upon the Infinite for health, for life, for strength, for everything. Live consciously in God, and know that to be in God is to be in health, because God is absolute health. Whatever you proceed to do, act in conscious unity with God; enter so deeply into the spirit of every action that you can feel the life and the power of the Infinite in that action. You thus place yourself in the spirit of God, and everything that you do will be done in that spirit, Accordingly, everything that you think or do will give expression to the spirit; that which is in the spirit will, through your thinking and living, come forth into the person; external existence will give form to internal truth, and the same reality that you have become conscious of in the within will constitute the only real to you in the without. The imperfect or the adverse will no longer seem real to you; sickness and weakness will not be recognized as having tangible existence; in fact, they will not even be recognized as tangible conditions; only that which is real will receive recognition at all, and the real is always well, always perfect, always true to the absolutely true.

As you place yourself more and more in the spirit of God, such terms as "weakness," "evil," "sickness," and "wrong" will mean less and less to you; your mind will be so permeated with that truth that is everywhere present in the spirit of God that untruth can find no room in your consciousness, You will be so deeply and so constantly impressed with the conviction that you are always well that all thought of sickness will be foreign to your mind. You will discern so clearly that great truth that "all is good in God and all is in God," that beliefs about evil will not exist in your world whatever. When evil is mentioned you have "ears that hear not," because the world means nothing to you. In the truth there is no evil, and you are in the truth. You are in the spirit of God, and the spirit of God is truth, therefore you are in the truth. Being in the truth, you are, in like manner, unconscious of beliefs about sickness. You have no beliefs about sickness, and you never think of the word. Even when adverse conditions are felt in your body, you never think of sickness; you do not call such conditions sickness; you give them no name whatever; the name of God is sufficient upon such occasions, and in that name you invariably find peace.

To live in the truth is to mentally dwell upon the truth; that is, when we are in the spirit of truth the mind is completely absorbed in the truth; we are conscious of truth only; in consequence, we cannot be conscious of that which is not truth. It is therefore evident that when we pass into the spirit of truth we pass out of every condition that is not of the truth. We can, when we are in the spirit of truth, know nothing of sickness, weakness or pain. That which is wrong cannot enter the world of truth, but must be left behind when we enter the world of truth. And herein we find the path to complete emancipation. Whatever the conditions of the body may be, enter the spirit of truth and you are out of those conditions. Where you go, mind and body will go also; therefore, when you enter the truth, mind and body will also enter the truth, and will pass out of every condition that is not of the truth. You cannot be conscious of two opposite states at the same time; nor can you live in two separate and wholly dissimilar worlds at the same time; when you enter the world of truth, you must necessarily sever your consciousness completely from the world of untruth; when you are so completely in a state of perfect health that you are conscious of the very soul of health, you cannot possibly know anything about disease; and you do attain this supreme consciousness of health when you are in the truth, because no mind can enter completely into the truth without becoming absolutely conscious of all that is contained in the truth.

Perfect Health

When the mind is absolutely conscious of any quality it becomes unconscious of everything that is outside of the world of that quality. To be conscious of the absolute is to be conscious of only that which is in the absolute; but such a consciousness does not narrow the mind or shut anything out from the mind, as many seem to think. The absolute contains everything that is real and true; therefore, when you enter absolute consciousness you lose your illusions only while you gain everything that real life has in store. When you enter completely into absolute consciousness you will forget sickness and evil; but those things we are more than willing to forget; and what is well to remember, as the number of people who have forgotten sickness increases, sickness in the world will decrease. When you blot out sickness and evil from your mind completely, you not only emancipate yourself but you will lessen the ills among scores, possibly hundreds and thousands. That we must think about disease, talk about disease and study disease in order to relieve mankind is not true. No one can ever know anything about sickness or evil. You cannot gain definite knowledge concerning empty space, nor can scientific facts be evolved from illusions. He who can completely forget all ills, is the greatest physician in the world.

The less you mention the ills of life the more you add to the comfort of life. He who gives no thought to the wrong must necessarily give all thought to the right; and he who gives his all to the right will perpetually increase the power of the right, not only in his own life, but in the life of the whole race. That which we think of we multiply; therefore, to forget the untrue is a great virtue; but we cannot forget the untrue unless we enter into the consciousness of that which is absolutely true. This, however, is not an attainment intercepted by difficulties; to be right is natural; to be wrong is unnatural; and to be natural is the easiest thing in the world.

Perfect Health

To be absolutely conscious of the real and true, is to be true to the normal consciousness of the mind; therefore he who becomes unconscious of wrong, and completely forgets all wrong, is not taking some new or extraordinary step in mental action; he is simply using the mind the way nature intended that every mind should be used. The mind was not created for abnormal action, and to act upon evil, to dwell upon evil, to think about evil, to recognize evil — all of these are abnormal actions. The function of the mind is not to create thought that is out of harmony with truth, but to create thought in the likeness of truth. The purpose of thinking is to elevate the mind into higher states of consciousness, and it is only such thinking as takes absolute truth for its model that tends to rise in the scale.

Think of absolute consciousness as normal consciousness; realize that to be unconscious of sickness and evil is natural; remember the great truth that the more wrong you forget the more good you will gain, and that the less you know of pain the greater your power to relieve others of pain. This may seem absurd but the fact is that you know nothing of pain only when you have risen entirely above the world of pain; and when you have risen into that supreme state of being, you are in conscious possession of that power that is greater than anything that is in the world. You can conquer pain when you are above pain, and when you are above pain you are in that consciousness of true being where pain has no existence whatever, not even in your memory.

What you think of as normal will soon become a permanent state in your mind, providing it actually is normal in true being. Therefore, when you think of absolute consciousness as normal, such a consciousness will soon become a real factor in your mind. Then you may, whenever you like, become so absolutely conscious of perfect health that all ills will be forgotten completely. You may take mind and body so completely into the realization of truth that your entire being will entirely pass out of that which is contrary to truth. Then your emancipation will be complete, and you will be free indeed. When you pray for health, do not simply ask for health. To continue to ask for health is to cause yourself to believe that you do not have health. But you are the image of God, and God is always well, therefore you are always well. You do not need health; you have, even now, absolute health; you do not have to ask for it; you already have it in abundance; believe that you have it, and you will realize its wholeness and power in every atom of your being. When you pray, enter into the spirit of God; feel that the spirit in you is the real in you, the all in you, and that the spirit in you is inseparable from the spirit in God. Then affirm with deep, spiritual conviction that you are in the truth what you wish to manifest; affirm that you possess in the real what you wish to possess in the actual. We should never separate the actual from the real in consciousness; the actual is that which appears; the real is that which forever is; but we should think of the two as one. They are one because the actual is always a reflection of the real. The real is the light; the actual is the coming forth of that light.

Think as God thinks, and God thinks only absolute truth. Live where God lives, and God lives only in the spirit of truth. To him who thinks the absolute truth, nothing is real but the world of absolute truth; and he gives conscious recognition only to that which is real. To live continually in the consciousness of the great truth that the real man is well, and that the real man is the whole man, is to think only health. What we are conscious of we think; and what appears in the personal man is the result of what we think of the real man. When every thought is created in the consciousness of health, every cell in the body will possess health. When the mind is full of health the body will be full of health, and every mind is full of health that is full of divine truth.

Sympathize only with the real, the true and the perfect. Select your mental companions from the world of truth only, and enter only those domains of thought that are illumined with the full light of the spirit. The absolute truth is not simply a remedy in the time of need; it is the very substance of life, and must be taken with every breath and with every thought as nourishment for true being. So long as human life is nourished with the truth, the human system will be actually filled with the power of truth; and there can be nothing less than perfect health — eternal health, where the truth reigns supremely.

Chapter 7

THERE are moments when we know not where to turn; when all remedies fail, and all mortal aid seems vain. It is not only the hour of need, but the hour of the greatest need, and also the hour of the greatest pain. To know where to go when such moments come will be the most precious revelation, that has even been given to man. It has, however, been given ages ago, but those who had ears to hear, heard not.

There are many little things that can be done in every hour of need, and they are all of value; but the one thing above all things is usually neglected; and this one thing is GOING TO GOD. When we are in trouble we generally resort to all sorts of means before we go to Him. Instead of believing Him sufficient, we forget Him entirety, until the hour of utter despair. And for this reason, millions of sad events have transpired that could readily have been prevented.

Temporary means have their value, but only in proportion to the life and power from within with which they can act. When our consciousness of higher power is limited, external remedies may help for a time, and to a degree, but when this consciousness becomes so large that higher power is brought forth with might and main, temporary means become wholly unnecessary. To realize that GOD IS SUFFICIENT, that His power can do all things, and that He is fully able to supply us, no matter how great may be the need — this is the great eternal rock upon which every life must establish its endless abiding place.

Though from this we are not to infer that to pray is the only thing to do in the hour of need; we may do everything that can minister in any way, but the first thing to do is to GO TO GOD and wholly depend upon Him. When we wholly

Perfect Health

depend upon Him, nothing further is required. He will prove Himself sufficient.

When your faith is not as strong as you wish it to be, use as many temporary means as you like, but remember that the higher life and power that you will receive by going to Him and depending upon Him — that is the remedy that will never fail. Do not trifle away your time with the lesser when you may receive the greater; and you invariably do receive the greater when you go to God first, depending absolutely upon Him.

Those who have not fully realized that God is sufficient, may, for some time, require temporary and external aid, and if they need this, let them have it by all means; no one must suffer, and whatever can relieve suffering, even but for a moment, should be used in faith. Besides, all things are from God, and all things contain, to a degree, His healing life. But things are limited in power and efficiency; therefore why should we continue to depend upon that which is small and uncertain, when we can go to God and receive from Him directly that which is limitless and faileth not?

When we grow in faith, we soon find ourselves in that beautiful state where difficult places are never met because His power and presence are ever with us to smoothen the pathway before us. And this high faith will come to everybody, who, in the hour of need, goes first to God, and depends wholly upon Him, regardless of what may come to pass.

These are the days of many changes in thoughts and methods; we are learning more of that unlimited power within us; and that this power can remove suffering and sickness of every description is being demonstrated daily; then why should we ever call upon external aid? To many, it seems wrong to employ material means when the greater spiritual remedies are always at hand; but in the presence of these conclusions, we often find that our prayers for healing are not answered, while external aid produces relief in many instances. And this fact is a problem that few seem able to solve.

The truth is, however, that power from on high comes to us according to our spiritual understanding and our nearness to God, therefore, while this understanding is undeveloped, we should not hesitate to seek temporary aid, if we think we need it; but the sooner we think that God is sufficient, the better. Because when we inwardly know that God is sufficient, He will prove Himself so to be. When sickness or adversity threatens, remember, "I AM thy God that healeth thee" Also, "I will never fail thee." And again," Depend upon Me, I will not forsake thee or leave thee, I AM thy Redeemer, I will care for thee." Full faith in these great statements will heal any one: and He will "raise thee up" from thy bed of sickness and threatening death, and "thou shalt be made whole" again and live.

When trouble comes do not forget that "I AM the Lord that brought thee out of Egypt." No matter how dense the darkness, how great the tribulations, or how hopeless the bondage, He can bring you out into the promised land of complete emancipation. It is a pleasure to God to take us away from our own self-created troubles, the only troubles we shall ever find, for the more we ask of God the more we please God; and He is sufficient, even in the hour of the very greatest need.

When we are in trouble we seldom think of God; we have lost faith in everything and everybody, and give up to fate. But this is the very moment when we should pray without ceasing, and consecrate every moment to the Most High. Go up into His presence when everything seems to go wrong; do not come down for a moment; keep your eye single upon Him, and think of nothing else. Have the faith that He is sufficient to cause everything to come right, and He will prove that he is sufficient. Ere long the clouds will break; the storm will pass away; and when the calm has come, we find that all things have worked together for good through every part of our recent experience.

Every person has frequently felt that he was not equal to the occasion; that he was losing ground and that failure seemed inevitable. He knew that a little more strength or reserve force, if he only had it, could carry him over the difficult places, and take him safely to the goal in view. But where may this added strength be received? At these moments, at this great hour of need, when our whole future seems to hang in the balance, we usually fail to remember that "they that wait upon the Lord shall renew their strength." Turn your heart and soul to the Infinite now, and you will receive at once that added power that can positively see you through.

Thousands of men and women have gone down in despair when the critical moment was at hand, when the time came that would determine whether loss or gain was to be their reward. But all of these people could have won a great and brilliant career by going to God in the hour of need and receiving from Him the power required to carry them through. God is sufficient; and it matters not how dark the day may be or how hopeless the goal in view; call upon Him for new power and He will raise you up unto victory.

There is possibly no hour that is more dreary than the one that comes when every friend seems to be lost; when we have no one to whom we can speak heart to heart. The whole universe seems empty and every moment an eternity of suspense. But at this hour of great need there is someone that is not far away, someone who can take away the burden, and relieve the heart of every sorrow and pain. This Great Friend may have been forgotten, nevertheless He is ever at hand, and ever sufficient; the very best friend of all, for "I AM with you always, even unto the end of the world."

When we go to Him and open our hearts to His tenderness and love; not a mere sentimental experience, but a real meeting face to face with the friend of all souls; when we do this, we become so filled with real love and sympathy that the very best of human friends will be drawn to us in large numbers. By seeking the friend of all friends, we receive His divine friendship, and in addition all the human friendship that we can possibly desire.

When we seem to be lost in bondage, mistakes and wrong, so we cannot find a single ray of light anywhere, we are not required to fall down upon our knees, and in agonizing petitions implore the mercy and forgiveness of the Supreme. Neither need we be afraid that we are lost, or that we have to pass through ages of darkness and sin. No, such thoughts are wrong, for wherever we may be, there God will be also; and whatever our condition may be, He is always sufficient. Do we believe this with the whole heart? Do we realize that the Infinite can, in one short moment, take us out completely from all the bondage and wrong in the world? Do we live in the conviction that He is sufficient no matter what may happen to us in the present or in the future? These are great thoughts to think of, for the moment we seek emancipation through Him, our days in bondage are numbered. The storm will soon be over; then will come the beautiful calm and the sun will shine again.

We make entirely too much of the adverse conditions we meet, and by giving so much thought to the threatening ills, we not only aggravate these ills, but we forget that "God shall wipe away all tears from their eyes." To live in this faith is to so live that tears will never come any more. We all realize that the hour of need is usually the critical moment, and what we do at this hour nearly always deter-mines what experiences we are to meet for days and even years to come. Therefore, we cannot give this hour too much right thought; we cannot use it with too much care and wisdom. But if the hour of need, "the hour of man's extremity and God's opportunity," is to become the turning point to greater things, we must call upon God and seek His guidance and power directly. No matter what other things we may do, His power and presence must be sought first. His help is the greatest of all, and with Him all things are possible. In the hour of need GO TO GOD first; depend upon Him, for He is sufficient.

Chapter 8

THE mind that would heal the sick must develop faith, love, soul-serenity and spiritual consciousness. His faith must be that faith that can go out upon the seeming void and always find the solid rock; his love must be that love that loves everything at all times, and from the heart, because it IS love; the calmness of his soul must be so deep, and so high, that he can truthfully say at any time "None of these things move me"; and his consciousness of the spiritual must be so perfect that he INWARDLY KNOWS that man is divine, created in the exact image and likeness of God.

However, these four essentials do not constitute the real power that heals; they simply awaken the real power, and are therefore efficient only as far as they are orderly combined with the desired object in view. The real power in healing is the coming forth of the spirit, the soul expressing itself through the body, the Word becoming flesh.

When any mind can awaken the spiritual life in others he can heal others; and every person can heal himself who can awaken spirituality in himself.

The spirit is perfect and whole in every manner; and the power of the spirit is greater than any force or condition that can possibly exist in the body; therefore, when the power of the spirit enters the body, every part of the body will be permeated through and through with health, wholeness and life; and so strong will be the force of this wholesome life from within that all sickness, weakness or disorder will have to take flight. When the spiritual nature of man is awakened, we turn on, so to speak, the light of his divine life, and as this divine life is health, absolute and invincible, the darkness of disease or disorder must disappear. But this divine life is not simply unconquerable health; it is everything that is perfect and true in the spiritual being of man; it is that universal light that eliminates all darkness; therefore, to awaken man's spiritual nature is to secure emancipation from everything that is adverse in human existence.

The spiritual nature of man is created in the likeness of God; it is as God is, and as God can neither be sick, weak nor out of order in any manner whatever, the spiritual nature of man cannot be sick, weak nor out of order. In brief, when the spiritual nature of man is awakened, he will express the likeness of God in everything. His body will be perfectly well, his mind will be sweet and wholesome, his character will be strong and beautiful, and his soul will live on the heights.

There are no imperfect conditions in mind or body that will not disappear, gradually or rapidly, as the spiritual life is awakened. "Greater is He that is in you than he that is in the world." It is the one only direct method of healing, while all other methods are indirect.

Indirect methods, whether mental or physical, do not always heal; usually they simply produce a temporary relief; but the one great direct method removes cause and effect and all; it brings forth a new life from the strong, wholesome, spotless within, therefore every trace of the old life, with its adverse conditions, must vanish absolutely. To live perpetually in the spiritual attitude is to retain perpetual health because there can be no disease in that which is spiritual, and so long as the mind is in a spiritual attitude the body will be in a spiritual condition.

When the body is in a spiritual condition it is immune from every disease, including all forms of contagious diseases; it is in that state where health is so strong and so positive that the negative actions of disease are simply powerless in its presence.

The chemical elements of a spiritualized body are sustained in the very life of the spirit, and the health of the spirit is unconquerable; nothing from without can disturb it. Its power comes from the Supreme Power and that power is irresistible, invincible and immovable. It is what it is, and nothing can cause it to be different.

To place the body in the condition of that health from within that is so strong that nothing can cause it to be anything else but health, is to secure complete immunity from all ills, and the body will be in this condition so long as the mind lives in the spirit; that is, in the spiritual understanding of its own divinity.

This spiritual understanding develops with the development of real spirituality and the awakening of more and more of the sublime spiritual life, and as this development continues, the power of health, wholeness and harmony will increase accordingly.

Chapter 9

And he said unto her, Daughter thy faith hath made thee whole. — Mark 5: 34.

THIS is the woman who had suffered many things from many physicians, and there are thousands today with a similar experience; but these thousands can all be healed, every one. Faith can do all things, and we all can have faith. This woman was healed by simply touching the hem of His garment; we can be healed in the same way. The Christ is here today; the presence of His spirit is within us and all about us; we may at any time touch the hem of His garment and feel that we are filled with His power through and through. Then we shall, as this woman did, feel in our bodies that we are healed; the adverse condition is dried up, withered away, vanished completely, and we are every whit clean and strong.

This is the inner working of faith; when we inwardly feel that we are healed, we ARE healed; whatsoever we inwardly feel, believing, that shall surely come to pass. Faith is not of the letter, but of the spirit; when we have faith we enter into the inner life of the spirit, and the power of that life can do and will do whatever we believe it can do. When we have faith we do not depend upon the outer, but upon the inner, and we thereby place ourselves in touch with the inner; we actually enter into the interior life and are therefore filled through and through with the supreme spirit of that life.

The spiritual life is always perfectly whole; when we have faith we enter into the spiritual life; and as we are no longer in darkness when we enter the light, we are no longer in sickness when we enter absolute spiritual health. When we are in the spirit, we inwardly feel that we are in health, strength and wholeness, and what we inwardly feel is true; it will come to pass; it is now coming to pass. The moment we feel health and strength in the spirit of the body, health and strength will begin to come forth; the turn for the better will come that very hour; if our faith is strong we shall be restored instantaneously, but in any event we will be made every whit whole.

To have the perfect faith and place in action the full power of faith, It is necessary to enter into the soul of faith; that is, the mind should recognize that interior spiritual power that animates the action of faith, and as we consciously come into perfect touch with this power, we INWARDLY FEEL the presence of this power. Then whatsoever we desire that power to do, believing, the same shall be done. "And all things, whatsoever ye shall ask in prayer, believing, ye shall receive."

When this woman touched the hem of His garment, Jesus "perceived in Himself that the power proceeding from Him had gone forth." Through her deep, strong faith, she placed herself in touch with the spiritual power that was so immensely strong in the divine personality of Jesus Christ; and as this power entered her being she "felt in her body" that she was whole. Her faith opened the way and placed her life in conscious touch with Supreme life; the power of the spirit proceeding from the Christ gave her wholeness and freedom.

But the same Christ is here today. The Christ is enthroned in every soul; by entering into the pure spiritual life of the soul we may touch the hem of His garment now, and the same power proceeding from the Christ shall come forth into us; then we shall also "feel in the body" that we are whole. Our faith has opened the way; we are in Him and He in us, and all is well.

Practical Self-Help

Practical Self-Help

Table of Contents

Chapter 1 - Learn to Help Yourself	204
Chapter 2 - Others Will Help You	207
Chapter 3 - The Two Great Factors	211
Chapter 4 - What You Should Do	218
Chapter 5 - You and Your Own World	220
Chapter 6 - Changing Your Own World	225
Chapter 7 - Results and Recompense	230
Chapter 8 - The Successful Mental Attitude	235
Chapter 9 - Full Use of Ability and Power	241
Chapter 10 - The Control of Circumstance	248
Chapter 11 - Effective Use of Thought and Action	253
Chapter 12 - Vital Principles in Self-Help	258
Chapter 13 - Building Self-Confidence	271
Chapter 14 - The Increase of Power	280
Chapter 15 - Equal to Every Occasion	284
Chapter 16 - Invincible Determination	292
Chapter 17 - Know What You Want	295
Chapter 18 - Special Rules in Self-Help	299
Chapter 19 - Building the Positives	313
Chapter 20 - The Courage to Go On	319
Chapter 21 - The Control of Things	325
Chapter 22 - There is Always a Way	328
Chapter 23 - Optimism That Makes Good	334
Chapter 24 - Act in the Present	340
Chapter 25 - Actions That Produce Response	344
Chapter 26 - Directing the Forces of Life	352
Chapter 27 - The Right Use of Life	355
Chapter 28 - The Most Helpful Principle Known Today	362

Chapter I

Learn to Help Yourself

The Principle. You are an individual. You have your own life to live; your own world to create; your own future to determine. And that you may accomplish these things, you must find yourself; you must learn what you are; what you can do; and where you can apply yourself to the best advantage. You must learn these things for yourself, and apply them yourself, for in the last analysis results depend upon what you think and do. Others may place facts and opportunities within your reach; but you must use them or nothing is gained or accomplished. In reality, others can do nothing for you that is of actual and permanent value. It is practical or effective self-help alone that counts. It is how well you apply yourself and help yourself that determines what your life, your achievements and your possessions are to be. But the idea of helping yourself should not be used in a limited or purely personal sense. You help yourself, in the best and largest meaning of the term, when you seek to apply your whole self; when you seek to be and do all that is in you to be and do. It is for that purpose, and to realize such an ideal, that the methods that follow have been formulated; and to take definite steps in that direction, this is what you should do:

(1) Make yourself the vital center of your own world. Every man lives in a world that is distinctly his own. This world is, in the main, created by himself; and it is so distinctly colored by his own individuality as to be wholly different from any other world. In this world of his own making he finds his opportunities. In this same world he finds those factors that he is to use in meeting his needs, living his life and realizing his aspirations. It is the use of those opportunities and factors, by the individual, that determines results for the individual. And to use those things in a manner to secure full service and full value, he must be their master. Here then is where you should begin. You should make yourself the vital center of your own world; first in thought, then in action. Think of yourself as the master hand, the one only ruler of everything in your own world. Do not think of yourself as the product of that world; but think of that world as being the product of your thought, your effort and your selection. You cannot help yourself to the fullest extent unless you crown yourself absolute monarch of your own domain, and take full possession of it all in the spirit of unconditional mastery.

(2) Depend, upon yourself. If you are to apply your whole self you cannot depend upon others. What is to be done in the direct use of the self you must do. In practical self-help it is not only tangible results that are wanted, but also the full scientific use of what is in your whole self. The object is not simply to get, but also to become; not only to increase the measure of external possession, but also to grow steadily into a greater personality. To depend upon yourself is to live, think and work in the realization of the fact that it is you that will have to do it. This will tend to draw out many talents and powers that have never been used before, and you will thereby become stronger, more able, more competent, and in brief, a greater man. Expect all results there-fore to come to you from your own efforts. Blame no one for your failures. Give yourself credit for your success. Others may have helped you indirectly; but unless you help yourself directly to the help that may come from others, and add thereto your own individual efforts, there is no gain for anybody concerned. It is the practice of depending absolutely upon yourself that counts in the long run; not only in securing definite, external results, but also in promoting the larger and more perfect expression of the best that is in you. The man who depends largely upon others will not make full use of his own self; and will, accordingly, permit many of his best talents and energies to lie dormant. To depend upon yourself, therefore, to the greatest possible degree, is to help yourself in the largest measure to acquire that additional power and ability that you will need to the full realization of your desires and aims.

(3) Use your whole self. But that which is used is not simply placed in action; it is applied for some definite purpose through which something greater and better may be secured. To use yourself according to the idea of practical self-help is to live and work to full capacity, and to live for. the largest and best that imagination can picture.

(4) Use what is contained in yourself for the continuous advancement of yourself. You are not helping yourself unless you are helping yourself to become more; and you are not helping yourself to advance unless you are constantly increasing that faculty in yourself that has the power to produce advancement. Everything that is in you should be applied with a view of promoting your own advancement. This would be self-help in the fullest and largest sense of that term. But you would, in this manner, not only become larger, more competent and more useful to yourself; you would also become a greater power for good in the world. True self-help, therefore, brings greater good both to the individual who fully helps himself and to all others with whom he may come in contact. Advancement, however, does not simply mean better positions, circumstances or advantages in the external world; it also means a decided and continuous improvement in yourself — in mind, character, personality, life and soul.

Chapter 2

Others Will Help You

Why the majority among men always act with the man who helps himself. The reason is that mankind is naturally attracted to that which is gaining ground, because there is a tendency in every man to want to gain ground, and move forward. The man who takes hold of things; who proceeds to do things, is complying with one of the greatest laws of life — the law of continuous advancement; and as every man feels more or less the prompting of this same law in his own soul, he takes instinctive interest in those who are succeeding in working out that law. For the same reason mankind is attracted to action, and therefore feels a desire to act with him who acts the most and the best. When someone is moving in the very direction that we wish to move, we naturally conclude that we will reach our goal in the safest and simplest manner if we go with him and act with him. We think that by helping him on his journey we will take the same journey; and in a measure we are right. It is wisdom to follow the procession when the procession is going where we want to go; otherwise not. But the man who is helping himself is doing the very thing everybody wants to do; and therefore a majority, or all who can, will go where he goes, and help him, directly or indirectly, to do what he has undertaken to do.

Why nature favors the man who helps himself. The man who helps himself applies himself. He thereby calls nature into action; and, accordingly, nature begins to act more and more with him. To him who would do much, nature lends much power. To him who calls into action all he has, nature will give more. This is the nature of nature. She lives for those who act, and she acts with those who desire greater action. The reason is simple. Whenever you call anything into action you call nature into action; and as nature is inexhaustible, you can call into action more and more of any element or power; nature will respond with the necessary amount. And he who aims to help himself more and more is calling nature into action more and more. He is, therefore, favored more and more by nature, as she gives her special attention to life and growth. She is not present where things are dormant; but the moment action begins, her life and her power at once rush in to aid in promoting the purpose in view.

Why God helps them that help themselves. It is the nature of infinite power to act — to work for the greatest and the best. There is neither pause nor misdirection in the actions of that power. That power is always doing something; and every man who really tries to do something will follow the law of infinite power. He will act in harmony with a greater power, and thus come closely into contact with that power. In consequence he will be helped by that power. Furthermore, when you help yourself you tend to enlarge your life; you are calling into action more and more of your talents and powers; and the larger your life the larger your contact with infinite life. You have become a larger channel of expression, and a large channel, when opened to a mighty stream, can convey far more than a small channel.

And again, when you apply all that is in yourself, you place yourself in a position where you can secure more. When you use all your life and all your power — that is, go to the limit, or outer rim, of your capacity, you place yourself in touch with the world of greater power. But you cannot come in actual contact with the larger life until you live to full capacity all the life you already possess. You cannot reach out beyond the circumference so long as you seclude yourself near the center. But the man who helps himself goes out into the larger fields of action, and frequently reaches out beyond the present circumference of his mind. He thereby comes in contact with greater power, and is more or less charged with that power.

A strange paradox. The more you help yourself the more help you will receive from all possible sources. This is the law herewith; and the converse of this law is equally true; that is, the more you help others, in the usual fashion, the less you help them, in the long run, and the less help and appreciation you receive from them. Daily experience is full of evidence to prove this fact; but instead of indicating that mankind is selfish and ungrateful, this fact indicates the very opposite. The moment a man begins to live exclusively for the world, the world begins to lose interest in his efforts and ideas. And it is to the credit of the world that such an attitude is always taken.

The fact is, you must live for yourself before you can live for the world, or be of real service to the world; but the man who lives exclusively for the world is not living for himself; he therefore is of no further use to the world, and the world wisely turns attention elsewhere. You must be able to help yourself before you can help man-kind; therefore mankind has no interest in the efforts or the ideas of him who does not help himself, knowing that his service has slight practical value. And the fact that the race wants practical value, not theories or speculation, proves that the race, as a whole, is reasonably level-headed, though individuals at times become confused. Then we must remember that when you neglect to help yourself you will grow less in power and usefulness; you will weaken and become a negative, ineffective entity, regardless of how good your intentions may be.

The world, however, is attracted only to the positive and the strong, because it is only positiveness and strength that can help the world and give service that has permanency and real worth. In this connection we should bear well in mind the fact that the only help that mankind really wants is that help that will help them to help themselves. For such help their appreciation is exceptional, and their gratitude unbounded. But help of the other kind, although sometimes accepted under extremity, is not wanted for long. We all feel that such help interferes with personal liberty, and tends to decrease the power and expression of individuality. And the fact that all normal minds instinctively refuse such help proves that the race is born with a spark of divine wisdom; and that we realize somehow that we are made, not to be carried upon the arms of others, but to create our own life, our own world and our own destiny.

Chapter 3

The Two Great Factors

In the science, of practical self-help, there are two factors that occupy the most prominent positions; and all results gained will depend upon how these two factors are caused to act, or caused to be acted upon. **These two factors are: The Human Entity and Environment; or, the man himself and the immediate world in which he lives.**

The human entity is, strictly speaking, the factor that acts, though it is almost constantly being acted upon, in a certain sense, by external surroundings. The actions of surroundings, however, are always indirect, while the actions of the man himself are always direct.

But man has the power to determine what effects all such indirect actions may produce in himself and in his world; he is therefore the master of the situation. He can cause any direct action in himself that he may desire, and he can admit or exclude what he chooses of all indirect actions from without.

To help himself man must cause only those actions to originate in himself that will result in actual self-help; and he must permit only such actions from without as will tend to increase or promote that same self-help. That is, he must govern the actions of the two prime factors. He must so govern himself — the human entity — that everything he does will be conducive to self-help — the whole self applied, and he must so adapt himself to his environment that the effect of that environment will tend to call forth into practical action more and more of what is latent in his whole self. To accomplish these things, however, man must understand himself and his environment. He must know of what the two prime factors are composed, and know how they may be so directed as to produce only such results as he may desire. And it has been stated that if man knew how to use his environment to the best advantage, and knew how to apply himself to the best advantage, he could accomplish almost anything he might have in view.

The various elements of which the human entity is composed can be grouped for convenient study as follows:

(1) The Physical Side. In determining what effect environment is to have upon human life, the physical side assumes a very important role; the reason being that this side of the human entity is the seat of sensation and the physical senses. And it is through sensation in general, and through the different senses in particular, that external surroundings produce their effects upon man. What we see, hear or feel tends to impress our minds with thoughts and ideas that correspond with what we have seen, heard or felt; and those ideas will, in turn, tend to cause actions, after their kind, in our own minds or personalities. The physical side must, therefore, be placed under perfect control so that only those impressions are permitted to enter the mind, through the senses, that tend to produce desirable actions.

To train the physical side to accept only the best that environment may suggest, ask yourself this question immediately you meet any circumstance, condition or event: "What is there in this circumstance that can add to the richness and the power of my mind, or that can serve the purpose of my life, in any form or manner?"

(2) The Mental Side. When man proceeds to act or originate any action from within himself, it is in the mental side that that action begins. It is also in the mental side that all those actions that are suggested from without make their first definite move. To illustrate, an impression from without enters the mind through the senses. The mind takes it up and transforms it into thoughts and ideas. Those ideas, through their natural tendency to express themselves, create desires to act; and if permitted to have their way, will proceed to act, the action in every instance being similar to that action in the without that suggested the original impression.

For example, you see a man doing something wonderful. You are impressed. You begin to think of those great deeds. That thought begins to act in your mind and causes you to desire to do something great. Then if you permit that desire to have its way you will actually attempt to do something great, or at least more than you have ever attempted before. In that case, therefore, you acted wisely in receiving the impression and in permitting all those things that came from that impression to have their way. But if you see a man gaining success by taking advantage of others, you are dealing with a different circumstance; and if you permit yourself to be impressed with what he is doing and permit those thoughts and desires that naturally come from that impression to have their way, you will be prompted to go and try to succeed in that way.

If you have taken control of the mental side, however, you can prevent that impression from becoming an action; and you can prevent all undesirable actions from becoming actions in your own mind. And this is decidedly important, because the more active an idea becomes in your mind, the more liable you are to want to carry out that idea yourself. Therefore whenever you find yourself thinking Of anything that you would not want to do, receive or experience in your actual life, proceed at once to think of something that you could welcome in actual life.

(3) Faculties and Powers. In practical self-help the first essential with regard to the faculties and powers we may possess is right use and full use. To use a faculty right, all the actions of that faculty should be constructive; that is, all those actions should work together for that particular thing which the faculty in question is trying to accomplish. And full use means the right use of all the power and talent that is in that faculty.

However, it has been demonstrated that the average person applies only a small fraction of the power and ability in his possession; and that most of the energy that is active in the average faculty is not directed upon the work of that faculty. But if all the energy in the human mind were applied constructively, and fully directed upon the work at hand, the average person could accomplish from two to ten times as much as he is doing now. His work would also be far better, and he would become a far greater man.

(4) Desires and Needs. What we need and what we desire invariably determine what we are to work for. It is therefore absolutely necessary to abolish all artificial needs and remove or prevent all abnormal desires. In practical self-help it is the aim to supply every natural need and fulfill every legitimate desire.

And in order that this may be accomplished, no efforts should be wasted upon needs and desires that have no rightful place in human life. For this reason we should desire only those things that tend to inspire the mind to work for the greater and the better; and observe moderation in supplying all normal needs.

(5) Ambitions and Aims. The force of the mind as well as the action of our faculties naturally follow the lines of our strongest ambitions; and when ambition is very strong it will tend to call forth practically all the powers and talents the mind may possess. It is therefore highly important that every ambition be inspired with the highest possible aim so that every force and talent called into action may work for something of great worth; and that every such ambition be given more force, more power and more determination.

And no ambition can be made too strong, provided its aim is very high. An aspiring mind cannot be too ambitious. That wagon that is hitched to a star cannot have too great a speed nor be propelled with too much force. In all such cases the greater the speed and the force the better. The force of every ambition is a building force, and when strong, concentrated and determined, will gradually build up sufficient ability to carry its own purpose through.

(6) Conditions and Tendencies. Every condition that arises in mind or personality may suggest thoughts or desires corresponding with itself; and every tendency in the human system may attract other forces into its own course. Conditions and tendencies may therefore determine action. But as such actions are not always desirable, it becomes necessary to observe all conditions closely, and exercise complete control over every tendency, whether it be physical or mental. It is through such control that habits and traits, whether acquired or hereditary, may be removed or changed as desired. And this is important, as the object is to remove what is not wanted, and constantly to change and improve what is wanted.

Whenever a condition arises that is not wanted we should imagine the possession of a condition that is wanted; then try to feel deeply the real nature of this new condition. All physical conditions, all mental states, and all moods may be changed or removed in this manner. Every unwelcome tendency may be immediately suspended by calling the mind's attention, at the time, to something that holds greater and richer possibilities. Attention will naturally go wherever the interest is deep and undivided; and a deep interest may be aroused in anything by simply trying to find, when examining that thing, the most interesting point of view.

(7) Activities — Constructive and Destructive. The human entity is constantly and literally alive with activities; and as many of these are destructive, or at least non-productive, it becomes highly important to know how all these activities may be so directed as to become building forces of the most efficient type. To this end it becomes necessary, first, to train the entire human entity to work for something, at all times, that has greater value and worth; and, second, to approach environment in such a manner that every impression suggested by what is discerned in that environment tends to inspire the mind to work for greater value and worth.

Illustration. You may watch a number of men working in a field. How is your mind impressed by that scene? It will depend upon your attitude toward such work, and what you are looking for. But you can hold any attitude you like and look for anything you like. You may therefore determine how your mind is to be impressed. You may think, as you witness that scene, that it is disagreeable work, hard work, unprofitable work, or that it is necessarily the work of undeveloped minds alone. In any case, such a view of the scene will not produce constructive actions in your mind, nor inspire your mind to work for greater value and worth.

But if your thought is turned upon the productive power of the soil, and how that power could be increased; how the soil could be so cultivated as to produce far more; or how the work of cultivating the soil could be improved, made more scientific, in brief, made a fine art — if such were your thoughts, that scene would impress your mind in a far different manner. The mental actions that were called forth by that scene would be thoroughly constructive, and the ideas gained at the time would give your mind a decided tendency to work for greater value and worth.

Chapter 4

What You Should Do

(1) Apply Yourself Constructively. This would imply the use of every active force in the system for some definite and valued purpose, and used in such a way as actually to produce the results in-tended. But only a fraction of the active forces in the human system, even among the most brilliant and most competent, is applied constructively, or for some definite and worth-while purpose. It is therefore evident that the man who will proceed to apply himself constructively will help himself to a remarkable degree.

(2) Change Your Nature According to the Demands of Your Ideals. There is nothing in the nature of man that cannot be changed. This is a fact that should hold a most prominent place in all thinking. And in all efforts to promote practical self-help this fact should accompany every action that may be taken. Whatever a man's ideals may demand, he can gradually change himself and modify his nature to correspond. There is there-fore no occasion for disappointment, regret or self-depreciation. No present condition need trouble his mind. It can be changed; and to believe this is to take the first step in that direction. The truth is that what we thoroughly believe we can do, we will eventually find a way to do.

(3) Develop Further What Is in You. If your powers and talents be small you can make them large. If your powers and talents be great you can make them greater still. There is nothing in human nature that is fixed; nothing that has reached its limit. Every quality and faculty in man is susceptible to development, and will respond to every intelligent effort that is made to promote growth. And the first two essentials in this connection are to desire, continuously and persistently, the further development of every faculty and power we possess, and to train more and more of our actions to become constructive. Here we should note that every action originating in the human entity will become constructive, provided the idea, thought or feeling that causes that action aims to acquire or produce something larger or better than what has been secured in that same field of action before.

(4) Perfect What Is in You. This would not constitute the working for an end, but the promotion of a process. And it would be the aim of that process to increase constantly the virtue, the quality, the usefulness and the worth of everything that you would try to perfect in your nature. Herewith it is highly important that the idea of perfection be distinctly understood, for perfection is the object and aim of everything that man may attempt to do. Every normal action in the human mind has perfection as its goal, and every idea that the mind conceives is born from the desire to understand more perfectly that which occupies attention at the time.

But perfection is not an end; to attain perfection does not mean to come to a standstill. Perfection is simply a step higher — as high as we can go just now; and every step in perfection can be followed — will be followed by another and another step, no matter how high we may go. If you are doing your best now, you are perfect as far as you have gone — you are complying perfectly with your present powers and capabilities; but as perfection is a continued process, you will, if you promote this process, constantly go farther and do better. To be perfect is to be all that you can be now — with the ever-present conviction that you can become more and more, on and on, for an indefinite period.

Chapter 5

You and Your Own World

Your own world, or what is usually designated as environment, is composed of the following factors, elements and conditions:

(1) All Kinds of People. The first and most important element found in the usual environment is the human element. And the way man adapts himself to that element and applies what he receives through his contact with the human side of his environment will determine largely how well, and to what extent, he will succeed in helping himself. In the first place, he should aim to secure the greatest good and the greatest amount of good from every shade of human nature that he may meet; but to promote that aim it will be necessary to give as little attention as possible to human defects and personal inferiority; to train the mind to search for personal worth in all human entities, and to appreciate that worth to the highest degree whenever found. In the science of practical self-help, the attitude of each individual towards the human race will be decidedly different from the usual, as it will be the purpose of the student of self-help to think of the race as a growing plant, and to examine that plant more and more closely with a view of finding its greatest possibilities.

(2) All Kinds of Things. The world of things may seem to comprise the larger part of environment, as it consists of almost everything that is not specially classified under any one particular head, and may include nearly all forms of tangible objects as well as circumstances and undefined conditions. And on account of its variety, the proper dealing with the world of things becomes a fine art; though it is an art which, when mastered, will mean immeasurable gain. In the study of this art, however, it is necessary first to realize that all things can help us if approached properly. Even those things that may seem to be against us will be found to be for us when approached from the right point of view. And to find this right point of view, in every instance, is one of the aims of this study.

(3) Building Material. The environment of nearly every man will be found to contain building material of all kinds; and with this material he may, when he knows how, build almost anything from a home to a destiny. Whatever man may wish to build, in his physical world, mental world, or spiritual world, he will find the necessary material in his own immediate environment. If he will only help himself to as much of that material as he can use, that part of his problem will be solved. But the solution of this problem is not found in the act of going out and appropriating, through any means whatever, the material that may be needed. We can appropriate without going out of our way. We may help ourselves to as much as we want. The question then is, how to use this material, be it physical or mental; and the answer is found in what may be termed "Constructive Application."

(4) Building Forces — Natural and Human. The building forces that are found in man's environment are of two kinds; those that exist in nature and those that exist in other people. A man who knows how to build can use, not only the constructive forces that are found in his natural environment, but can also call forth constructive forces from others — forces that would otherwise remain dormant. To inspire and direct other people to build for greater things than they would have been capable of if left to themselves is a high art, and one that is practiced both extensively and effectually by those who have gained prominent positions. And the results are two-fold. The man who can call forth the building forces of others will enrich the lives of those people as well as his own. He will naturally receive a part of the increase, while the others receive the remainder.

By helping others to help themselves he has promoted his own self-help on a large and extensive scale. And this is always the case. In dealing with the building forces in his environment, man should therefore aim to call forth, for practical use, those forces that exist in nature and those that are yet dormant in the minds of his fellow men. But in doing the latter his ruling desire must be, not to help others to help him, but to help others to help themselves. If his sole aim be personal gain his power to call forth the building forces in others will be greatly decreased. The selfish man cannot inspire others, nor can the self-centered man reach out and awaken those greater forces in nature that may exist in the larger and finer realms of his environment.

(5) The Finished Product. How to use, to the best advantage, the many forms of the finished product existing everywhere in our environment is another vital problem. Every finished product, whether physical, mechanical, mental, intellectual, artistic, esthetic or spiritual, holds possibilities for practical use in many ways; and the man who can fully appreciate and appropriate for actual self-help, the sum total of what human effort has completed to date, is on the way to the helping of himself on a very large scale. This idea gives us a new view of what the world has done, and reveals possibilities for human enrichment that are practically unlimited. And here we may add a very important rule. Never look upon what the world has done without asking yourself what that same thing can do for you.

(6) Demand for Talent. Among the many factors that are found in man's environment, one of the most prominent is that of demand for talent. This demand is persistent everywhere, and as the demand for the best talent is not only exceedingly strong, but constantly growing, the art of supplying this demand will be found to be an open gate to one of the richest fields in practical self-help. There is no one way through which man can help himself so much as that of improving his ability to that degree where he can answer successfully the constant call for more ability. But in trying to improve his ability he must consider the nature and purpose of the two prime factors in his life. He must learn to apply himself, and learn to use his environment. And here it is well to remember that it is just as necessary for man to use his environment properly, if he wishes to improve his ability, as it is to apply himself properly. Indirect actions from external surroundings have just as much power to advance or deter the faculties of the mind as have those direct actions that originate in the mind itself.

Illustration. You may be living in a neighbor-hood where people have little or no ambition, where great deeds are almost unknown and where the ordinary is considered good enough. You may have considerable ambition yourself, but you are constantly being discouraged from carrying out your greater plans. In the course of time you give in to those adverse suggestions from the human element of your environment, and later find your ambition practically gone. If you should then examine your mind psychologically you would find that those faculties in which your ambition originated have weakened to a marked degree, and that your ability to do what you were ambitious to do has decreased to less than half of what it was. And the cause was simply this, you permitted your environment to put a damper on your ability. The result was that both your ambition and your ability disappeared. But if you had, on the other hand, turned those adverse suggestions to good account, by becoming more determined to carry your ambition through, you would have aroused more and more of the latent power of your mind until your ability and capacity would have doubled.

(7) Opportunities. In practical self-help the art of taking advantage of every opportunity is vitally important. Every man's environment is actually full of opportunities, and to take advantage of those opportunities that can be mastered now, while constantly preparing for greater ones — these are the two problems. And the solution is found in a dearer insight into your own present capacity, and a better understanding of the needs and demands of the world in which you live. But do not wait for opportunity. She is already waiting for you. Do not go out in search for better opportunities; search for methods through which you may fit yourself for better opportunities. When you are ready for the greater, the greater will be ready for you.

(8) Obstacles and Difficulties. These two elements are present to a greater or lesser extent in nearly every form of environment; but to the man who aims to help himself in every conceivable manner there are no difficulties and no obstacles. Every difficulty is an opportunity — an opportunity to call forth energies that have never been used before; and every obstacle is rich with possibilities — possibilities that you can develop for your own use if you will. In practical self-help the idea is not to try to overcome difficulties, but to try to use them; not to try to avoid obstacles, but to try to get out of them the good they may contain; and they all possess much good. In fact, an obstacle is simply a bundle of good things misplaced, and you can make those good things your own, thereby helping yourself, by placing them where they belong. When you try to avoid an obstacle, you not only miss a valuable opportunity, but you permit yourself to be mastered by conditions and things in your environment. Environment, however, was not made to master man, but to be used, directed and mastered by man.

Chapter 6

Changing Your Own World

It is in your power to change and improve your own world, so that the elements of that world will serve you better — help you to help yourself. And to that end, this is what you can do:

(1) You can so adapt yourself to your surroundings that every idea, thought, impression or suggestion received will be favorable. And make this your rule: Whatever you see, look for some-thing that you can use; and whatever you meet, ask yourself how it can be improved.

(2) You can convey favorable impressions to others. The value would be two-fold. First, you would call into action the most helpful elements and forces in yourself; and second, you would call forth the most helpful elements and forces in others. And he who helps much will be helped much in return. We can do nothing that is good without receiving more and more good of the same kind. Therefore you should aim to make every word and action give encouragement and inspiration to others. Talk health, happiness and prosperity. Be optimistic in all your speech. Never give expression to a pessimistic thought, and never act in an attitude that indicates depression or disappointment. Look for the best and say so. Expect the best, and put forward your best efforts to make that expectation come true.

(3) You can act constructively upon all things. The basis of such action is to try to turn all things to good account. And the best method would be to have some greater purpose in view, and try to make all things you meet serve that purpose.

(4) You can act in harmony with all people. This is highly important, as harmony increases the power of the one who is harmonious, and tends to convert obstacles into new and better plans. But to be in harmony with everybody does not necessarily mean to agree with everything. When two people agree to disagree, and do so harmoniously, they may continue in just as perfect harmony with each other as when they agree to agree. And all that is necessary to agree to disagree is kindness, character and self-possession. However, in case you cannot get into external agreement with others, continue to be internally harmonious. Feel harmonious and give your attention to those chief essentials that will promote most perfectly the best interest of all.

(5) You can convert building material into any finished product desired. The belief that you can finish only certain products and make actual use of only certain kinds of material is not true. There is no limit to what man can do with the raw material that may be found in his environment, be that material physical or mental.

(6) You can convert obstacles into opportunities by proceeding in the conviction that if those forces and possibilities that are latent in every obstacle were developed and applied, you would gain much in an external sense, and would, at the same time, call forth forces and talents in yourself that have hitherto been dormant. And you can take advantage of any desired opportunity by adapting yourself now to the ones that are nearest at hand, and by preparing yourself in the meantime for the ones that are richer and greater.

(7) You can control circumstances and improve your environment by acting, first, upon yourself with a view of making yourself stronger and more efficient; and, second, by acting constructively upon the chief factors of that

Practical Self-Help

circumstance in which you are living at the time. To illustrate, we will suppose that you are living in an undesirable neighborhood, the chief factors of which are unwholesome, depressing, and even sickening. To control and change your circumstances, your first step will be to improve yourself so that you may increase your earning capacity, thereby becoming able, either to move or to improve your surroundings.

Your second step will be to act constructively upon the chief factors of your immediate environment. If your place of abode be dreary and cheerless you can make it a place of sunshine and joy; and this you can do without extra expense. If everything about the place is monotonous, you remedy that matter by introducing new and novel modes of ornamentation, none of which need add to your expense. If your place is a "sore eye" in your sight, you make it a "color spot" in your neighborhood. And what is the result? You live in a new world where you are; you have changed your environment to a considerable extent without changing your locality; you are gaining encouragement and inspiration from your successful efforts at "transformation," and the experience will enlarge and enrich your mind. You also give enjoyment to others. You have changed and improved the individual factors in your environment, and have thereby gained more individuality in your community.

You have placed yourself in the fore in that particular place. Many will note this, and when it is learned that you have taken special pains to improve your ability and efficiency, as well as make the best of what you have, you will soon be invited to go elsewhere — to go where opportunities are better, recompense larger and surroundings more congenial. The world is ever looking for those who are succeeding in making the most of what they

Practical Self-Help

have; for it is just such men and women that are wanted where much can be turned to more.

But to make the best of what you have is not to let well enough alone and be satisfied. To make the best of what you have is to try to bring out the best that is in what you have, and try to improve that best constantly. To illustrate further, two men own adjoining farms. The one neglects everything except the mere act of sowing, reaping and marketing. The other tries, in addition, to make everything about his place look attractive. His houses are painted; his machinery is protected from the weather and always looks new; fences are in repair; the lawn nicely mown; the shrubbery well trimmed; his horses well groomed, etc., etc. He keeps his place in this condition at practically no extra expense.

He is acting constructively upon the chief factors of his environment, trying to bring out the best that is in them, and improve them as much as possible. What is the result? His environment is an inspiration, and an incentive to better work. And as better work always produces greater results, his power and means still further to improve his environment are constantly increased. Then we will also suppose that this man is trying to improve himself, both in understanding and in the application of scientific agriculture; and we begin to realize how the use of the two essentials in the improvement of environment — the increase of ability and efficiency in the man himself, and constructive action upon the chief factors of his surroundings — will naturally and unfailingly improve that environment.

(8) You can direct the building forces in your environment; both the forces of nature and the forces of those people with whom you may come in contact. To do the latter, the first step is to call for originality in everybody; to encourage all minds to create new and better ideas; and to aim, in all transactions with others, to help them to help themselves. To do the former, the first step is for man to make of himself a building force. The more constructive a man becomes in his own actions the more power, insight and skill he gains with which to apply constructively the building forces in his environment. The man who can build with his own power has found the secret of constructive action, and he can apply that secret just as effectually to forces in his external world as to those in his own mind or personality.

Chapter 7

Results and Recompense

It is how well man applies the two prime factors in practical self-help — The Human Entity and Environment, that will determine the results that he is to gain from his efforts. These two factors, as they act and react upon each other, will constitute the real cause of all results to be gained, whatever his work may be. These two factors, therefore, must be taken into account in every action and in every undertaking, and his aim should be, first, last and continuously, to use them both as fully, as constructively and as scientifically as possible.

The man who tries to apply and improve himself, but who neglects to act constructively upon the chief factors of his environment, will secure only partial results. The same is true of the man who tries to use and improve his environment, but who neglects to apply and improve himself. Results in his case will be only partial. To secure the greatest and the best results, therefore, the full use of both factors must, as far as possible, enter into every action, and the improvement of both factors must be promoted constantly.

And as a special rule you should aim to make full use of everything in your environment; make full use of everything in yourself; and aim, in all your thoughts, actions and efforts, to improve both yourself and your environment. Try to improve yourself so that your actions may be better; and try to improve the thing acted upon so that your actions may work to better advantage. Regarding recompense, the application of these principles will reward the individual in many ways, chiefly as follows:

Practical Self-Help

(1) The Expression of Self. The more man tends to draw forth what has worth within himself, and the more he causes himself to act, with definite and worthy aims, upon the elements of his environment, the more fully he will express himself. And there is no greater recompense than that of realizing that the worthy and the superior in your own nature is coming forth into living and tangible expression. When man does not aim at the full and constructive use of himself and his environment, only fragments of his better nature will be called forth. He is therefore living a fragmentary life, and enjoys but a fraction of the greatest of all recompense.

(2) The Enrichment of Life. This is another valued gain that comes directly from the same cause — the full and constructive use of the two prime factors — as the effort to act more fully and more completely at all times tends to increase the measure of life, and also to improve the quality.

(3) The Enlargement of Life. In the helping of one's self, there is nothing that is more important than the constant enlargement of life; and the reason is simple. The larger your life becomes, the more you will have to draw upon, and the more you will have to work with. That results may be increased in proportion is evident. The mind that acts along a few lines only and to a partial degree will be small; but the mind that tries to act along more and more lines, and tries to act as fully as possible along every line, will naturally become large. We understand therefore why the full and complete application of the two prime factors will tend to enlarge life continuously.

(4) More and More to Live For. He who aims to live for much will have much to live for. There will be no end to the increase, and in the last analysis, it is more and more to live for that we all want. It is this that constitutes one of the greatest in the world of recompense. If there is but little to live for, the reason is that no constructive effort has been made to live for more. But no one can succeed in living for more until he tries to apply the best that exists in himself upon the best that exists in his environment. When a man will cause all the elements in himself to act for some definite and valued purpose, and will proceed to act intelligently upon all the elements in his external world, he will soon have so much to live for that his mind cannot fully encompass them all. When one joy has served its purpose, a thousand better ones will be waiting.

(5) Happiness, Pleasure and Contentment. The greatest pleasure of all, the only real satisfaction and the deepest feeling of joy, comes only to him who lives in every part of his being, and lives for everything in his world. The steady gaining of ground along all lines of ambition and aspiration can alone produce genuine and lasting happiness. And such a measure of happiness will surely come to him who applies himself fully, and in all things.

(6) External Possessions. The steady increase of external possessions will naturally come to him who fully applies the science of practical self-help; for the real meaning of self-help is the whole self applied; and he who applies his whole self will steadily become more and more competent. He will therefore work himself gradually and surely up into those positions in life where recompense is larger and opportunity greater. All legitimate wealth has been gained through the man applying himself intelligently upon one or more of the elements of his environment. So, therefore, all wealth or increase in external possessions can be traced to the practical and constructive use of the two prime factors,

(7) New and Better Surroundings. As the man grows larger and more worthy, he will not only be attracted to

Practical Self-Help

better things in his external world, but will gain the power to produce them. Another valued recompense, therefore, to be gained in this manner, will be that of coming into better, richer and more beautiful surroundings at the beginning of every new step in advance in his life. And if he takes full advantage of the whole science of self-help, he may take steps in advance at frequent intervals.

Desire For Reward. As the element of recompense is a natural part of practical life, we cannot master this element unless we understand its deeper cause and real meaning. And so we ask: Why does man try to improve himself, advance himself or help himself? Why does he try to call forth the best that is in him, and why does he try to act to the best advantage upon everything in his external world that may make for growth, promotion or enrichment? It is the desire for reward — reward in its largest meaning — a desire that is a necessary part both of the purpose of life and of the real nature of life.

Cause of This Desire. The desire for reward is found in that deeper feeling in human nature that naturally wants its own; and in that finer consciousness that instinctively knows that reward will add to the value and worth of life. This desire does not originate in selfishness, as usually defined, but in the soul's realization of the fact that the creator and the thing created are one. And inseparably coupled with the realization of this fact is the feeling that it is not only man's prerogative but his unquestioned duty, both to himself and the race, to create to the full capacity of his power.

Effect of This Desire. The effect of this desire, as it is more and more completely fulfilled, is to give man the ability to live for more, and the power to secure more to live with. His gaining of reward, not only externally, but in all phases of his life, gives him the power to apply himself more effectually, and in the living of a still larger and richer life. The effect, therefore, of this desire, is not only good, but leads directly to the highest good.

Basis of This Desire. The real origin or basis of the desire for reward is found in man's inherent tendency to work for greater and better things. The nature of life is to want to live more; and to live more we must be rewarded so that we may have the means with which to promote life on a still larger scale. The purpose of existence is to move forward into the greater, the richer and the more perfect; and it is the recompense we receive at every step that gives us the ways and means to take the next step. The desire for reward, therefore, is natural and the gaining of recompense necessary.

Chapter 8

The Successful Mental Attitude

The necessity of always proceeding in the right mental attitude is a matter that has until recently been largely ignored. But when we analyze the various elements that are naturally expressed in the average, as well as the special, mental attitude, and note their effects, we conclude that the right mental attitude is of the highest importance. Whatever we do we will naturally proceed in a mental attitude of some kind; and as this attitude will affect us, and through us will affect our work, it is evident that in order to secure the best effect possible we must proceed in the best mental attitude possible. Then we must also remember that if we are to apply the whole self we must apply all the elements of the mind; and apply them to the best advantage. This, however, we cannot do unless every mental attitude is right; because every mental attitude, be it right or otherwise, will express certain elements of the mind. The wrong attitude will misdirect those elements or forces of the mind, which it tends to express, and will not only prevent the best application of the whole self, but will also produce detrimental conditions in mind, character and personality — conditions that will be in the way.

To proceed in the right mental attitude the following lines of thought and action should be closely and faithfully observed:

(1) Have faith in yourself; have faith in the undertaking, and have faith in the outcome desired.

This attitude will bring out into positive action more and more of yourself, and will tend to keep your thought and attention upon your work until it is finished. It will also cause others to have faith and confidence in you, which fact will enable you to secure their co-operation as desired; and no undertaking of real worth is possible without the co-operation of others.

It is always true that the more faith you have in yourself the more faith others will have in you. And we know that the most pronounced failures in the world were caused by the fact that those who were back of the undertaking did not have faith enough to see the thing through. Their faith did not hold out, so therefore they abandoned their project, and possibly when one day more would have brought a glorious victory.

(2) Continue in a joyous and positive expectation.

Expect everything to go right. Expect the best from yourself. Expect the best from everything and everybody. Expect the results desired. This will tend to call forth the best that is in you, and will place you in perfect harmony with all things, which is greatly in your favor. It will also make your actions more alive, more energetic, more persevering and more constructive. Expectation is always a rising attitude, and when positive tends to cause the mind to rise up, to move forward, to press on, and do. To expect anything, with an expectation that is positive and alive, is to arouse the mind to action, and to cause the forces of the mind to concentrate more and more upon the effort to produce the thing expected. In fact, positive expectation invariably leads to perfect concentration, and tends to draw all the available energies of the human system into the line of concentration. It also draws out more power and ability as it urges the mind to work more thoroughly, and with more enthusiasm, for that which is expected.

The joyous attitude tends to encourage, to prompt, to elevate, to inspire; and tends to heighten the effect of all action. The more joy there is in an action, the more life, power and go there is in that action. The joyful action is charged, so to speak, with energies of a rising nature, and therefore has the power to use the greater things. But the joyless action is weak, almost empty, and cannot get above the ordinary. It is therefore evident that a mind that lives and works constantly in the joyous attitude has taken advantage of a principle of unusual value.

The fact is that the more you expect, the more you will get, provided that expectation is joyous, positive and continuous; for happiness is to the talents of the mind what sunshine is to the flowers and the trees.

(3) Desire persistently that you may do your best; that everything will respond properly to your efforts; and that you will secure the results expected.

When your desire for anything is strong and persistent you arouse a great deal of extra mental energy, and that energy always tends to act upon, and thereby develop farther, the very faculty, which, when developed, can produce the thing desired. In brief, a strong, persistent desire for wealth tends to direct this extra energy upon the faculty of financial ability. A strong, persistent desire for greater success in the literary field tends to direct this energy upon the literary faculties, and so on. A desire for results along a certain line will therefore give more life, energy and working capacity to those faculties that can, when made stronger, produce those results. Accordingly, the attitude of persistent desire, when present in any undertaking, will give added power and ability with which to promote that undertaking. It will also make the individual more persistent in his determination to succeed, which means much; and it will tend greatly to attract the attention and cooperation of others. People are readily fascinated by persistent efforts; and are naturally drawn where the action is the most positive, the most powerful and the most determined. Therefore the greater your desire to realize a certain aim, provided that desire is expressed in action, the more people you will attract who will want to aid you in making that desire come true.

(4) Think that you can. Convince yourself that you can do what you have undertaken to do.

There are many dormant cells in the brain and many inactive forces in the mind, which ought to be aroused, and which can be aroused by the deep and constant thought that you can. So that by thinking that you can, you get more to work with, and thus gain a decided advantage. Nothing can be done until we first think we can. We cannot move a single muscle until we consciously or subconsciously inform the will that we can. But the will has never been used by anyone to full capacity. It can place in action many forces and elements that we have never used before, if we only convince ourselves, deep down in the heart, that we can. And so we shall, by thinking more and more that we can, constantly add to the power and the capacity of mind, and personality.

(5) Live, think and work in the optimistic attitude.

This attitude gives the mind the upward look; and it is the mind that looks up that has the dearest thought, the best ideas, the largest vision and the most perfect ideals. The optimistic attitude fixes the mind, not on failure, but on success; not on weakness, but on strength; not on loss, but on greater gain; not on the limitations of the past, but on the richer possibilities of the future. And the mind always thinks of those things upon which its attention is fixed. He who fixes his attention upon failure will think failure; he will fill his mind with the idea of failure, thereby producing the fear of failure as well as causing the mind to become more negative. But he who fixes his attention upon success, greater strength, greater gain and richer possibilities, will not only make his mind richer and stronger, but he will also inspire his mind to work for those things.

To fix attention upon the silver lining, and to look only upon the brightest side of things, is to give the mind more light; and the mind that thinks in the light can think far more clearly, create far better ideas, and evolve far better plans and methods than the mind that thinks in the darkness. However, the pessimistic mind, the discouraged mind, the despondent mind, the dissatisfied mind, the critical mind, the unappreciative mind — such a mind thinks in mental darkness, and cannot see anything exactly as it is. But the more you are imbued with the living sunshine of the optimistic spirit, the more you inspire your mind to work for the larger, the greater and the better.

(6) Love your work with all your mind, with all your heart and with all your soul.

Love every factor connected with your work; or at least, look constantly for the good that is in every factor, and in every person connected with your work. We give our best to that which we love the best; and as it is our purpose and desire to give our best to our work, at all times and under all circumstances, it is strictly scientific to love our work with all the love that is in us, no matter what that work may be, or in what surroundings that work must of necessity take place. Here we should note, with special attention, that the factors of environment respond the best to him who loves his work, because his approach is better. And this is vitally important, as the way the thing acted upon responds to our action —

that is what determines largely what results we are to secure.

(7) Give the building attitude to every thought, to every feeling and to every action.

Aim to make every action a growing action; every thought an expanding thought; every tendency an enlarging tendency; and every purpose a broadening purpose. Think of the way before you as becoming wider the farther you go; think of every channel of action as becoming deeper the farther it goes; think of every new field as becoming larger and every new world as more immense; think of every new thought as bursting forth into a multitude of larger thoughts; and think of every new idea as becoming the mother of a host of greater ideas. In brief, train every attitude of your mind to move forward and outward in every direction, having increase — every imaginable manner of increase — constantly in view. You thus tend to enlarge your ability, your capacity, and all the powers and faculties in your possession. And that such an attitude will be found invaluable in anything we may undertake we can realize perfectly.

Chapter 9

Full Use of Ability and Power

If you would help yourself to the greatest possible degree, then purpose to make full use of all the ability and power you possess. Aim to be all that you can be in every thought and action. Give your best to your work; and, literally, turn on the full current of all that is in you. Give constructive expression to the full capacity of mind and personality; and to this end, give special attention to the use of The Conscious Mind, The Subconscious Mind, Concentration and Will.

The Conscious Mind. The sum total of all the faculties and states of mind that we employ in general conscious action constitutes the conscious mind; and its full use may be secured through the cultivation of positiveness in thought and action.

(1) Positive thought knows what it wants to think and what it wants to do, and proceeds accordingly with the full force of mind. Positive thought goes directly and with determination to the goal in view; it never hesitates, falters nor doubts; it decides upon its purpose, and never hesitates to carry it out regardless of feeling, advice, suggestion or appearances. And to train the mind to employ such thought whenever action of any kind is desired, is to promote more and more the full use of the mind.

(2) Positive action is that action that is filled with the element of go. And when positive action is combined with constructive action, the action will not only go to work with all the energy in its possession, but will go to work intelligently for the realization of some definite aim. Action of real value, therefore, is secured upon the work in hand, and in addition, a strong tendency to promote the full use of the conscious mind has been created. Besides, the more elements and forces you call forth into positive action in mind or personality, the more unused elements and forces you arouse for further action. To use fully what is now in activity is to call more and more into activity. He who goes to the limit with what he has will always get more. He who is doing his very best every day is invariably doing better every day.

The Subconscious. That vast mental world that lies beneath and within the world of the conscious mind is termed the subconscious; and although its vastness makes it impossible ever to employ the whole of it, still as much of the subconscious as we can fully grasp at every step of our advancement should be fully applied. And to proceed, all action in mind and thought should be deeply felt, as deep feeling goes underneath ordinary mental life and arouses the subconscious. The subconscious should be directed to give its life, its power and its full assistance to everything we undertake to do, even the least important; and whatever is done, the whole heart and mind should be given to that work. Aim to use the whole mind — conscious and subconscious — whenever the mind is used for something definite, and expect the whole mind to respond. Think, act and feel with the whole mind, and think, act and feel with the full capacity of the whole mind. This will promote the full use both of the conscious and the subconscious, and will call into action an ever-increasing measure of ability and power.

Concentration. The purpose of concentration is to focus, upon the one thing we are doing now, all the ability and energy we possess; and is therefore indispensable to the full use of the mind. To apply concentration successfully the two methods given herewith will prove very effective:

Practical Self-Help

(1) Whenever attention is directed upon any subject or object, the actions of the mind should be as deeply felt as possible. When the actions of attention are deep, perfect concentration comes of itself; and a constant desire to deepen those actions will give them more and more depth until full and natural concentration may be secured.

(2) Whenever attention is directed upon any subject or object, the mind should try to find something interesting in connection with that subject or object. This will cause the mind to become interested; and when the mind is deeply interested, we invariably have perfect concentration. But when there seems to be nothing of interest, an effort should be made to find some-thing of interest; and such an effort will invariably create interest. Furthermore, to train the mind to act in the right mental attitude is to aid greatly in the cultivation of a full and perfect concentration. In fact, the lack of concentration is usually due to wrong mental attitudes, and is therefore a matter that is easily remedied.

The Will. Every faculty must be willed into action before it can act. The same is true of all the forces and functions in the human system. No voluntary action can take place until we will it so; and the force of every action depends largely upon how much will we put into it. The importance, therefore, of using the will to full capacity whenever we will to do anything is evident. And it is also evident that the full use of the will in all mental endeavor will naturally promote the full use of ability and power.

(1) The first step in the full use of the will is to make the will deeper, larger, more firm and more determined. And this is accomplished by making it a point to will with all there is in you.

(2) Make it a practice for a few moments several times every day to try to will into action more energy and more ability. This will not only strengthen the will, but will greatly increase the working capacity of the mind.

(3) Make it a daily practice to try to increase the efficiency of all your faculties by pushing them forward with the will; that is, try to will them into fuller and more determined action. Take each faculty in turn with this object in view; practice faithfully, and positively expect results.

(4) Use the will frequently and extensively in trying to push up all your faculties and forces into a higher and finer field of action. This will tend to heighten the actions of your whole mind, and will thereby improve the quality as well as increase the quantity of your mental power.

(5) Use the will only upon yourself — upon the best in yourself, and with a view of causing higher, greater and more efficient action in every power, faculty, talent, force or function you possess.

Facts About the Will. The power of the will is the power of the individual ego or self to initiate action anywhere in his own system; or to act through some element, force, function or faculty in the system, and having a definite purpose in view.

(1) In the building up of the will it is highly important to act upon the principle that the will to be real will power must act through, and not merely upon, these elements or forces that are concerned. The will acts through the deeper or inner states of an element, force or faculty, and is directly concerned with the cause region of life, thought and activity.

Practical Self-Help

(2) The will develops as definite actions through forces or faculties are increased in number and frequency, and as the consciousness of the individual ego becomes more keen and alive; that is, when we know what the will is and where it comes from, and, in that knowledge, increase the application and the range of the will continuously.

(3) There are many reasons why the will re-mains weak, but these are chiefly to blame: Mental vagueness as to the nature and functions of the individual ego; uncertainty as to purpose in life or action — acting with no definite object in view; permitting external factors to take prolonged hold of mind, thought or feeling; giving full right of way to habits, desires or tendencies; and living and acting according to systems prescribed by others.

(4) In the development of real will power, you should emphasize repeatedly the fact that you are the individual ego — the real self that lives, thinks and acts — that initiates, directs and governs; and realize more and more deeply that the ego acting through any force or element in your system, with a view of initiating further actions or greater actions — this is an act of the will.

(5) Deepen more and more your consciousness of the ego; and deepen your power to feel the will actions of the ego; that is, train the mind to know what is actually taking place in the field of the individual ego as that ego thinks, wills, initiates and directs. And the mind will respond readily to any new form of training or realization if properly prompted and encouraged.

(6) It is very important to realize that the use of the will involves no desire to control action in the usual sense of that term; but involves the desire to originate new actions according to purpose. In the right use of the will you do not

Practical Self-Help

try to compel forces or elements to be different; you create new actions and conditions; you will into action the new and the better according to your aims and ideals.

(7) To build up the will and extend its range, it becomes necessary to decide definitely as to purpose, even in minor matters, and to act promptly and firmly through the elements and forces involved; that is, we must know what we want to do along every line; then go and do it with a will — a simple practice that develops real will power to a marked degree.

(8) A scientific study of the will leads to many startling conclusions; and among them is this, that nothing can happen to an individual unless he wills it so — unless he gives permission to actions from outside sources, or initiates these actions himself — the latter being a will action of personal choice and the former a will action of personal consent.

(9) All actions that originate from individual choice are first willed into being or expression; and all actions that are produced in the mind of the individual by external suggestions or influences — these arise because the individual will has willed to give permission, or has willed to step aside so as to give these external influences right of way. Thus we understand that whatever may happen to us, we have, either positively or negatively, willed it so. And what an "awful" truth this must be to those who have been in the habit of shifting responsibility elsewhere.

(10) A great factor to emphasize is this, that you the individual ego can will to initiate, or set in motion, any force or group of forces, or any mode of activity desired in any part of the system at any time. You will conditions in yourself to be what you may plan or purpose; and therefore we

understand how you can will to be well and powerful; how you can will to change and improve every condition or circumstance in your world; how you can will to succeed and accomplish more and more; how you can will to create your future and master destiny.

(11) In the right use of the will, you control yourself, not by trying to change, suddenly, all present actions in your system, but by originating a group of new interior actions — more perfect and more positive actions in the within that will presently come forth and produce the conditions you want in the without.

(12) When you weaken the will you also weaken your power to be, to live, to achieve and attain; and we always weaken the will when we give in, or give up. But when you build and strengthen the will, you increase largely your power to accomplish what you have in view and make real your ideals. And you always strengthen the will when you proceed to see the thing through, working with all the faith and power you have in your interior possession.

(13) In our study of the will we must eliminate the belief that a strong will is forceful or commanding or demanding; or that such a will acts necessarily in sledge-hammer fashion; for such is never the truth. The great will moves easily, but with a well-defined, determined purpose; and it is gentle, but powerful; kind, but invincible. The great will is always serene, but deep and positive, with tremendous capacity and range — a calmly, orderly-moving avalanche of constructive power.

Chapter 10

The Control of Circumstance

To further personal advancement and accomplish what we have in view, the art of dealing with circumstance is one of imperative importance. Results depend so largely on how the individual takes hold of, and controls, the elements of environment; how he adapts himself to, or relates himself to, the active factors in his own world; and how ably he can modify, change or control his circumstance. Briefly, how well he can act upon the world of conditions and things; and how well he can call forth the best that is contained in conditions and things. It all depends on the man and his world; what these two possess, actually and potentially; and how these two act and respond to each other. It is herewith that we find our chief problem in successful self-help; and to solve this problem the following methods and suggestions will go a long way:

(1) Consider the elements of your environment; that is, the conditions and things that exist where you live and work. Then arrange and rearrange those things in such a way that you can work with them and act upon them to the best advantage. There is room here for a great deal of deep study and practical analysis; for the fact is that you feel better, and can work better, when the elements and factors in your immediate environment are arranged in a certain way. And if you can arrange things in a setting where all things and all persons give up their best, with a natural response, you are controlling your circumstances, and achieving something of marked importance.

We should note, herewith, that the elements of environment may make or mar the life and career of almost anyone — depending upon how those elements are arranged,

Practical Self-Help

and how the individual adapts himself to the arrangement. A certain setting of things in your place of work may give you mental stimulus; while another setting of those same things may give you mental inaction or indifference. Certain friends and associates give us inspiration and self-confidence; others give us pessimism and self-depreciation. But you can select and arrange what is to constitute your environment and associations; and to that degree you not only control your circumstances, but you help yourself to secure far more out of everything that comes your way.

(2) When you proceed to act upon or work with things, make the best approach possible. And here is a wide field for profitable study.

But to be brief, you will make the best approach and secure the best results when you proceed in the attitude of faith, harmony, self-confidence, definite purpose, determination and controlled enthusiasm.

(3) When necessary, adapt yourself to environment as far as possible. When conditions are not suitable, make them so. Know that you can. Never let adverse conditions influence your thought, your conduct or your plans. Do not permit anything in your environment to control your mind. Think, feel and act as you have planned; and change your plans only when you yourself decide to do so. When you are about to change your mind, ask yourself what it was that prompted that change. If you find that it was external conditions, proceed at once to modify that change and make it better, provided it was good in the first place. Thus you revise your own thought, and you take your mind, at the time, above the influence of environment. But if you find the change suggested not to be good, refuse to make the change. This practice will train the mind to select every line of thought and action with greater care and wisdom.

(4) Adapt your environment to your needs as far as you can; and every effort in that direction will make you more successful in applying this principle. Study your environment carefully, and examine its chief factors with a view of finding how they can be so changed as to respond more successfully to your efforts. You will discover many changes that can be made to advantage; and every moment of thought given to the matter will prove most profitable. The habit of leaving the larger part of our external surroundings to themselves, with no thought of change or improvement, must not be permitted. Every element in our surroundings, and every factor connected with our work, should be changed and improved as frequently as possible; but always with the idea that the change will better serve our new and greater needs.

(5) Make the best of every circumstance or condition while it lasts; and aim to get all the value, all the experience and all the constructive discipline you can out of every adverse circum-stance. Do not wait for adverse conditions to spend their force and disappear. Use that force yourself. Turn it to good account. Put the enemy to work — to work for you; that is the only scientific course to pursue whenever an enemy appears, be he animate or inanimate. To illustrate: A certain boy refused to study in school but persisted in whittling up the desks instead. He was taken out and given practical instruction in wood-carving and soon became an expert. A certain woman had a husband with a terrific temper.

She could not cure him and soon found herself having fits of anger whenever he did. In trying to overcome this tendency an idea struck her. She resolved she would test herself and see how long she could remain unmoved during her husband's violent moments, and how pleasant she could actually feel during the test. She soon began to take delight in this rigid practice, and finally developed a remarkable character. And the change in her worked a miracle in the husband; for his temper disappeared.

(6) Control your circumstances by constantly increasing your creative power so that you can gradually improve those circumstances. The more competent you become the more you can accomplish; and the more you accomplish the more power and means you will have with which to improve your circumstances. This is how circum-stances are controlled — gaining freedom from the lesser by growing into the greater; and he who adopts this method, with a definite purpose, will positively realize the change desired.

(7) Adapt yourself in such a manner to those people that you meet in life, as to secure their attention, their appreciation and their cooperation. Aim so to act that the largest number possible will be in harmony with you. Avoid actions that antagonize, that mentally confuse or disturb others, that discourage others, or that tend to deprecate your worth. And do nothing that will make others lose confidence in you. To succeed, you need the confidence of others; and the more people there are who believe in you, the better. Make yourself an adept in the fine art of being in harmony with everything and everybody; and you have solved one of the greatest problems in the world as well as realized one of the highest of attainments.

Finally, in trying to place your environment in a condition where it can be acted upon to the best advantage, and where it will respond most successfully to your constructive actions, always have these three things uppermost in mind: First, seek perfect harmony with everything in your surroundings, both animate and inanimate; and persist in being harmonious, whether other things are so or not. Second, aim to arrange and re-arrange everything in your surroundings in such a manner as to give you inspiration, and call forth the best that is in you. And third, try to improve constantly both the appearance and the efficiency of every element and factor that plays some part, great or small, in your immediate surroundings or in your work. When you have done these three things you have placed your environment almost completely under your control; and it will respond more and more to your positive efforts in constructive application.

Chapter 11

Effective Use of Thought and Action

(1) In the realization of the purpose we have in view in this study, the right use of thought and action becomes absolutely necessary. Results can only follow action, and before there can be action there must be thought. Thinking must be constructive and progressive in order to be right, and in order to originate actions that are constructive and progressive; and every action must follow a constructive and progressive system in order that every force applied in action may build itself, as well as build those things for which the action has been directed to work.

(2) Constructive thinking is thinking for results; that is, placing in action only such thoughts and mental states as tend to work for the results expected. And here it is well to remember that every thought placed in action in the mind, and every mental state held in mind, contains a certain amount of energy which will either work for or against the purpose in view, depending upon whether or not it be constructive. All mental action that is constructive is favorable, and tends to work for whatever the mind has in hand at the time; but all mental action that is not constructive is detrimental, and tends to prevent the mind, in a measure, from working successfully for the object in view.

(3) In placing in action the right mental states — states that tend to build — it is only necessary to encourage such states of mind as have an upward and onward tendency, and to avoid all others. In brief, entertain faith instead of fear, harmony instead of discord, hope instead of doubt, optimism instead of pessimism, confidence instead of discouragement, expectation instead of uncertainty, encouragement instead of

criticism, kindness instead of anger, justice instead of revenge, co-operation instead of antagonism, determination instead of instability, the larger vision instead of worry, enthusiasm instead of depression, the attitude of perseverance instead of the attitude of delay.

(4) Every state of mind has its effect upon character and ability, as well as upon every action employed in actual work. Wholesome and upbuilding states of mind, if given full possession, will strengthen character from year to year, and will constantly increase ability and working capacity. Besides good states of mind will tend to prevent waste of energy and vitality, and accordingly give mind and body better health and greater endurance. In fact, so vitally important is the cultivation of right states of mind that no other mental state should be permitted for a moment, no matter what the occasion might be.

(5) To cultivate constructive thinking, every mode of thought should move towards the object that is to be realized or worked for; and every thought should contain the building impulse. And this impulse may be given to every thought if the mind, at the time the thought is created, is animated through and through with a real desire to build, develop and advance. Every mode of thought that works with you in your purpose and aim is constructive; and likewise, every thought that aims at good work or greater work. To think of what you do not want, what you fear, what you dislike, or to think of anything that is detrimental in any way, is to create thought that is not constructive. And such thought will not only waste energy, but will tend to misdirect the various actions of the mind. To train the mind in constructive thinking, think of what you want, what you desire to do, what you are determined to accomplish; think of what is good, what is wholesome, what is satisfying; think of the greater, the better, the more perfect and the ideal; and think of yourself as achieving what you wish to become.

(6) To secure constructive action in mind and personality, every action should be conducive to the results that are expected; that is, every action should not only aim to work for those results, but should have a building tendency. And every action can be given that tendency by the mind itself, if the purpose to build is fully expressed in that mental action that originates and promotes the personal action. Whenever you think of action, your purpose and desire to build should be so strong that your building thought invariably takes form in action. All thought tends to take form in action, especially if the thought is strong and persistent; and the nature of the action will correspond with the nature of the thought in each case. Therefore, if we have a strong desire to give every action a building tendency whenever we think of action, every action will be given that tendency, and every action will become constructive.

(7) Every action that takes place in mind or personality should be animated with a positive desire for greater and better things. And no action that does not have such a desire should be permitted. Even pleasurable actions should be enjoyed with the idea that they will renew life and power, and prepare the mind for better work, higher attainments and still greater enjoyment. Here you may well ask yourself now if you have ever tried to give the building tendency to any of your actions. Then ask yourself how much more you might expect to accomplish if all your actions were constructive—filled with the building tendency.

(8) Thought and action are progressive when all thought and action are working toward the larger, the greater, the ever-growing ideal; when thinking tends to enlarge and develop itself as it proceeds; when mental action gathers increased intelligence and force as it promotes its own action; when every new idea contains the power to produce several greater ideas; when every mode of thinking tends to become richer, stronger and more extensive every step of the way; when every action of the mind contains the latent power to become larger and stronger the farther it goes, and to produce greater results the farther it goes.

(9) Make it your definite purpose to act towards the larger. Animate every thought and action with a persistent desire to become larger and larger as it proceeds. Act towards the greater in the same way. Inspire every action with the aim to produce greater and greater results, and fully expect this aim to be realized. To act towards the larger and the greater is to concentrate attention upon some worthy goal that is constantly becoming larger and greater the farther the action proceeds.

(10) When you begin to work for the realization of your ambition, concentrate all your actions upon the highest goal of that ambition. Then as you continue, picture that goal in your mind as becoming larger, greater and more wonderful the farther you go. Thus you have, not merely a great goal to work for, but a goal that is ever becoming greater. And you train your mind, in consequence, to reach out farther and farther for the greater. You will not move in a fixed groove, but in an ever-widening pathway; you will transcend limitations again and again; you will outgrow yourself at frequent intervals; you will call forth and apply more and more of the whole self, and you will fulfill the leading purpose of self-help — to help yourself to help yourself more.

(11) Have greater efficiency in view at all times and under all circumstances. Give all thoughts and actions the tendency to become more and more efficient the longer they work or act. Do not simply aim to be efficient. Make your efficiency progressive, so that the more efficient you become in your work, the more efficient you will become in the art of increasing your efficiency. This is the progressive idea; and every thought and action should be made alive with the spirit of that idea.

(12) Think and act towards the perfect, and picture in mind the perfect as a state of perfection that contains possibilities of innumerable degrees of higher states of perfection. Have such an idea of the perfect always in view, and cause all things and actions both to become perfect in themselves and to produce the more perfect as they proceed.

(13) Think and act towards an ever-growing ideal; that is, an ideal that is ever becoming more ideal. Do not simply have ideals; have ever-growing ideals, or idealizing ideals. To simply have ideals is to take the mind up to a certain point and then stop; and at that point the mind will begin to circumscribe its ideals; or rather to make them fixed and final entities. But when this occurs the ideal is no longer ideal; it is simply an opinion or a mere habit of thought and cannot inspire the mind any more. Every system of idealism, therefore, must be a progressive system; and all thought of the ideal must be progressive thought; which means that the mind must not only try to see the ideal but also try to see the greater and the more ideal that such an ideal might contain. Thus every outgrown shell is left the very moment it is outgrown, and higher forms assumed, to be again superseded by forms that are still higher and more wonderful.

Chapter 12

Vital Principles in Self-Help

The application of the following principles should be made a permanent part of all thought and action; and a working basis will be established upon which the larger development and the further expression of the whole self may be promoted:

(1) Place yourself on the strong side of every proposition. Whatever happens or whatever you meet, seek invariably the strong side, the positive side, the side of constructive action; and place yourself firmly on that side. Act with that which moves forward, that which builds up, that which works for the larger and the better. When things go wrong do not become disturbed or disappointed. Such states of mind are on the weak side. Be determined to make things go right; and proceed in the positive conviction that you can. You thereby place yourself on the strong side. And to place yourself on the strong side of every circumstance or event you meet in life is to increase constantly the strength of your own mind and character.

When things are against you, have more faith than ever before that you can make all things be for you; and act according to that faith with all the life and power that is in you. When you meet failure do not give in, do not weaken, do not decrease your ambition. On the contrary, make yourself more ambitious than ever before, and be more determined than ever before to carry your ambition through.

When you do not get what you want, do not reconcile yourself to fate and resolve to be satisfied with what you have. Renew your strength and your ambition, and proceed with all the power you have to secure even a greater prize than you sought previously. When you find yourself in discord do not act on the side of discord. Act with harmony at all times. The side of harmony is the strong side, and you are always on the side of harmony when you are harmonious in your own thought, feeling and action. The deeper and the more perfect your consciousness and attitude of harmony the greater your strength, your capacity and your power.

When you have lost something that you highly prize, do not permit yourself to feel the loss, and do not regret what has happened. Proceed with the purpose to gain something that is better, and that has still greater worth; and know that you can. When better things are coming into your life, do not fold your arms in the belief that you need not act just now, as everything is going right. To assume this attitude is to become negative; and the negative attitude is weakening, so that you will soon lose hold upon the good that has been gained. Instead, take full possession of those better things with a view of making them still better. When things are going right proceed to give them more life and power in the same right direction. When things are moving forward give them an extra push forward again and again. When things are coming your way increase your activity so as to cause them to come more rapidly and in a greater measure. Thus you are always on the strong side — the side of growth, advancement, increase and enrichment.

When you meet good opportunities do not expect those opportunities to put you through. Take vital hold of the situation and put those opportunities through. You thereby not only secure everything that those opportunities have to give, but you also prepare yourself for still greater opportunities. In like manner do not expect influential friends to push you forward. The having of such friends is an advantage and may give you a desirable opening, but do not wait to be pushed forward. Proceed to push yourself forward, and proceed with so much strength, courage and efficiency that you prove worthy of even better things than were offered at first. Thus you make yourself a successful candidate for still better openings, which will shortly appear in your onward path.

Do not permit yourself to be carried away by adversity. To drift with the stream no matter whether the stream may be good or ill is to place yourself on the weak side. You are always on the weak side when you do not assert yourself positively for the purpose you have in view, and act with your whole self in furthering the work of that purpose. To be on the strong side, work positively for the good, even though you may be in the stream of adversity. And work positively for the better when you are in the stream of prosperity. Never be carried away by anything, but aim to take everything with you into the fields of greater increase and greater good.

(2) Proceed with the conviction that you can, and continue unceasingly in that conviction. The more fully convinced you are that you can, the more of yourself you apply. When you do not think that you can, you hesitate and hold back a large portion of your ability and power. When you are convinced that you can, you give expression to all the power and talent that is active within you. To give expression to all the power or ability that is active in your being is to call forth into expression more and more of that power or ability that has previously been inactive. To use all that you have is to get more for further and greater use. To apply all that is in action is to arouse more into action. Much gathers more; full capacity produces greater capacity; the law of increase promotes increase; to him that hath shall be given. When you are convinced that you can, all your elements and faculties will become imbued with the same conviction and accordingly will work with you with full force in doing what you are convinced you can do. And no man can fail when all the elements and faculties in his being are working with him to full capacity.

The man who proceeds in the full conviction that he can, will apply in his work from ten to fifty per cent more ability and energy than anyone else of equal ability or power who does not consciously apply this law. The attitude of "I can" tends to place things in action. It is the attitude that calls together all the energies of mind and inspires them all to act, to work, to create, to press on, to achieve. He who thinks he can needs no encouragement. He knows what he is and knows what he can do. He has real self-confidence; and to have confidence in self is to concentrate more and more energy upon the development of self. Conceit is shallow, and is based not upon the consciousness of the superior man within, but upon the one-sided development of the superficial man without. Real self-confidence is based upon the discovery of the greater powers within. And therefore, he who has real self-confidence knows that with such powers to back him up he can positively do whatever he thinks he can do.

(3) Combine the full use of what you possess with a constant effort to develop more. The fact that you may not possess much ability or power need not disturb you. You can develop more and more; in fact, as much as you may need to realize your ambitions. And in the meantime if you will make full use of what you already possess, you will accomplish far more than many others who may appear to have twice your ability and capacity. Back of every mind there is an immense subconscious world, and from this world we can call forth any amount of ability, talent and power. There is no reason therefore why any mind should remain small; and the only reason why any mind does remain small is because the greatness of the subconscious is not developed for practical use.

We steadily grow into the likeness of those mental pictures that we have formed of ourselves, and we become in the real what we positively, persistently and continuously think that we are in the ideal. Nature has given man sufficient power to accomplish anything he may desire; and this power will increase as the nature of man develops into the vast field of those greater possibilities that are inherent in human life. The secret is be all that you can be, and you will secure everything that you may desire; and the more you bring forth of what is in you the more you will be; for in actual living we are, both in mind and personality, what we express in actual living.

The majority, even among the most energetic, apply only a fraction of what is in them. Much of what is in them remains inactive, and much of what is in action is wasted. The opportunity, therefore, for the man who will apply all that is in him is great indeed. The path that leads into the greater life, the life worthwhile, is based upon the constructive use of all the principles and laws in the being of man. In other words, it is idealism in all things; and idealism in all things means the right use of all things. The result must necessarily be the best of all the good we have in view.

(4) Change yourself to correspond with the change you desire in your environment. The various elements, factors and conditions that you find in your environment, and that compose your environment, are similar in every respect to that which is active in your own nature; and these are the reasons why: First, some of those things you have selected, and like selects like; second, some of those things you have attracted, and like attracts like; third, others you have created, and like creates like; fourth, still others you have modified or changed, and like causes produce like effects; and fifth, the remainder you have permitted to remain as you found them. Here we should remember that what we permit to remain as it is invariably corresponds to certain things that we permit to remain in our own nature.

To illustrate, the father who permits recklessness in his children has a certain amount of recklessness in his own nature. The woman who permits uncleanliness or disorder in her home has some of those conditions in her own mental makeup. The business man who permits questionable methods among his employees has those same traits in his own character, even though he may successfully hide them from public view. The gardener who permits weeds to grow has a tendency in his own nature to let the useless and the wasteful have their way. The young woman who permits ungentlemanly speech or conduct among her male companions has similar weaknesses in her own character, though in conduct she herself may seem innocent and good.

One of the principal reasons why the many fail to realize their ideals is because they are not ideal in all things. A portion of the mind is working for ideals, while the remainder is perpetuating the ordinary and the inferior. The house is thereby divided against itself. The roses are checked by the weeds. The ascending forces are counteracted by the descending forces and very little is accomplished. Ideals, however, need the best of care. Weeds can grow without any care, but not so with the roses. If we want the most highly developed flowers to grow in the mind, we must provide conditions that favor the growth of such flowers; and the necessary conditions are those conditions that are ideal; conditions that tend towards the lofty, the perfect, the sublime and the beautiful.

That which is active in the world about you is similar in every respect to that which is active in the world within you. The word "active" is important in this connection and will explain many seeming exceptions to the rule. There may be things in your environment that may not seem to correspond with your own nature. For example, you may love the beautiful, and yet be living in a house where the beautiful is practically absent; and the reason is that the power to produce the beautiful in the material world is not active in your own being. You may love harmony and be a man of peace, and yet be living and working where discord and confusion are almost supreme. Again the reason is that your power to produce harmony and peace in your own world is not active in your nature or has not been positively asserted. In that case, your desire for peace and harmony are mere negative qualities, and every negative quality permits the existence of its opposite.

If there is anything wrong in your environment, you may know that the opposite of that wrong is simply a negative quality in yourself; but if you make that quality positive in yourself the external wrong will begin to disappear. It will not disappear mysteriously, but will disappear because you have gained the power to act upon your environment in such a way as to change that wrong and make it right. Suppose there is poverty in your home. The reason is, that your power to supply a competence is either negative or only in partial action; but if you make that power positive and thereby increase your efficiency many times, your recompense will increase accordingly and poverty will disappear. Or, you may love to have friends but are practically without friends. The reason is, your quality of friendship is negative. No one is attracted to you because it is only the positive that can attract.

Your friendship is not in action and therefore cannot cause response. It is only love that begets love; but dead love cannot beget living love, and that which is hidden cannot be admired. When you make the quality of friendship positive, however, you become a good friend in reality. That is, your friendship is given expression, and those who live in your own world will discover the living quality of your friendship and be attracted to you accordingly. Or, suppose you desire certain opportunities but do not have them. The reason is, your ability is too negative to make itself felt in the world of that opportunity. But when you become a positive power in that world, applying your ability to the fullest capacity and to the highest efficiency, the greater opportunity you desire will soon be forthcoming. When we understand this principle we shall find that whatever becomes active within ourselves will invariably create or attract its kind in our environment. The secret, therefore, is to determine what we wish our environment to be, and then to give positive action to everything in ourselves that corresponds to the new environment desired.

Here we should note the law that no change can take place in the man unless that power within him that can naturally produce that change is made active. And from this law we learn why so many minds remain unchanged regardless of the fact that they almost constantly wish for such a change; but a mere wish is usually negative. It may dream of the better but does not go to work to produce the better. The same is true of many ideals held in mind. They are not made real because they are not active. They continue in a state of negativeness and do not come forth to act upon the real.

The ideal of a beautiful home can become real only when it inspires positive, constructive and creative activities in those faculties and powers of mind that can earn, produce and build such a home. The same is true with regard to every ideal we may wish to make real in our environment. We must make that ideal so active within our own minds that it produces full and constructive action in those powers of mind or personality that can produce, in the outer world, what we have pictured in the ideal world.

When in the midst of changes it is well to remember that every change constitutes an open door to something better, but if we permit the mind to be confused we shall fail to see this door and thus lose a valuable opportunity. Changes usually mean excitement, divided attention and scattered forces; therefore the new openings that are hidden in every change are not discovered. To take advantage of every opportunity that a change may offer, the mind should be perfectly calm, while attention should be used as a searchlight, so to speak, constantly watching for the very best that the new conditions may hold in store. When we enter any change fully expecting to find an open door to something better we shall positively find it. The mind that expects the better is wide-awake to the better and will know the better the very moment it is in view. The subconscious mind should be trained to expect improvements from every change and from every new experience, because when this is done all the elements of life will be directed by the subconscious into the channels of improvement. What the subconscious is trained to do it invariably will do; and it is through this law that man may attain and achieve practically anything he has in mind.

(5) Direct every element and force in your system to work with you for the purpose you have in view. It is only when this principle is applied that we carry out the idea of self-help — to apply more and more of the whole self; and whatever we undertake to do we must always bear this idea in mind. To direct every force and element in your system to work with you, you must have a definite purpose in life, and this purpose must be felt so deeply that it becomes an ever-present factor in consciousness. In fact, this purpose should be impressed so deeply and so thoroughly upon the mind that you never think without thinking of this purpose; that you never desire without desiring the realization of this purpose; that you never express your ambition without giving to this purpose the full life and power of your ambition.

When any purpose, desire or ambition is so deeply felt as to be felt in every fiber in one's being, and is so strong that it stirs every atom in one's being with its force and power, then all the elements and forces in the system will follow the line of action of that purpose, desire or ambition, and will work for the object held in view. And to apply this principle we should note the following:

a. The purpose in mind must be so strong that the force of that purpose predominates over all the otter forces in the system.

b. The force of that purpose must be so deeply felt that it is keenly felt and constantly felt in every part of mind and personality.

c. All thought and all action must be concentrated upon the goal which that purpose has in view; and that concentration must be so strong that the goal in view comes vividly before the mind the very moment any thought is given to the future.

d. A number of times during each day the mind should deeply desire that every element and force in the system work with full capacity for the purpose in view; and every night before going to sleep the subconscious mind should be directed to carry out the demands of the same desire.

e. Imagination should be trained to picture all the forces of the system moving in harmony towards the goal in view, and working together for the realization of that goal.

f. At frequent intervals the will should apply its ruling power upon the entire system; and should at such times will every part of the system to work for this purpose. This action of the will should be calm, deep, positive and determined; but quiet and gentle, with a firm conviction that its efforts are continually producing results.

g. The entire system should be kept in poise so that all energy may be retained in the system and applied with full capacity in the work at hand; and here we should remember that poise is produced by a feeling of peace in the system, blended with a feeling of power. Poise is power in peaceful action. Poise is peace in powerful action.

At first it may seem impossible to direct every force and element in the system to work for the purpose in view, because it may not seem dear how the mind can get tangible hold of all its elements and forces; but after every possible effort has been applied for a few months in producing such results — especially through desire, imagination and will — the increase that will be noted in capacity, endurance and power will be nothing less than remarkable. All mysteriousness of the process will disappear, however, when we learn that it is the nature of all the elements and forces of the system to work with the strongest ambition, and to work for the realization of the purpose of that ambition. The principle is to make your cherished ambitions so strong and so determined that its presence tends to arouse to action every atom in your being; and all that is in you will work for you.

(6) When you do not get what you want, change your mind and want something better. The fact that you do not get what you want, provided you have persisted for a reasonable length of time, is usually conclusive proof that your desire has not been moving in the right direction. To change your mind, therefore, is the proper course; but that change should never be towards the lesser. It should invariably be a change towards the greater and the better. The fact that you have not secured what you wanted does not prove that you are not good enough or able enough. In many instances you are both good enough and able enough to secure something far better; and in every case you have it in you to secure something better.

You may have the desire to move a certain rock, but have not the physical power. Should you therefore continue to permit that rock to remain in your way? Not necessarily. You may have the mental power to construct and apply a machine by which that rock may be removed with ease. Or, you may have a certain position in view, and have spent years preparing for it without results. What is the reason? Most likely you are not adapted for that work, and to get into it has been up-hill work. It has been like removing an immense rock with your bare hands; but you may have talents which if applied would give you entrance to a far better position. Thousands of people have failed trying to win a small place in life when they actually had the power and the talent to win a place many times as large and with one fraction of the effort.

If you are alive and ambitious you can almost say with a certainty that you have the power and the ability to gain something much better than you have received or wanted up to date; and therefore you are safe in proceeding to want something better. But there is another side to this matter that is more important than the first. When you proceed to want something better, you call into action the greater and the higher powers in your being. You thereby place yourself in a position where you can apply more and more of your whole self; and it is this that will enable you to realize your desires and make your wish come true. For it is the truth that there is enough in any man, provided it is placed in full constructive action, to enable him to realize any normal or rational desire.

When your life has failed to give you what you wanted, then give your life an opportunity to work for something else, and always something better. The tendency of everything is to want to work for the better. It is the same with the powers of your own life and mind; and we always succeed the best when we follow the higher tendencies of nature. Furthermore, to proceed to want the better and work for the better is to renew life, mind and thought; and the complete renewal of your entire being becomes invariably the open door to a new world where the greater and the better are at your command.

Chapter 13

Building Self-Confidence

Believe in your whole self, and inspire every element in your whole self with the conviction that you can do what you believe you can do.

Believe in your whole self, not simply in a part of yourself. Have full confidence in everything that is in you. Believe in every fiber in your body. Believe in every cell in your brain. Believe in every talent in your mind. Believe in every power in your soul. Have unbounded faith in every element in your being, from the outermost states of physical existence to the very deepest depths of your marvelous interior nature. This is self-confidence in the fullest and truest sense of the term.

To have faith in those talents and powers that are tested and tried is not sufficient, nor is it sufficient to believe only in those parts of your nature that you can see or feel. That part of yourself that you can weigh and measure is but an atom compared with the vastness and immensity of your whole self. Believe in the vastness and immensity of your whole self, and you will bring those great interior powers forth into tangible action. You may be conscious only of a small part of all that is in you, and you may believe in that small part, but in that case your greater self is lying dormant, and, therefore, instead of living a great life you are simply sustaining a mere personal existence.

You may be ambitious, and you may have ideals, but if you believe only in a fraction of yourself you will not gain the power to reach your goal; and here we find one of the reasons why so many fail to make their ideals real. When you express confidence in yourself do not simply think of that part of yourself that you are conscious of; think of your entire inexhaustible being, and let your mind feel the very spirit of that thought. Think not simply of the working capacity of every atom in your system, but of the limitless power that exists back of every atom, and that is ready to express itself through every atom.

To think constantly and deeply of your larger self is to cause consciousness to penetrate more deeply into the richer mental realms that exist within you. In consequence, your conscious, active mind becomes larger and larger, thus growing steadily both in ability and working capacity. But this deeper thought and recognition of your larger nature will be very limited in practical value unless you thoroughly believe in that which you are thinking about. Confidence excites to action invariably. When you believe in yourself you not only arouse that in which you believe, but what you arouse you bring up to the highest state of efficiency. The more confidence you have in yourself the greater and better will be your work, because it is the nature of confidence to bring out the best. The very moment you thoroughly believe in yourself, you cause the very best in yourself to become alive. Why confidence acts that way is a deep psycho-logical study that is not the question just now; but the fact that confidence does act that way is a fact of extraordinary importance. Real self-confidence, however, does not simply arouse the best, the strongest and the greatest that may be found in the limitations of the outer personal self. Confidence will arouse the best, the strongest and the greatest wherever we may place confidence. We therefore understand how much we shall gain when we learn to believe thoroughly in everything that may exist within us.

The great within of every mind is a mine of fabulous wealth, and we are just beginning to explore this vast domain. Every imaginable power and possibility is being discovered in this great interior realm; therefore we have an abundance within us in which to believe. Modern psychology is demonstrating daily that we have thus far only touched the outer rim of the subconscious, and what is hidden deeper down, or if you prefer, higher up in the mind, is marvelous indeed to think of.

We are not confined, however, to the mere thought of this rich interior life. Thousands are turning more and more of this inner, superior life to practical use; and everybody can. Real self-confidence is one of the secrets — belief in the vastness of your whole mind, conscious and sub-conscious, and faith in all the powers that the great within may contain. Include your whole self whenever you express confidence in yourself, and do not fail to express that confidence in your every word, thought and deed. Live in the very spirit of this deeper, larger, greater confidence; and whatever you undertake to do, proceed with full faith in all that can possibly exist within you. Do not simply believe that you can; but let that faith touch the very soul of every atom in your being. The great purpose is not simply to believe in the shell of your being, but also in the kernel, to know that the kernel of your being can bring forth the mightiest oak of human greatness that your most inspired imagination could possibly picture.

You must learn to know and feel that there is a greater man within. You must believe in this greater man. You must let the penetrating power of your faith go into the very life of this greater man, and make your confidence in this greater man so strong that you can actually feel the marvelous power of this greatness within you thrill every atom in your being. Then you will begin to develop self-confidence that is really worthwhile.

Then you will begin to call forth the powers of your whole self, and every day you will find yourself becoming greater and greater in mind, thought, life and soul.

We are now in the midst of a period where we feel, more than ever before, the need of exceptional self-confidence. The civilization to which we be-long has undertaken a task that is monumental; that is, the building of a civilization to conform with the new ideal; and than this, nothing greater was ever attempted in known history.

For this extraordinary piece of work — what we are seeing through now and what we shall see through later — we shall require the most thorough application of the best we possess; the best we possess in mind, talent and energy, as well as the best we possess in material wealth and equipment. To the application of the latter we are giving expert attention, guided as we are in this respect by men of wide knowledge and experience; but the former needs further and better attention. Decidedly so. To that part of the program we must address ourselves more extensively, and with a clear insight, giving the subject the full force of what we know now.

We must get definite and positive hold of all that we are in mind, talent and capacity, and apply these with thoroughness and science; and to this end we must have self-confidence — a self-confidence that Is deep, great and powerful, and based upon an undaunted conviction that we positively can see our purpose through.

If we would be our best, and think and work with the best we can secure or develop in ability and power, we must have unbounded faith in what we are, what we have, what we can do; but the majority are not in possession of such a faith; therefore they apply only a fraction of their possible energies and talents; and the reason why is readily explained.

We know that practical men everywhere advise freely on the necessity of self-confidence; and young men and women are admonished again and again to believe more thoroughly in themselves; but in their attempt to act upon these valued precepts, they meet with a very discouraging situation, and do not get very far.

When a man who has not accomplished very much is advised to have more confidence in himself, he may try for a while; and he may through such an effort stimulate his mind to some degree; in consequence, he may improve — say five, ten or even twenty per cent in force, action and ambition. This is encouraging, but is only temporary in its effects.

There is always an after effect from mental stimulus; that is, where it is only stimulus and where there is no added self-knowledge or development as a foundation. And when this reaction comes, the man in question feels less energetic than before; he may realize that some gain was made, temporarily, in force and working capacity; but after repeated attempts with the ever-recurring reactions, he can see no real gain in himself.

At this point he may take a general survey of himself; and in a partly critical attitude will ask himself if there really is anything about his personality or mental equipment that is deserving of added self-confidence. He takes note of the fact that he has not accomplished very much; that he is only average, to judge hastily, in ability and working capacity; and that he has discovered nothing unusual about his mind or leading talent. Briefly, he can find nothing exceptional about himself, then how can he have exceptional confidence in himself?

Practical Self-Help

That is the vital question in this important field. "How can he expect more and more from something that appears to be only average?" And how could anyone expect the large from that which seems to be small? Like causes produce like effects. Results are remarkable only when the factors applied are remarkable. These are statements generally accepted as conclusive; and, therefore, they who feel themselves to be average only, cannot with any degree of enthusiasm believe themselves to be more. It is such a situation that the majority face when trying to build self-confidence. They take a general view of the objective side of mind and personality; and as they do not find very much there, on the surface, to depend upon, they remain in their usual condition with slight prospect of future advancement.

We all know that there is not very much on the surface anywhere; and if we are to depend upon that only, or depend upon occasional spurts of mental stimulus, we will neither build self-confidence nor feel encouraged to attempt what is be-yond the commonplace. The problem, however, that we meet herewith is readily solved; and the solution is not only effective but wonderful to the greatest conceivable degree.

To build self-confidence, the first principle is to know positively that you can; to know that you can be more; that you can do more; that you can secure and accomplish more; and to be absolutely convinced of the fact. But where and how can we secure such knowledge? We must begin with something definite; we must have something to believe in that can, at the first test, prove itself to be true; we must find something in our mental equipment in which we can place our utmost confidence and faith. And when we have found this one in-dispensable element or factor we shall have a solid foundation upon which to build; we may build and rebuild according to higher ideals and larger requirements, proving ourselves equal to every occasion, and we may look forward to a future of continual advancement.

Modem research into the true nature and actual possibility of the mind holds the answer that we are looking for; and this answer is not only affirmative — affirming a great fact with power — but is truly extraordinary in its import and range. Indeed, it is a ringing message of hope, assurance and rejoicing — a declaration of unbounded significance to the ambitious and wide-awake everywhere.

The facts are these, that back of and beneath the surface of objective consciousness there are fields beyond fields of latent energy, and regions within regions of greater possibility. Briefly, there is more in you — vastly more — than you ever dreamed. Thus far you have dealt only with the outer stratum of your Whole Self; you have called into action only the surface energies of your own mental dynamo; and all the while the "more" that is in you has been waiting to help you do the great and the wonderful.

When you know these things — and they are indisputable facts — then you have something in which you can place unbounded faith; then you have something in which you can have confidence to the utmost; then you can, with soul-stirring enthusiasm, believe in yourself and in your future; and you may entertain such a confidence, such a faith, regardless of what present conditions may be. To build self-confidence, therefore, you begin right here. You build your foundation upon the fact that the deeper regions of your mental world hold possibilities that are nothing less than marvelous; and you proceed with your building by calling forth, for practical use, more and more of what these deeper regions hold in store.

Practical Self-Help

When you are advised to have more confidence in yourself, you do not turn first to present personal capacity; you turn first to the "greater some-thing" that is in you; and in that "greater some-thing" you place your utmost confidence; in fact, knowing what you do — what you are in your Whole Self — you feel perfectly free to place enormous confidence in the full power and the latent possibility of this Whole Self — what you may well think of as the Wonderful Self — the all of you.

Herewith we may with much profit call to mind that richly poetic and deeply scientific statement, "Straws upon the surface flow; he who would seek for pearls must dive below." And so we are not discouraged if there be straws — mostly straws — floating about on the surface at the present time. We know that there are "pearls" below in the depths of the mental wonder world; and we have the power to go down and get them.

The majority, however, have dwelt in mind too much on the surface; and having noted that there are mostly straws on the surface, they have seen nothing in which to place confidence. This may be your condition; and if it is, you know the remedy. Consider the pearls below; consider the vast re-sources that are latent in the deeper regions of your mind; consider the "layers beneath layers" of potential energy held in store in the same wonder world within; then lay hold upon those energies and resources; dive for the pearls.

You will not do so in vain; you will find what you seek; you will positively succeed. Then you will have tangible evidence of the fact that there is more in you than you ever dreamed. Then you will know absolutely that you are, in your deeper, greater self, a mine of possibility — rich beyond calculation. These discoveries and such convictions will give you more confidence in yourself than you ever conceived of in the past. And the more confidence you have in your larger self the more life, energy, talent and power you will call forth from the vast resources within. This, in turn, will increase self-confidence still further, resulting in added achievements with steps upon steps of personal advancement.

Thus you will build self-confidence steadily and surely, and advance continually in your life and your work. You will become a living, growing power in your world, and whether you apply your-self for personal achievement, or take part in that greater task that we all are determined to see through successfully; you will be a tower of strength, and a constructive force of tremendous value.

Chapter 14

The Increase of Power

Give your whole self to your life, to your thought, to your purpose, to your work; and know that the more you give of your whole self the greater becomes your power to apply your whole self.

The idea that we must save ourselves, save our power, save our faculties and save our energies, is entirely too prevalent; and is founded upon the belief that our supply of everything is limited, therefore we must take care of it and save it; but to save power is to lose power. It is only the power that is used that is multiplied. It is only what we place in action that produces increase.

To give ourselves freely to what we think and do is to develop ourselves more and more until we become practically limitless in capacity; but to save ourselves is to limit ourselves more and more until our capacity contracts into almost nothing. "When power or talent is held back it becomes in-active; and power that is changed from activity to inactivity is wasted.

What we suppress we destroy; what we try to hold in reserve becomes dormant; and when power or a faculty becomes entirely dormant, it usually requires a great deal of time to arouse it into action again. What is active in the human system now should be expressed and used constructively now. If we cannot use it to advantage in one way, we should turn it into a different channel and use it some other way.

We do not gain power by hoarding power. Hoarded power gradually wastes away. We gain more power by putting to work the power we have. It is the full expression of power that draws forth more and more power from the limitless source of the great within.

The same is true of ideas. That person who keeps his valuable ideas to himself will soon lose consciousness of the inner truth of those ideas, and will also lose his power to gain more of those ideas, because when ideas are suppressed, then that faculty that discovers ideas becomes inactive. The average person lives in the fear that he will do too much and weaken himself thereby. In con-sequence, most of his power is suppressed; and it is this suppression that makes him feel weak whenever he thinks he has done too much. When we work in the conviction that the energy we use generates more energy, we shall never feel weak. Instead, our working capacity will steadily in-crease, and we shall be able to do whatever we are called upon to do. We shall have the power to do what we want to do, and our capacity will be fully equal to our ambition.

We must not conclude, however, from this fact, that a person should do nothing else but work. There are only twenty-four hours in the day. Seven or eight of those are for sleep; and seven or eight more for study, recreation and enjoyment; but when we do work, we should work in the conviction that we are generating energy faster than we are using it. When we work we should give our best selves and our whole selves to that work, knowing that we are backed up by limitless power.

When we work in this manner, we shall not only accomplish a great deal more, but our efforts will have greater worth, and we will enjoy every moment. To live in the belief that you can do only so much, that you must be careful with yourself and save as many steps as possible, is to make yourself weaker and weaker every day. It is to separate yourself from the greater powers within you, and to impress your subconscious with the idea that you are weak, limited and insignificant. In consequence, the subconscious will cause you to become weak, limited and insignificant. The subconscious always causes us to become what we think we are. This is the law. Tell the subconscious that you are weak, and you will receive only a limited amount of weak power from the great within. Tell the subconscious that you are strong, and you will receive all the power from the great within that you can possibly use. The subconscious will give you whatever you positively and ceaselessly claim as your own.

That person who is constantly watching himself so he will not overwork will feel overworked most of the time; while that person who goes about his work in the conviction that he has the power to do it all will never have occasion to think of overwork; he will feel equal to every occasion and enjoy it. He will give his whole self to his work, and that is the reason why.

When we are called upon to do something more than usual, we should go and do it. We should give ourselves to it, knowing that there is no limit to the self we have to give. We should never think of extra work as a burden, nor should we feel that we must limit ourselves today so as to save energy for tomorrow. The best way to provide more energy for tomorrow is to use well all the energy we can generate today.

Invest wisely what you have today if you would realize increase tomorrow. To live in the realization that there is abundance of power where our present power came from, and that we can draw upon this greater source for as much as we can use, is to place the system in that position where it will naturally call forth, from the layers upon layers of power that are latent within, all this energy that is required at any time for any work we may have in hand. It is the law that the more power we use the more power we generate; therefore we should never try to hold back our energies or faculties. On the contrary, we should express them all as fully as possible, and aim to apply the whole self in everything we do.

There is a marked distinction, however, between using power and wasting power. A useful action draws forth every power, while a wasteful action does not; and too many of the actions of man are wasteful. That is why his activity makes him weak when it ought to make him strong. To make every action useful, make it a point to work, act, think and live in poise. Be in harmony with yourself and with your surroundings. Try to make every action constructive, and have greater things in view. In this manner the longer you live the stronger you will become.

Chapter 15

Equal to Every Occasion

Depend upon yourself, and proceed in the conviction that your whole self is equal to every occasion that may arise in your life or your work.

To depend upon a part of yourself is to have doubts and to hesitate; but to depend upon your whole self is to know that you are equal to every-thing that you may meet or be called upon to do. To depend upon a part of yourself is to express only a fraction of the power you possess; but to depend upon your whole self is to express more and more of the power you possess until you actually find that you are equal to any occasion.

That which you depend upon in yourself you call into action; and the more of yourself you depend upon when you act, the larger, the stronger and more effective will be that action. To apply your whole self in every action, you must think of your whole self whenever you act, and deeply desire the whole self to come forth into that action. This practice, if continued in all actions, will gradually develop activity in the whole self; and the capacity of your mind and personality will increase in proportion. Our object is to bring out the best there is in us; to apply the whole self; and also to so relate ourselves to others that we may be instrumental in calling forth the best that is in them; but to do this we must observe closely the great principle that no one can be his best unless he learns to depend upon himself.

A person becomes strong by using his own powers, and he develops through the expression of his own inherent capabilities. No one can learn to walk, physically or metaphysically unless he is, taught to stand upon his own feet; and no one can learn to think constructively or progressively until his mind acts independently of all other minds. These are great principles, but they have been almost wholly neglected, both in self-development and in the training of others.

In depending upon yourself, however, the idea is not that you should depend upon yourself for everything that you need in life, or that you should expect others to depend upon themselves in the same manner, and thus refrain from giving them your best. To depend upon yourself is to depend upon yourself in the application of what you may have secured in life; that is, you should gather material and wisdom from every source possible, but you should depend upon yourself in the use and the application in your own world of what you have gathered.

All good things should be given and received in abundance, whether they come from the physical, the intellectual or the spiritual realms; but they should be given and received not with the intention of easing life, but with a view of enlarging life. The only ease is that which comes from greater capacity. We lighten the burdens of others when we help them to bring out their own superior strength. We should not try, therefore, as a rule, to shield others from difficulties, but" we-should" try to make them so strong that difficulties become mere playthings in their hands.

We grow by attempting to do the larger and the greater, and not by frittering away our time with what is usually called a "soft snap." However, when attempting the more difficult we should proceed gradually, step by step, and never overreach, because overreaching usually brings unfavorable reactions.

Practical Self-Help

Everything that tends to make a person de-pendent tends to decrease that person's ability, and consequently makes life more difficult for him to live. On the other hand, everything that tends to bring out the person's own individuality will increase his ability, capacity and power; and he will thereby not only make his life easier and more agreeable, but will accomplish a great deal more in his chosen vocation. Make men and women strong, competent and highly individualized, and you need not be anxious about their life, their circumstances or their future. Such people will have gained the power to change their circumstances and create their own future; and no obstacle can prevent them from becoming what they wish to be. To such people troubles are not troublesome, because they are overcome at once and trans-formed into opportunities.

And what is more, when a mind gains sufficient power to master his own fate, there will be few disagreeable things in his life, because after all, the ills of life come only through mistakes; and when we gain sufficient capacity and power to live life as it should be lived, mistakes will be reduced to a minimum, and troubles will practically cease to exist in our world. When we see a strong soul in the midst of a large experience, which from our narrow viewpoint may appear to be a serious trouble, we usually feel sorry, but such tears are frequently in vain. In most instances he is thoroughly enjoying the experience, and will come out victorious, with greater power than he ever possessed before. Wherever we may go in life, we see the great value of mental and moral strength, the ability to depend upon one's self, and the ability to meet every occasion with an individuality that is invincible; therefore, it should be the purpose of all training to make every individual both self-reliant and self-sufficient; in brief, to give him the power to apply such a great measure of his whole self that he can always depend upon himself. Whatever an individual is called upon to do, that he should be able to do himself, without depending upon anyone. He should not only be willing to depend upon himself, but he should have the capacity and the power to see the matter through without seeking unnecessary assistance from others. All educational institutions should base their efforts upon this purpose; and when they do, a most remarkable service will be rendered to the race.

In our efforts to improve ourselves, we usually depend upon some person who is supposed to understand the process better than we do, and there-by make ourselves dependent upon his mentality. In our efforts to instruct others, we too often take such a deep, sympathetic interest in their welfare that we make them dependent upon us. This is especially true of young minds that are very susceptible to the influence of sympathy. Such minds are not permitted to act independently, but are constantly being interfered with through the over-wrought anxiety that we constantly hold over them. The true course to pursue is to teach the young mind the principles, laws and methods; and then give him the privilege to work them out through his own individual application. Let him understand that you expect him to work out the matter himself, and he will, if he has any ability; and lie usually has far more ability than he is given credit for.

The average child is made to feel that he can do practically nothing, and is thus made mentally dependent from the very start. This means daily interference with the progress of the new mind. Though the child be dependent to a degree in the beginning, nothing should ever be said or done to impress the idea of dependence upon the child's mind. The dependence of the child is temporary, and should be viewed as a passing something to which we should not give serious thought.

The true use of sympathy is extremely important in this connection, because it is through sympathy that we can understand a child sufficiently to direct that child, and it is through the wrong use of sympathy that we make the child wholly dependent. When we are in sympathy with another mind, we can intuitively feel the present needs of that mind, and can be of real service; but if our sympathy goes farther than that, unfavorable results will follow.

Here we should note that children who receive the most care and attention are always the weakest in body and the most dependent in mind; but it is not difficult to understand the reason why; though when we do understand the reason why, we realize how important it is for every mind, regardless of age, to learn the art of depending upon himself. Parents frequently declare, "We do not want our children to go through what we have gone through," and accordingly they proceed to make the lives of their children as free from care as possible, often shielding them from experiences that are indispensable to the fullest expression of real life. Later on, such children usually turn out to become mere leaves in the whirlwind of circum-stances, and are thrown here and there, giving constant anxiety to friends and relatives.

The idea is not, however, that we should place hardships in the pathway of the growing mind, for hardships have no place whatever in any life. The idea is that, instead of trying to shield children from the problems of life, we should teach them to become so strong that they themselves can readily master those problems. Instead of eternally watching young people lest they go wrong, we should help them to become so strong that no power on earth can lead them astray. We should make them strong enough to stand by themselves, and then hold neither fear nor anxiety over their sensitive minds any more.

Practical Self-Help

At first sight it may seem noble of parents to prepare an easy life for their children; but is it not far more noble to teach children to become so strong and so competent that nothing in life is difficult? Here we should ask ourselves which we would rather be, a puppet in a soft snap, or a mental giant with sufficient power to master any-thing, to be equal to any occasion, and to fill with comparative ease the highest positions in life.

When we are training children, large or small, this is something we should consider well; and as the same law is applicable to all minds, we realize the great value of changing all systems of training, both those that apply to others and those that apply to ourselves, so that mental dependence may be reduced to a minimum, and the power to depend upon one's self developed to the highest degree.

In religious life, the idea of dependence has been expressed in a most detrimental manner. In fact, religious and moral education tends almost entirely to make a person dependent, and is consequently directly responsible for a large share of the wrong that is done in the world. There is no glory or mark of manhood in periodically sinning and repenting, because the former is always the result of weakness, while the latter is nearly always the result of fear as to future consequences. But there is glory in becoming so strong that temptations are powerless in your presence; and when the mere thought of sin is so far beneath you that it never touches your invincible character; and we all can reach this height, even in this world. The principal reason why so few have thus far reached this height is because we have not taught people to depend upon themselves in obtaining moral and spiritual strength. We may have told them to be strong, but we have not taught them how they can go and do it themselves.

No person can become strong until he is taught to depend upon himself in this matter, because the power that is in him does not come forth until he begins to use that power through himself; but he cannot call his own power into expression, so long as he is told that he is wholly dependent upon something else. Religious and moral instruction, therefore, to be true to man must adopt this new principle; and when we examine the real purpose of religion, we find that it does not teach us to depend upon authority, or upon the Supreme, but to work with the Supreme. It is not the purpose of the Supreme to make helpless dependents out of humanity. The purpose of the Supreme is to make each individual soul so strong that it becomes invincible in the midst of all sorts of conditions.

We have told people again and again to over-come sin; but a weak character cannot overcome sin. Such a thing is a psychological impossibility; therefore if we wish to help people to overcome, we must help them to develop a strong character; but this they cannot do until they are taught to depend upon themselves.

We do not mean, however, that man is to ignore the Infinite, nor ignore the assistance he may receive every day from his fellow man; nor do we mean that man should ask the Infinite to do it all, as millions have done to their sorrow. The principle is not to depend wholly upon the Supreme, but to work with the Supreme, and likewise not to depend upon any one person, or any group of per-sons, but to work with everybody.

In the realm of intellectual training, the same great possibilities exist for the application of these principles, and everyone who understands should do his utmost to hasten the day when they will be universally employed. In the beginning, however, the true use of sympathy is the first essential. We must sympathize sufficiently with people to know their needs, but we must not sympathize in such a way that we interfere with the free, independent actions of their minds. To be deeply interested in everybody without disturbing the independent thinking of anybody is the object, and also so to relate ourselves to others that we cause them to express the best that exists within them.

It is evident, therefore, that one of the greatest essentials in practical self-help, and in the full application of the whole self, is to learn to depend more and more upon yourself; and to this end think of yourself as equal to every occasion; feel that you are, and be determined to prove it. Proceed in that attitude and with that conviction, and your power will gradually increase until you realize that you are master over every situation.

Chapter 16

Invincible Determination

Base your actions, your desires, your feelings and your moods, not upon external indications, but upon your own invincible determination.

No external indication must be permitted to suppress the self, and no external indication must be permitted to determine your aims, desires, feelings or moods. Maintain the mood that is most conducive to good work, even though all your circumstances may tend to produce the opposite mood. Continue to feel the way you want to feel, regardless of the fact that all surrounding conditions may tempt you to feel the reverse. Persist in the desire that is uppermost in your mind and dearest to your heart, even though there may be nothing at hand just now to indicate the fulfillment of that desire. Hold firmly to the aim you are determined to see through, no matter how many circumstances or events may seem to prevent you from realizing your ambition now. In brief, give your own determined self full authority to decide what you are to think or do, and permit nothing external to influence your attitude or movements for a moment.

This is absolutely necessary, and the reason why is found in the fact that the expression of yourself will decrease if you permit external conditions or events to influence your thoughts, aims or feelings; while on the other hand this expression will greatly increase if you give yourself full authority to determine what your aims or desires are to be.

The more fully the whole self determines what every action of mind or body is to be, the stronger and larger becomes the expression of the power of the whole self in every action. The converse of this law is also true; therefore the man who permits himself to be influenced by external things, and who thinks and acts according to what his environment may suggest, will express less and less of the power of his self in his actions; and this is why such a man always becomes weaker the longer he lives, losing ground steadily, while the man who applies the above law becomes stronger and stronger every day.

There are a number of people, especially among those who are engaged in creative work, who are unable to do anything of worth unless they are in the mood; and as they do not know how to place themselves in the desired mood, a great deal of valuable time is lost. In the average person the desired mood comes unconsciously, from causes that have been produced unconsciously, therefore there is no control whatever over any phase of the process involved; but this process can be con-trolled, and the desired mood can be produced at will at any time.

What is termed the proper mood is that state of mind wherein the subconscious is ready to act, and the conscious mind or outer mind is ready to be acted upon or through. When this condition prevails, you not only feel like doing what you want to do, but you feel that you can do it well. All conditions required for exceptionally good work are present. Genius is alive, and the personality is in the proper attitude to give expression to the power of that genius. The proper mood, therefore, may be produced directly by causing the subconscious to become highly active at the time when the work is to be done, and by causing the outer mind to become responsive to the sub-conscious at the same time. To produce the de-sired subconscious action, the subconscious should be impressed with regard to what is required some hours before, or the day before the work is to be done; and while the work is being done the outer mind should give full right of way to the genius from within.

Whatever you wish to do in the near future, direct the subconscious to give full expression to this power at the time when you wish to be in the mood; and the proper mood will invariably be produced. While impressing the subconscious, have dearly fixed in mind what you want done and when. Then direct the whole of attention upon that inner, finer mentality that permeates your entire being, and with deep, strong feeling desire to impress the within with the object you have in view. What you impress or direct the subconscious to do while in this state of deep, strong feeling, that the subconscious always will do. This is a law that is exactness itself, therefore the mood for good work, or any kind of mood, may be produced whenever desired. Instead of waiting for the mood to come, you can make it to order as required. The power of the subconscious is limitless, and can do whatever it is properly directed to do.

Chapter 17

Know What You Want

Know what you want. Then continue to want what you want with all the power that is in you.

The application of this principle bears directly upon the idea of self-help; that is, the full application of the whole self; and the reason why becomes evident when we examine the mental process involved in the action of desire. When we desire something definite, we naturally concentrate the forces of mind upon the goal in view, and the more fully we concentrate the forces we possess, the larger and stronger becomes the expression and application of the self.

Here we should remember that those forces that are scattered do not call forth additional forces, while forces that are concentrated invariably call forth new forces with added energy and power; and the more of that which is in us we call forth into action, the more of the self we apply in every action. Another reason why this principle bears directly upon the self-help idea is found in the fact that there is no action of the mind that goes so deeply into the interior realms of mentality and personality as the action of desire; and there is no action that tends so much to arouse the larger life within. Therefore when we want what we want with all the power that is in us, we tend to arouse and make alive our entire mental world; and this is our purpose. To apply the whole self we must make alive everything that exists in the vast domain of the whole self.

In addition, the power of desire when full, persistent and strong has special value, as it tends to arouse and develop those very forces and faculties that will enable us to secure what we desire. It is literally true that we shall finally get what we wish for, if we only wish hard enough; and to wish hard enough is to give so much life, so much determination, so much depth and so much soul to our desire that we arouse into full action those forces and faculties within us that can fulfill that desire. There is enough power and talent in the mind of any man to enable him to realize every normal and rational desire he may entertain, provided all of that power and talent is constructively applied.

To make constructive application of the power and talent you possess so as to change everything in your life for the better, never ask yourself what your future is to be, but ask yourself what you want your future to be. Then focus all your energies upon that one supreme goal. You create the future you want when every force in your being is directed to create what you want; and the principal reason why so few accomplish what they have in view is that some of their energies are directed to create the bright and the growing side of life, while the rest of their energies are either scattered or permitted to create what is adverse and detrimental. The average person builds with one hand and tears down with the other. That he should accomplish little or nothing is therefore evident. But in practical self-help we learn to apply both hands in the building process, so that all the power we possess is used wisely in working for those desires or ambitions we wish to realize.

When you know what you want, proceed to work for what you want with all the force and ability you possess, regardless of circumstances. The fact that there are no immediate signs of your securing what you desire should never influence your mind. You can get what you desire when you become large enough to produce or command what you desire; and your whole self is large enough to produce or command any desire. Whether or not you are to get what you want, therefore, depends entirely upon how much of your

Practical Self-Help

whole self you apply; and in this connection we should remember that we tend to suppress the self and hold back this power whenever we hesitate to work for what we want, or live in the fear that we may not secure what we want.

We should also remember the converse of this fact; that is, the more we work for what we want the more of the self we apply in that work. Accordingly, that work will naturally be more successful, and will take us another step nearer the goal of our cherished desire. When we work for what we desire and give our whole life to that work, we build ourselves up, so therefore, the gain is great, even though the desire itself might not be realized. For this reason it is the height of wisdom to work even for desires that seem to be entirely beyond us. Our efforts to reach them, if full, persistent and strong, will build us up to such an extent that we shall finally become giants in mind and soul; and when we reach that lofty state in the scale, we shall find that those desires are not beyond us anymore, but are easily within reach.

The ruling idea must always be the full application of the whole self; and everything that will tend to bring out into constructive action more of the self should be practiced both faithfully and persistently. To work for what we want, whether or not there are any indications of our getting what we want, is one of these important essentials. And here we should remember that indications are but reflections of our own life, power and activity. If the weak man should desire some greater thing, the indications in his favor would not be perceptible. According to appearances, no one would decide that he would get it; but if a strong man should desire that particular thing, the indications would be that he could very readily realize that desire. The indications, therefore, in each case depend upon the man; in fact, are the direct results of what is active in the man. The weak man, however, can make himself stronger and stronger by applying more and more of his whole self, and therefore make the indications more and more favorable until those indications declare positively that he can secure without fail the greater thing desired. Thus we understand how man can change and control his circumstances practically at will.

If there is anything wrong or unfavorable in your circumstances or your life, blame no one but yourself. Do not look in the external world for the cause. Look into your own mind. Look at yourself and the way you are using yourself. You will there find the cause in every case. External conditions are invariably reflections of what is going on in yourself. Circumstances are the results of what you are doing with yourself, and how you are applying yourself; and the way the world meets you is the direct result of the way you meet the world. Indications of every description are produced by yourself. When those indications are unfavorable, it is because your use of yourself has not been favorable.

Change yourself, and indications change to correspond. Improve yourself and the use of yourself, and indications will very shortly become more favorable. Meet the world in a changed mood, and the world will respond with the same changed mood. It can all be traced to yourself. Therefore, act as you like; improve yourself as you like; meet the world in any way that you like; and apply as much of yourself as you like. You are complete master of the situation, and can therefore receive in return what you like. The secret is to know what you want; and to apply more and more of yourself in the realization of what you want. This action will make you larger, greater and better in every sense of those terms; and like attracts like.

Chapter 18

Special Rules in Self-Help

(1) At all times and under all circumstances aim to express and apply your whole self; that is, everything in yourself that is active; and aim to make more and more of yourself active through every method available. Whatever you do, results depend upon how much of yourself you apply, and how well that application is made.

(2) To apply the whole self literally means to turn on the full current of your life, ability and power; and the first step in this direction is to desire deeply and constantly to turn on the full current in yourself; and to think with conviction and feeling that the whole current is being turned on in everything you do. Begin the day with a deep, positive determination to apply all that is in you every moment and in everything you undertake. You thereby train your system to apply more and more of the ability and power that is active within you; and you also cause more ability and power to become active in your system every day.

(3) Always think of work and action as tending to give you more strength, greater endurance and greater ability. Expect your work to build you up and to call forth more and more of your whole self. The mental attitude you entertain in connection with any action, physical or mental, will tend to modify the natural results of that action to correspond with the nature, the purpose and the tendency of the attitude. Therefore, if you work in a mental attitude that expects weariness, from work, the influence of that attitude will produce more weariness than the work itself. While if you work in an attitude that expects physical and mental growth from work, the influence of that attitude will give every action of your work a tendency to add strength and capacity to mind and body. Accordingly, weariness will be reduced to a minimum and the expression of the self increased.

(4) Undertakings that seem difficult, if approached with undaunted faith and courage, will invariably call forth power and ability in yourself that were not in action before. Thus more of the self will be expressed and applied, and the capacity to undertake greater things will be secured. To look upon a difficulty as a difficulty, or an adversity, is to hold back a large percentage of your power; while to look upon every difficulty as an opportunity through which you may express and apply more of yourself, is to increase to a great degree the measure of your active power.

(5) When you seek to apply more of the self, proceed to exercise every power, every function, every muscle, every fiber and every atom in your being. Aim to use everything that is in you; to use everything fully; and to use everything right. And a deep, persistent desire to use all that is in you in this manner, combined with a positive determination in the same direction, will even at the outset increase the action of every element in your being from ten to twenty-five per cent.

(6) Whatever your work may be, continue to move forward. Do not hesitate. Do not delay. Continue to move on. Move slowly, if you are not absolutely certain of your ground, but always continue to move. Resolve to see your purpose through to a finish, and have the courage to proceed regardless of circumstances. It is the man who is stronger than adversity, and who proves himself superior to all circumstances, that invariably wins even though a thousand failures threaten to engulf his purpose or plan.

(7) Positive action is necessary to the in-creased expression of yourself. Be positive in all thought and action; and this means, to give your whole life and the fullness of your whole life to everything you think, say or do. There is no better or simpler way to train yourself to apply more and more of what is in you, than to make it a point to express in your every action, physical or mental, all the life and power you possess. To apply this rule be calm and determined in every thought and action. Feel positively the fullness of your life in every thought and action. Desire persistently to express the greater man within you in every thought and action. Will to apply all there is in you in every thought and action. Press on with all that is in you in every thought and action; and whatever you do, enter into it with all your mind and heart and soul.

(8) Give all your qualities the best possible setting, the best possible opportunities for expression, and the fullest life and action from within yourself. In brief, so live and act that every quality you possess will not only have a fair chance, but the best possible chance; and you will soon find that those qualities will serve you twice as well, and more.

(9) Rise superior to your position if you desire something better; and you will invariably secure something better. Do your work so well that anyone can see that you are fitted for a more important work; and when this discovery is made you will have more opportunities for advancement than you can use. The demand for the more competent in all fields of action is many times as large as the supply. And to rise superior to your position, proceed to apply more and more of yourself in your work. Apply all your ability and genius even in detailed or trivial matters. You will thereby prove your greater worth and give your ability a fuller, a larger and a more efficient expression. Never think of your present work as menial or degrading. All work is noble in itself, but may appear ignoble when performed by those who think they are serfs. Look upon your work as a path to advancement, to increase, to greater things; and everything you do will help you to advance.

(10) When you fail to realize your ideal in your life or your work, the cause will invariably be found in your own attitude; either in a lack of expression in yourself, or in a misdirection of that expression. If you have not secured the higher position you desire, there is either something deficient in the way you apply your ability, or there is something wrong about the way you think or approach your work. If you do not think of everything you do as a stepping stone to greater things, your idea of your work is not right; and if you do not apply all that is in you to what you are doing now, you are not on the path of advancement.

(11) When you do not secure results in one direction, turn about and apply all your ability and power in some other direction. Refuse to feel depressed or discouraged at any time, as such states always decrease the power of the mind.

Instead, increase your faith and determination with every seeming failure, and know that there are a thousand other places and opportunities open to you.

(12) Moments of inactivity are necessary. Do not count such moments lost. If you are ambitious, and are pushing to the front, such moments are but nature's method of preparation for greater things. Frequently, when the outer mind seems barren and inactive, the subconscious is working out something of decided importance which will come forth later to enrich and build up your life.

(13) Every man when prompted and encouraged to do better work, will increase his efficiency from ten to fifty per cent; and the same is true of your organs, muscles, powers, functions and faculties. Therefore, encourage and direct every atom in your system to be up to the mark. Expect everything within you to become more efficient; prompt everything within you to become more efficient; and continue in the positive faith that greater efficiency is being realized throughout your entire system.

(14) When your environment is adverse, remember that no wrong can affect you unless you permit that wrong to impress itself upon your mind. What you dwell upon mentally will impress itself upon your mind. What is impressed upon your mind will become thoughts, mental actions, desires, and in many instances physical actions. Accordingly, to dwell mentally upon the wrong is to produce wrong thoughts, wrong desires and wrong actions both of mind and body; while to dwell mentally upon the right, the good and the greater is to produce superior thoughts, noble desires, and actions of mind and body that tend to build and enrich the whole of life.

When there is adversity or discord in your home, in your place of work, or in your environment, do not permit your mind to dwell upon that matter, nor even think for a moment of what is wrong about you. Instead, turn your whole attention upon the supreme goal of your ambition, and look so intently for the most interesting factors of that ambition, that you become completely absorbed in its powers and possibilities. Your mind will thereby work up more and more to the goal of that ambition, and ere long you will find that you have entirely moved out of the discord and the adversity with which you were previously surrounded. To continue to think of the wrong and mentally live with the wrong is to continue to remain in the wrong; but to think of the right and live mentally with the greater good of the right is to grow out of the wrong and enter into the world of the right.

(15) When you do not seem to have desirable opportunities, the reason is that you are not improving yourself. Improve yourself steadily, and you will become a better opportunity to the world. And he who becomes a better opportunity will meet better opportunities at every step of the way. The man who improves himself will be wanted where still further improvement can be realized; and the man who does better and better work will have the opportunity to go where still better work is in demand, with advancement in recompense as a natural sequence.

(16) When your individuality seems weak and you cannot feel that there is anything of ac-count within you, turn your attention to the fact that all the power and possibilities of the greatest of human nature exist in your own system. Then dwell upon this fact constantly. Try to feel that it is true. You will soon become conscious of the more that is in you. Then you will begin to show greater richness and power in your mind and personality; and you will feel more and more the adding of quality and worth to every fiber in your being.

(17) When everybody is in discord about you, remember that you need not be in that discord, because you have the source of harmony within yourself. Try to feel this harmony in your deeper nature, and try to live and think in touch with that lofty realm within your own soul that is always calm and serene. Then be harmonious within your entire system. Express harmony in everything you think, say or do. Others will soon discover that you are in harmony, and will soon enter into the same state! Thus you may still the troubled waters in your environment by becoming still, harmonious and self-possessed in yourself; and thereby prevent much wrong in the life of others as well as in your own.

Practical Self-Help

(18) When life seems barren or dreary, remember that the source of riches may be found in your own interior nature. The well-spring of joy, power and contentment is ever full to over-flowing in your own mind and soul. Then place yourself in conscious touch with this vast reservoir within. You will soon find a decided change for the better in your entire being; and as you change, all things in your outer life will change to correspond. Suppose you have no friends. Then remember that the source of real friendship may be found among the finer elements of your own higher nature. Place yourself in touch with this source and awaken your own true friendship. You will, from the very beginning, become a better and a better friend; and as you become a better friend, good friends in abundance will want you for a friend. Apply this same idea to everything in your life that is not what you wish it to be.

(19) When you have lost everything do not think of the loss. Think instead of those factors in yourself, and in your environment, that produced the gain; then remember that those factors can be applied again, and more successfully than before, because your past experience will give you the power to cause those factors to produce far greater gain, and in less time. There is always a way out, no matter how difficult the position, or how hard the times; and if you turn on the full current of your mind and life, the way will be opened in every case. The secret at such times is to apply the whole self and all that is active in yourself. When you do this the possibility of failure is entirely removed, and you can positively turn the tide in your favor.

(20) Have definite plans before you proceed with any undertaking. Know what you want to do and how you are to do it. Then proceed with the positive determination to push those plans through. Add enthusiasm, and results will follow as expected. A large percentage of the failures in life are due to no other cause than this — that so many act without definite plans. Such a course wastes energy, and it is wasted energy that constitutes the greatest obstacle to attainment and achievement.

(21) When you are disappointed about results, remember that the securing of better results demands a fuller and better application of your ability and power. The feeling of disappointment, however, tends to decrease the application and expression of the powers of the self, while the actions of faith, courage, persistence and perseverance invariably increase those powers. The more determined you are to succeed, and the more faith you have in the possibility of success, the more ability and power you call forth with which to promote your success.

(22) When you wish to secure favors or positions, be your best, look your best and express your best. The more of yourself you express, provided that expression is orderly, self-controlled and pleasing, the more you prove there is in yourself; and the people who have the most in them are the ones selected for the best places.

(23) When you are in a position where competition is so keen that the chances of each one reaching the top are less than one in a thousand, remember that every step you take in the improvement of yourself will add to the value of your own life. And to advance in worth, in power, in usefulness — in brief, to apply more and more of the self — that is your purpose. No matter how many applicants there may be for an important position, the fact remains that the demand for competent men and women is much larger than the supply. The man, therefore, who improves himself and makes himself more efficient, will not only gain far more from his life, but will positively advance to better positions in the world's work.

(24) That which is best suited to your own nature and demands will, when realized, give you the greatest happiness and add the most to the value and welfare of your life. Nothing should be selected, therefore, with a view of imitating or outdoing others, but always with a view to serving your own best needs — for greater service to the world.

(25) Be orderly, neat, attractive and refined in your dress and personal appearance. This will invariably cause you to appreciate yourself better, which in turn will tend to call forth your better qualities in a larger measure. To make a good impression upon others is one of the many ways by which you can act to advantage upon your environment. The people you meet or associate with constitute one of the principal factors in your environment; and it is therefore highly important that the impression you make upon that factor be favorable to the greatest degree.

(26) Associate as far as possible with people who fully appreciate your worth and your work, and who do not hesitate to express their appreciation at every available opportunity. When we receive appreciation our minds become more active along the lines of our work, and a strong tendency towards still better work is produced. And so strong does this tendency become at times, that most ambitious minds can accomplish almost twice as much as usual if fully and wisely appreciated.

Realizing this fact we should express our appreciation of others whenever we feel justified in doing so. No good work should be noted without a word of appreciation; and for those who are doing their very best our appreciation should be most enthusiastic. But we should never indulge in mere flattery, nor be too free with our compliments. Our words of praise should be merited, and should always be sincere.

Sincere praise is always inspiring to those who receive it and deserve it. If all who deserve appreciation received all the appreciation they deserve, there would be ten times as many competent people in the world as there are now. Efficiency among the majority would be improved fully one hundred per cent, and deeds of real greatness would be multiplied many times.

(27) Associate mentally with the great souls and the great deeds of human history. Think much of the great, the noble and inspiring. Use your spare moments in this most profitable manner. Through this practice you create superior thoughts. You enrich your mind. You add quality and power to your thinking and thereby become stronger, more able, more competent and more worthy. We steadily grow into the likeness of that which we think of the most. Therefore, if we would rise in the scale, we must think much and frequently of those who have reached the high places in life.

(28) When others do not appreciate your efforts at once, remember that it takes more time for the race to discover the value of the extraordinary than the ordinary; so be patient and self-sufficient, and glory in the fact that your work is already above the average. Appreciation positively will come and may come almost at any time; and when it does come the reward will be many times as great. Do good work, the very best of which your whole self is capable. Full appreciation and adequate reward must follow. The best things come slowly and require more time and effort, but it is the best things that make life worthwhile.

(29) To live and work with people who are antagonistic to your belief and plans is a circumstance that becomes comparatively easy when you apply the correct idea of freedom, and realize that no circumstance can stand in the way of a great soul, a worthy idea or a meritorious plan.

Practical Self-Help

Remember that every person has a right to his own views; and also that you need not express your views in order to carry them out. The proper course is to live them, and by so doing prove your superiority by deeds and results. In a reasonable time others will recognize the superiority of your plans, and be glad to give them full right of way.

(30) When you meet exceptional opportunities before you are prepared or feel competent to take advantage of them, there are two things to bear in mind: First, all good opportunities continue to come again and again to the man who is making his life count in the world. If the time is not ripe at first, it will be later or in due time. Second, it is possible to prepare yourself on very short notice, and thus take advantage of exceptional opportunities without delay. It is remarkable what you can do when you think that you can, and are determined to do your utmost. But at such times use good judgment and never hesitate. The man who hesitates, and makes it a habit to hesitate, will never accomplish anything worthwhile. It is the man who makes himself equal to every occasion, by applying everything that is active in his whole self, that secures the best opportunities, and that moves forward with the greatest measure of real success. The growing, determined mind will not find it necessary to wait for exceptional opportunities, because he creates such opportunities as he is ready to use them.

(31) In practical self-help there is nothing more valuable than effective ideas. Ideas can change anything. Ideas can improve anything. Ideas can change defeat into victory, failure into success, adversity into prosperity, loss into greater gain, a useless life into a rich and remarkable life. No matter what your conditions may be, if you produce better ideas those conditions will change for the better, and the reason why is simple. There is no way that you can help yourself more than by producing greater, better and more effective ideas. Therefore, the aim should always be to secure better ideas, and to train the mind to become an expert in the creation of ideas that have exceptional value. The more the mind is exercised in the formation of efficient ideas, the more efficient the mind becomes in the creation of such ideas. Therefore, exercise the mind in the formation of practical ideas; ideas for doing things better; ideas on the way to make things better; ideas on how to change and improve everything in your life. Thus your mind will become so efficient in this respect that it will always be prepared to produce the right idea when emergencies appear; and in the meantime those improved ideas will add greatly to your welfare in every other respect.

(32) Before you consult others on what to do give your own mind the fullest opportunity to apply its power in solving the problem. You can usually get better ideas for yourself by engaging the full power of your own mind than by consulting others. Therefore, use your own mind first. This will give your mind most important exercise, and your power to produce ideas will be developed. After giving your own mind the first opportunity in this respect you may consult others.

Thus you may secure ideas that you can combine with your own; and such combinations nearly always prove more valuable than the individual ideas secured from either source. The greatest and most successful plans in the world of achievement have, in most instances, been the result of combinations of ideas contributed by several brilliant and highly active minds; that is, each individual concerned gave his own mind directions to produce the best ideas possible in connection with the plan; and later the best ideas from all those minds were combined into a new plan which proved to have all the essentials required.

(33) When you have obligations to meet, and are not prepared to do so, the situation should always be met on the strong side. Do not worry. Do not be disturbed. Have no fear. Remove all depressing states of mind. Be determined to meet your obligation. Have the faith that you can. Declare again and again that you must find a way. Call upon the elements of your mind to aid you, to give you ideas, plans and effective methods; and positively demand results. You will in this manner gain remarkably in mental power, character, positiveness and personal worth; and you will, with hardly a single exception, find a way out. In fact, it is practically impossible to find an incident where the victory was not won in this way; but where the way out was not found at once, the loss in material things was slight com-pared with the gain in mental power. And to gain mental power is not only to become able to regain what was lost, but to add much more in days to come.

To worry at such a time is to destroy the power necessary to find the way out. At such a time you need ideas, plans and methods; and to find these the mind must be dear and strong. And when the mind continues to be dear and strong, the necessary ideas or plans will certainly be found, provided all the elements of the mind are called into full determined action. When you find yourself in a difficult place do not despair. Do not get ready to give up. Do not think of going under. Be strong. Be firm. Be positive. Be determined, and go to work with all there is in you to form ideas and plans through which you may find the best way out. At such times do not worry, but create greater ideas instead.

(34) When you cannot carry out your favorite plan proceed at once to try some other plan. Direct your mind without delay to work out something better. Declare that you must have it. Lose no time regretting what was not possible. "Let the dead bury its dead." Your mission is to act among the living — to do things. Therefore, when you find that certain things do not respond to your efforts you must proceed at once to act with other things. The coming of failure has turned many a man into a far richer and greater field. In fact, all failures act in this way in the lives of those who determine to do great things. If you fail in one direction you may know, if you are doing your best, that there is something greater in store for you in another direction. In the life of a great soul the closing of one door is invariably followed by the opening of a larger door; and every soul is potentially great. The secret is: Be true to all that is in you; and be all that you can be now.

Practical Self-Help

Chapter 19

Building the Positives

Make it your constant effort and aim to cultivate the positives. Train yourself to express in thought and speech only those things that have a decided tendency toward the larger, the better and the more wholesome in life. Do not permit a single thought or a single word that points downward, because the way your thoughts and your words go you will also go.

Train yourself to express only positives and you will, through that one thing alone, grow steadily in health, strength, power, ability and efficiency. Every positive action in your system is a building action, while every negative action is the reverse; and the reason why is found in the fact that the positive action deals with quality while the negative action deals with the absence of quality. When you think of anything as being difficult or impossible you admit to yourself that you are not equal to the occasion. You cause your mind to dwell on the absence of sufficient power instead of upon the presence of sufficient power; and you thereby weaken yourself. No one can bring forth all the power that is within him so long as he thinks about his lack of power; and that is what you do when you complain of things being difficult or admit the possibility of defeat.

When you criticize others or feel dissatisfied about yourself you are likewise dwelling upon the absence of quality and power. You are not bringing out the superior. You are simply impressing your mind with the inferior. In other words, you are filling your mental store-house with cheap material, and such material is not only valueless to you, but stands in the way of your gathering better material.

The more room we give to the inferior the less room we shall have for the superior, and vice versa.

Never think or say that anything is difficult. Affirm constantly that all things are possible, and live in the conviction that you will have the power to do whatever you are called upon to do. Never feel dissatisfied with what you have done, but continue to say, I will do better. Never admit the possibility of defeat. Keep your mind positively upon victory and resolve to transform all present conditions into victory. Never criticize or find fault under any circumstance. Do not take the negative path. Take the positive path. Instead of calling attention to the defect, call attention to the possibility of improvement. In this manner every imperfection we may meet can be met with-out giving any thought to the weak side; and when we give all our thought and attention to the strong side, the strong side will steadily grow in strength, value and efficiency.

To feel anxious or worried is to deal with the absence of power. It is to believe in the lack of power, because no person would feel worried if he felt that he had the power to carry through what he had undertaken. However, we must not attempt to displace worry with indifference. Instead we should live in the positive conviction that we can reach the goal in view. We do not eliminate the cause of worry by simply ceasing to have thought of failure. The secret is to think about success, and to be so determined to succeed that there is no longer any room in the mind for thoughts of failure. We remove the negative condition by introducing the positive state; and the positive state is always the opposite good of that which is detrimental, inadequate or undesired.

When we come to a place where we seem utterly unable to see our way through, we may think we are justified in being anxious; we may think we have grounds for fear and that we cannot be blamed for being worried or feeling discouraged; but the truth is that it is just such circumstances that demand all the faith, all the power and all the positive determination that we can possibly arouse. Even if we should fail for the time being, we have become so strong during the experience that we are fully prepared to turn the temporary defeat into a great and permanent victory. However, if we continue to express the positives and the positives only when we enter so-called trying times, we shall pass through and out of such times with flying colors in every instance. That person, however, who never permits a single negative to exist in mind or personality will never fail. He will not even meet temporary defeat. He may find places at times that will demand all the faith, all the courage and all the energy that he can possibly arouse, but he will continue to move forward.

But to bring out the positives when we meet difficult places is not all that is necessary. It is necessary to bring out the positives at all times. Eliminate negatives in your mind and you will not have to meet negatives in your circumstances. Cause every mental action to be a building action and tomorrow you will always be greater and better than today. Do not be down in your mind and you will never be down in your fate. There will be no downward tendencies in your life so long as there are no downward tendencies in your thought or speech. When you have begun to move upward and onward in your mind, you have also begun to move upward and onward in your life and your destiny.

When every thought and every word gives expression to the power that makes for greater things, everything you do will build for greater things; but to call forth building power we must not dwell mentally upon the lack of power. Instead we must give all thought and attention to that which contains power, abundance of power, and possibilities for greater power.

Have no regrets. Let the past go and proceed to make the future better. Know that you can, and be determined to do what you know you can do. Do not be sorry when others are in trouble, but do something tangible to help them out. Grief is a negative and wastes energy. To develop practical helpfulness is a positive and develops energy. Never fear the worst. Never think that you fear the worst or ever permit yourself to say so. Always expect the best. Think so at all times and say so whenever you are in the company of those who enjoy wholesome speech. When you are in the company of those who may not understand the principle of wholesome speech, say only what is necessary and continue to think positives with all the power and conviction of your soul.

Never think or say that things are going against you; that you are not able to do what you want to do; or that fate is unkind, or that life is too short. Such ideas cause the mind to dwell on the weak side, the lesser side, the undesirable side; and we are invariably drawn into those conditions that we think of the most. Do not admit that things are against you, even though they may seem to be. Think nothing about it, but do think about the great fact that when you become greater than things all things will be for you, no matter what you may wish to do. And also remember that you immediately become greater than things the moment you begin to express positives and positives only. It is therefore an easy matter to cause things to take a turn.

When you seem to be unable to do what you wish to do, give your positive attention to the great fact that you can become what you wish to become. The reason why you cannot do what you want to do is because you have failed to become as much as you have the power to become. Give your

Practical Self-Help

present thought, with full positive action, to what you desire to become, and the opportunity to do what you desire will shortly follow.

Do not feel disheartened because fate seems to be unkind. Do not weep over the failures of the past or the limitations of the present. Do not think of what you have failed to get. Begin to think about what you have the power to give. Then proceed to give the best to the world; and as surely as the universe is in motion the best will begin to come back to you.

To think that life is too short is to dwell upon the limitations of life, the lack of life and the final absence of life. To live as we wish to live, how-ever, we must steadily grow into more life, richer life and better life. Therefore, every thought and word should convey the idea of limitless life and be inspired by the feeling of a perpetual increase of life. Never think of trouble. Never look on the dark side. Never feel suspicious. Never feel hurt. Never think ill of a single creature. Never talk sickness to anyone. Never mention bad luck or even think of possible misfortune. Never take a pessimistic view of anything. Never admit that you are tired. Never say that you feel bad. Never admit weakness of any kind. Never pay attention to defects in others. Never say that you are only human. Never say that there is always something wrong. Never think that the results you expect can only come after a long, hard pull. Never lose faith in yourself or anyone else. Never contemplate the idea of giving up. Never pity yourself or feel sorry for "poor me." Never think of anything as being hard or fixed or limited. Never think of any condition or circumstance as being, greater than yourself, and never think of any obstacle as being insurmountable. These are all negatives, and as all similar expressions of thought or speech are also negatives, anyone can readily discriminate between the negatives and the positives in whatever may be thought, said or done.

When you express the positives you talk health, happiness and harmony; you talk peace, power and prosperity; you talk virtue, wholeness and superiority; you emphasize the greatness of man; you mention only his good qualities; you think only of his better and stronger side; you live in the conviction that you have the power to grow out of any condition into a superior state, and you act accordingly; you direct your whole attention upon the greater possibilities that exist within you; all your thinking is trained to bring out the greater; and all your energy is used in building up the greater. You know, therefore, that your life and your destiny are in your own hands; and you not only bear that fact in mind at all times, but you so live and work that that fact becomes a reality in every part of your own sphere of existence.

Practical Self-Help

Chapter 20

The Courage to Go On

To begin, it is necessary to remove the principal obstacle in the way; that is, the fear of the future, and we accomplish this by realizing that the tasks of tomorrow are not one-half as difficult as they may seem from the viewpoint of today. When we think of that which is to come we usually transform our imaginations into mental telescopes and what we see is thus made larger and brought closer to our present position. Being so large we think we must give the matter much thought; and being so near we think we must attend to the matter at once. In consequence, we generally give future tasks several times as much thought as necessary, and we begin preparation weeks and months before we have to, thereby wasting time, energy and previous thought, simply because we did not see the thing where it is and in its true size.

Sometimes the task looks so large that we fear to begin; we have doubts as to our ability to carry it through; we do not feel equal to the occasion because we have magnified that occasion several times over through a misuse of imagination. In this way people frequently live for weeks in dread of something that they have to do because it looks so large and so difficult; but when they come to do it there is nothing to fear at all; there are no difficulties connected with it, and they find it to be one of the easiest things they were ever called upon to deal with.

The magnifying power of imagination is the cause of this confused state of affairs; and through this very thing millions of people either stumble outright or have started on the down grade. To be able to see one's self and everything pertaining to one's self as it really is; and to be able to see one's work as it really is, these are most important attainments.

You cannot do justice to yourself today unless you can correctly measure your present capacity; and you cannot properly approach your work un-less you can see that work as it actually is — no larger and no smaller than it is. You may be far greater than your work. You may be equal to far greater occasions than the ones you daily meet, but you may not know it. You may be looking upon your work through the magnifying glass of abnormal imagination. This makes your work look large and difficult, and you fear it. You therefore look upon yourself through fear, and through that glass you appear to be much smaller than you really are.

Nine people out of ten habitually magnify their work and belittle themselves. They do this unconsciously; in fact, they have inherited the habit and usually do not know that they have it. Occasionally we find a man who takes the correct view in this matter, but in too many instances he retains this correct view only for a short time. The nearer he comes to the real occasion, the more he tends to refer to the wrong view, until he comes to think that the work is hard and that he himself is incompetent.

To secure the best results from every occasion, both the action and the thing acted upon must be seen and understood as they really are. When the coming task is easy we cannot afford to give it a great deal of thought or preparation; and when it is hard we want to know it so that we can prepare ourselves thoroughly; but we cannot properly prepare ourselves to meet the difficult so long as we live in dread or fear. To dispel this fear, how-ever, it is only necessary to realize that we are equal to every occasion that we may meet upon our onward path.

Practical Self-Help

We are never called upon to do what we are not able to do. This is one of the great laws of life. What comes to us comes because we ourselves have at some previous time sent the invitation. Things do not come of themselves, and other people can never give to you what you do not willingly accept. When we are equal to great things we will be called upon to do the great and difficult. Therefore, when the difficult does come, we may know that we are fully equal to the occasion.

We can state it as a general rule that every person is the equal of every action that comes into his life. There may seem to be exceptions, but upon close examination we find these to be only temporary modifications that are usually too insignificant to change the results. It is therefore thoroughly unscientific for anyone to fear the future or to tremble in the presence of any occasion he may not have met before.

If we were told that we had to tie our shoe strings tomorrow and had never done so before nor seen anyone else do it, we should possibly lie awake most of the night worrying about how we would ever get through with such a difficult undertaking. And although this conclusion appears to be absurdity itself, nevertheless there are a great many people who spend sleepless nights thinking about how to do things that prove just as simple as tying shoe strings. A great many, even among the most competent, spend days, nights and weeks turning things over in their minds that could be handled perfectly upon ten minutes notice. But people would never do this, however, if they could see their task in its true nature, and know themselves sufficiently to realize that they are equal to every occasion.

Imagination, or rather the wrong use of imagination, is to blame for all this, but the whole matter can be remedied by training imagination to act in its own legitimate realm. To accomplish this in the simplest manner possible, train yourself to live constantly in the conviction that you are equal to every occasion that comes your way. Practice will prove that this is the truth, and the man who makes it a practice to meet every occasion with the thought that he is equal to it will never fail to turn action to good account.

When doubt comes up and you begin to feel that possibly you have met your Waterloo, remember the great law that like attracts like. You have attracted something difficult because you are able to handle the difficult. You have been called upon to take up the new task because you are ready for it; and going at it in such a spirit will always produce success. In addition, your imagination will be daily trained into normal action. In this connection, however, we may well ask what it is that causes the Waterloos in life, if it is true that like always attracts like; but the answer is simple. To say that you are equal to an occasion means that you can cooperate to advantage with that occasion and thus produce satisfactory results.

It does not mean that you have met something to fight or resist. The average person, however, thinks that life is a battle and he proceeds accordingly; but he thereby misapplies his power, and it is the mistake that leads to failure. He may be making a battle out of his life by fighting every difficult occasion that is met, and because he fights he meets many a Waterloo. In constructive work failure comes only when we are so afraid of the occasions we meet that we do not cooperate with them properly; and we fear them because they appear to be larger and more difficult than we supposed, due to the fact that we look at them through the magnifying glass of an abnormal imagination.

He who takes advantage of every opportunity; who is always at his best; who views all things correctly; who does

Practical Self-Help

not give unnecessary time to trifles; who does not fear the difficult; who knows that he can do whatever his own sphere of existence may call upon him to do — to him there is victory in every case. He will not have to turn back or go down. He will never meet defeat, be-cause he is complying with those requirements from which all victories proceed.

The majority are creatures of habit, though it is neither necessary nor desirable that any one should be; and on that account we usually find it easy to do things to which we are accustomed, even though they may be very difficult. But what we have never done before usually seems difficult though it may in truth be simplicity itself. The reason why is that we have entered into right relations with those things to which we are accustomed, and have adapted ourselves to the requirements. Accordingly, we are always prepared, and such work comes easy. In brief, the subconscious supply is always at hand; and to fill that particular place in life has become second nature. When we meet something difficult, however, we are unable to comply with the requirements at once. We are not adapted to the new work. We have not trained the subconscious to respond. We have not formed the right relations; and it is necessary to be properly related to our work before it can be done as it should be done.

Here we find the great problem in this connection; how to relate ourselves properly to every occasion that is met; and to solve this problem we must first remove the tendency to magnify our work and belittle ourselves; for with such conceptions of things we cannot see anything as it is, and cannot produce proper relations between ourselves and our work. To cooperate with the occasions we meet under such false conceptions will only result in misfits; and here we find one reason why so many people are in the wrong place, working at things they are not adapted for. To give your best to your work you must properly relate yourself to your work;

and to relate yourself to your work you must see yourself as you are. You must also see your work as it is; but all of this is simple and is readily accomplished by removing all kinds of belittling and magnifying processes.

And although this may seem to be an immense study, you can simplify the matter by living constantly in the conviction that you are equal to every occasion that you may meet in life. This conviction when thoroughly grounded in the sub-conscious will remove the two undesirable processes just mentioned; and will establish right relations between yourself and every new occasion that you may meet. Accordingly, you will know that you are equal to every occasion; and when this discovery is made, you will have removed practically all the difficulties that may exist in your pathway. Then combine this conviction with a group of well-developed positives, and you will have the courage to go on; to go on at any time and under any circumstance; to go all the way — to go to the apex of your highest vision.

Chapter 21

The Control of Things

When we know what we want and begin to press on with all the power and faith in our possession, we may look forward with joy to the coming days. What we want we shall receive, because things will take a turn and the turn will be in our favor. Things always take a turn when we are determined that they shall. Things invariably obey when called upon to do so by a mind that makes itself invincible.

When all things appear to be against us we are against ourselves, and when things seem to be slipping away the reason is that we are neglecting to hold ourselves in that strong, positive, masterful state where we belong. Things will do for us what we are doing for ourselves. That is always the nature of things. We originate action whether in the right or in the wrong. Things merely imitate what we are doing. Therefore, we may cause things to do whatever we desire.

We do not have to control things nor command things. It is only necessary to control ourselves and command ourselves. What we are determined to do, things will proceed to do. Things always follow the strongest force. And we become the strongest force in our own world when we determine, with all the power we possess, to do what we want to do.

There is no fate that cannot be changed, because fate is but the result of the actions of things, and things will change their actions when we proceed to change our actions. As we act so will things act. This is invariably the rule. Then, we find that adversity is simply the result of a disordered mind, or a mind that has not caused all of its actions to move towards the one supreme goal. But when we know what we want, and give our undivided attention to what we want, all the powers of mind will work together for the object in view; mental order will prevail; and adversity will pass away because only that which is orderly can live with an orderly mind.

The orderly mind is always firm and positive and works unceasingly for some greater goal. The disordered mind is the inactive mind. It does not possess itself. It has no definite object in view. It has not brought all its forces together to work for any definite purpose. It is unsettled and undecided. Its forces are confused. Its attention is divided. Its thoughts are scattered, and therefore can neither control itself nor determine the actions of those things that may exist in its environment. When the mind is inactive, unsettled or out of order, the actions of things will move in the same confused manner. Accordingly, adversity and trouble will be the result. But when we change the movements of our own minds the movements of things will change to correspond, and all things will work with us to promote the object we have in view. When we produce the desired turn in the mind, things will take a similar turn. We shall then find the desired turn in the lane and we shall go where we wish to go.

What we create in the within we meet in the without. Those external conditions into which we are drawn always correspond with those internal conditions that we previously created. For this reason, the mind that ceaselessly and positively desires a change for the better will invariably find a path that turns toward the better. This is a law that cannot fail; but the mind in question must know what it wants, and must want what it wants with all the faith and power in its possession.

To produce the change we desire we must keep the eye single upon the mental picture of that change. We must live in the mental world of that change. We must expect it with all the faith that we can arouse, and we must determine to produce it with all the power we possess. We shall find, if we proceed in this manner, that the desired. change will be produced. The mind is the master; and when the mind asserts itself in the full power of its supremacy things will obey.

When circumstances are adverse and the future looks dark there is no occasion for sadness or gloom. Fate is in the hands of man, and when we determine to create a better fate, to get out of present conditions, to find the freedom we desire, to secure the opportunities we desire, and proceed with all the faith and all the power in our possession, things will take a turn. This is how we control things, because things always obey when directed to do so by a mind that makes itself invincible.

Chapter 22

There is Always a Way

Whatever we may wish to accomplish, the way will be opened and the necessary opportunities will be found, if the will be sufficiently strong and properly applied. The reason why is found in the fact that the will controls and directs every faculty of the mind; and the stronger the will the more efficient will that faculty become that is necessary to carry out the purpose of the will. Suppose you desire to gain a better position in your particular field of work; you see no opening, however, as the way is not dear; but you do have a will to find a way. In consequence, the faculties that you employ in your work will be spurred on to greater effort and higher efficiency. You will thus not only become more valuable, but you will so increase your strength, determination and personal power that everybody you come in contact with will be most favorably impressed. Accordingly, you will have taken the first step in opening up the way; and it will only be necessary for you to proceed along the same line to open wide the way that you actually desire.

When the will is strong, those faculties that you are using at the time become strong in proportion; all the latent ability that those faculties may contain is aroused and placed in action, and you become far more competent than you ever were before. Therefore, when you positively and continually will to succeed, you steadily increase your ability, your power and your working capacity along that line where you desire to succeed; and you will surely forge to the front. You will arouse all the power that is in you, and there is enough power within you to overcome any obstacle or adversity you can possibly meet.

Practical Self-Help

Suppose you are in the midst of confused or detrimental circumstances, and do not see your way out; but you remember that where there is a will there is always a way; and you become positively determined to apply that principle in finding your way out. You live constantly in the deep, strong feeling of "I Will." While in the spirit of that will you are ever looking for the way; and this is what happens: There is a faculty in the mind that is usually spoken of as finer insight, or the power to do the right thing at the right time. When you strongly will to find a way out, the power of your will begins to arouse this finer insight. Your understanding is pushed up, so to speak, above the clouds of confused circumstances, and you begin to see clearly what to do next in order to get out of your trouble. Your idea factory begins to work, because it has been made alive by the determined efforts of your will; and when you begin to get practical ideas on the problems of the hour, the happy solution is near at hand.

Though the present may be as dark as pitch, and everything may seem to be against you, be determined to find a way out. Have a will to know what to do, and remain eternally in the very spirit of the deepest and strongest powers of that will. You will thereby make alive your finer insight; your discernment will become clear and strong; your understanding will rise out of the darkness of the cellar, into the sunshine of the upper story; that faculty that invents plans and methods, ways and means, will go to work with a will, and will work in the light because you have willed your whole mind up into the light. By having a will to find a way, you make alive those faculties that can see the way, and you also arouse sufficient power to carry out the plans presented.

To secure the best possible results in the working out of adverse or limited conditions, as well as working up into larger, greater worlds of attainment and achievement, we should concentrate attention upon the finer insight of the mind whenever we will to rise in the scale. In other words, when we will to find a way up towards the goal in view, we should think deeply of that finer discernment in mind that has the power to see the way we want. We thus apply the power of the will directly in giving greater brilliancy and efficiency to all those faculties that lead the way toward greater things.

To illustrate further, we will take a young man with tremendous will and ambition, but no opportunities in sight. He is living in a small worthless world with no paths leading out into the greater world of his dreams. He is in that place where there seems to be "no chance," and he has no visible or tangible means with which to go where he may find a chance. Thousands are in his position. Most of them stay there all through life, not because they have to, but because they have not a will to make a way out. The young man with a will, however, finds the way out, and this is how he goes about it. The walls have ears. If you are a power, someone is going to find it out. You will not have to work miracles nor exercise some mysterious force over present undesirable conditions.

When someone discovers what you are, you will at once be wanted where opportunities are greater, and where opportunities for further advancement are still greater. When your will is immensely strong within your limited world, you will become so strong that your power will be felt outside of your limited world. Strength will not stay bottled up very long, especially if that strength keeps on growing stronger; and the man with tremendous ambition and will is constantly growing stronger. He may be bottled up for a time where there is no chance, but he will not stay in that condition very long. The cork of cramped environment will soon blow up. His life will be felt on the outside; his voice will be heard far beyond the limitations of his sphere; and the world always stops to listen when real power proclaims "I Will."

There may be thousands of opportunities almost within arm's reach, and you may not feel strong enough to lay hold of any of them; but if you have the will to go out after those opportunities, you will gain the courage to try, the power to take hold, and the mental capacity to make good. The power of the strong, positive, unwavering, determined will, brings out all there is in you. That is what the will is for; and by training the will to promote more thoroughly its real purpose, you gain conscious possession of the real quality of greatness.

The man who is alive with power can never hide from the world of achievement, not even though he may be in the wilderness of the desert. If you have power you will make a stir of some kind, and the effect of that stir will be felt everywhere. Be negative and few will know there is such a person as you; but be positive and everybody will know that you have existence. They will also know that there is something in you, and it is such persons that the world is looking for every day.

The world of demand attracts its desired supply. Be that desired supply and you will be drawn to the world where you are in demand. This is a great natural law, and it is universal in its action. It is very simple, however, in its action regardless of the fact that it seems mysterious. Be something, and no matter where you are, the world will find it out. Then, the way to pastures green will be open to you. By having the will to be all that you can be, you will naturally gravitate into those environments where your greater ability and power can be turned to practical use. The strong positive actions of the will have in this manner actually created the necessary way.

When you set up a positive action in yourself you become a center of attraction. You not only stimulate the powers and faculties of your own being, thus making yourself more competent, but you also stimulate interest in yourself. You will be watched by everybody, admired by the majority, and a few will single you out as the man that is wanted in some larger place. So long as you are negative, however, you attract nothing, not even attention; but the moment you become alive with will and determination, everybody begins to take an interest in you. You will thus be found by those who are looking for men of worth, and thereby find the way you wanted because you continue to have the will.

The world is not interested in darkness; and the negative person is a light turned down very low; but the whole world is interested in light; and the positive person is a light turned up with full blaze. Such a person can be seen at a great distance; and as everybody needs light, everybody will go where they can secure light. Therefore, the moment you turn up your light, you will have any number of opportunities to make real use of your light whatever your talent for giving light may be. And here we should remember that it is the power of a strong, determined will, the will to make a way, that turns up the light of every talent we may possess. The stronger your will, the more brilliantly will the light of your mental faculties shine, and the more power you will have to focus that brilliancy where the greatest results may be gained.

Whatever you wish to accomplish, make it a point to will to succeed, and think deeply of those faculties you are using at the time. You thus give added power to those faculties; and greater ability and power expressed through any faculty always opens the way to greater opportunities. If you are in the business world, think deeply of business ability whenever you will to succeed; and have a will to succeed at all times. Apply the same method if you wish to succeed in salesmanship, mechanics, literature, music, art, oratory, or any vocation whatever. The power of the will is thereby concentrated directly upon those faculties that you are using in promoting your advancement; and in consequence you will advance steadily and rapidly — sometimes with leaps and bounds.

Chapter 23

Optimism That Makes Good

The sun shines constantly whether we can see the sunny side or not. In consequence every cloud has a silver lining at all times and under all conditions; and what is true in the physical world is also true in the metaphysical world. The sun of boundless life, limitless power and innumerable possibilities is ever shining in the life of every individual. No matter how dark things may seem to us in the present there is a sunny side to the circumstances in which we live, and we have the power to find it.

To find the sunny side it is only necessary to keep it constantly in mind, because we are invariably drawn into those conditions and circumstances that we think of the most. There is no mystery about this law. It is as natural and as simple as the simplest fact that we ever knew, and anyone can prove it to be true. When we see the silver lining we should keep the mental eye upon it constantly. We thereby concentrate our whole attention upon the brighter, the greater and the better. In consequence, we not only create the greater, the brighter and the better in our own minds, but we are also drawn into the happier conditions of the sunny side.

When we cannot see the silver lining we should imagine that we see it. We should picture it and concentrate our whole attention upon the brightness of that picture. We should do this in the full conviction that the silver lining is there. Though we cannot see it just now we should know that it is there just the same, and we shall have the same result as we would if we actually did see it. The reason why is simple because we create those conditions in ourselves that we think of the most. There is no circumstance, however adverse, that does not contain some valuable power or some rich possibility that we can gain possession of and use in the present. Though the cloud of adversity may be dark, it has a silver lining. Beyond the darkness there are better things in store. And by keeping the eye single upon the silvery side, we pass through the darkness, arriving safely in the world of better things.

When we concentrate the whole of attention upon the silver lining, whether we can see it or not, and are determined with all the power we possess to reach the better goal we have in view, we cause everything, both in ourselves and in our circumstances, to work with us. We are turning all things to good account. We are causing all things to work together for good, and that which was against us will change and be for us.

To keep the eye single upon the silver lining is to keep the mind full of brightness, wholeness and power, and such a mind can never fail. It is the mind that becomes depressed that goes under, and the reason is that the depressed mind is weakened, thereby becoming wholly incompetent to cope with its circumstance. Besides, such a mind continues to work in mental darkness thereby making mistakes at every turn. The mind, however, that continues to concentrate attention upon the silvery side of all things will continue in mental dearness. It will make few mistakes. It will see dearly how to act, and being in the upper story will have the necessary power to act. The mind that dwells on the right side is always strong, vigorous, energetic and brilliant. Such a mind, therefore, has the mental clearness to know what should be done under every circumstance, and also has the mental power to do what it knows should be done.

The path to every high attainment and every great achievement is an ascending path. The mind that would rise in the scale must continue to go up; and the mind that concentrates the whole of attention upon the brighter and the greater is constantly moving toward the upper regions of thought, life and action. In such a mind all the forces are building forces. Therefore steady advancement both in attainment and achievement must invariably follow.

When everything looks dark and no silver lining is in sight, the average person will begin to give the whole of attention to darkness and despair. In consequence, the mind goes down into weakness, confusion and failure. This, however, can be easily prevented by creating a silver lining in imagination, and then concentrating attention upon that bright picture with full faith, determination and power. Give the mind something bright to think of and it will move upwards. It will rise out of darkness into the silvery brightness on the upper side. It will leave adversity behind. The victory will be gained and the coveted goal will be a dream no more.

It is not sufficient to hope for the best. It is not sufficient to be cheerful and optimistic. It is not sufficient simply to say, think or feel that things will come out all right. In addition, something tangible must be done to make things come out all right. The mind that simply hopes that things will change for the better is not using its power directly in producing that change. Hope is only passive. It looks in the right direction, but it does not act. It means well, but to change fate something more will be needed besides good intentions. The proper course to pursue is to turn hope into faith and combine faith with work and ability; then proceed to change conditions, circumstances and things as you wish them to be. You can. He who combines the highest faith with his greatest ability and the most thorough work may reach any goal in view.

Practical Self-Help

The average optimist is simply a prophet of better times; but that is not sufficient. In addition to being a prophet of the true, the greater and the ideal, you must do something definite and something tangible to make your predictions come true. And in this connection you should constantly bear in mind the great fact that you positively can. When the outlook is bright an opportunity is at hand, but opportunities do not materialize into tangible results unless they are acted upon with persistence. To say simply that the future looks bright, when present indications are full of promise, is not sufficient of itself to produce brightness in the future. Good indications must be developed and turned to good account before their promises can be actually fulfilled.

The hopeful expression of the average optimist if not worked out into practical action may become sounding brass, nothing but empty words having no power one way or the other; though on the other hand no effort can act to the best advantage unless it is expressed through an optimistic attitude. It is real live optimism combined with real live doing that produces results worthwhile.

The pessimistic attitude darkens the mind, lowers the quality of intelligence and mental power, and causes fully one-half of the energy of the system to be wasted. The pessimist naturally makes more mistakes than the optimist because the former lives in the lower story of mind while the latter lives in the upper story. There is more light in the upper story of mind; the view is larger; the outlook better; the quality of intellect finer; judgment better; understanding more exact; the actions of mind more rapid and thinking more harmonious and dear. It is therefore evident that no person can afford to live in any other than the upper story of mind. And to become a real optimist is to enter this upper story.

Practical Self-Help

When the optimist does not simply fed optimistic, but is inspired with a strong, irresistible desire to make his bright hopes come true, he will positively succeed in reaching his goal. And the reason is that the optimistic attitude is a superior attitude; it has finer intelligence and more power. But those qualities must be turned into real constructive action before the greater vision of this superior attitude can be made real in practical life.

The man who faces the light of a brighter future will feel optimistic; but if he is not moving towards that light with all the constructive power of his being he will not inherit the brighter future he has in view. The average optimist sees light ahead, but he is usually standing still. Things may look rosy to him; he may feel hopeful, and he may try to inspire hope in others; but in too many instances that is all. He is standing still, viewing the promised land, but is not taking a step towards that land. For this reason his dream will not come true, and he will not share in the good time coming that is just a little farther on.

The optimism that is worthwhile is the optimism that makes good; in other words, that attitude of mind that not only sees better things, but that also does something substantial to make things better. The prophet that deserves honor even in his own country is the prophet that makes his predictions come true. Anyone can have visions of the new, the beautiful and the ideal; but it is the mind that makes its ideals real that commands the attention and the admiration of the world. It is such a mind that renders real service to the race, and his reward will be great indeed.

In every vocation in life the pessimist is at a disadvantage, while the optimist, if he applies himself properly, is absolutely certain to have things come his way. The pessimist confuses his mind and wastes his energy, while the optimist, by rising into superior states of mentality, illumines his mind and increases both the force and the capacity of his energy. The pessimist is always in bad luck of some kind because his mind is too dark, and he fails to see dearly where and when to act. The optimist, however, is always in good luck because his mind is higher up. He sees what is going on in the world and therefore, even unconsciously to himself, does the right thing at the right time.

The spirit of this age is optimistic. The best minds in the present refuse absolutely to speak or think of the dark side; but another step is required. Simply to feel optimistic is not sufficient. We want an optimism that acts, that does things, that produces results. The mind that sees the greater possibilities of life, that keeps the mental eye single upon the brightness of those greater possibilities, and then proceeds with all the power of life, thought and action to realize those possibilities — that is the mind that is thoroughly worthwhile. It is such a mind that we all should cultivate, because such a mind not only has the power to see the greater, to predict the coming of the new and the better, but also has the power to make this prediction come true — to cause the new and the better to be realized in practical life here and now.

Chapter 24

Act in the Present

What seems possible now should be done now, because what seems possible now is possible now; and to put present possibility off into the future is to lose an opportunity that the present alone can employ. To wait for a more convenient time is to be a servant of failure, because the more convenient time never comes to him who simply waits. We create our own circumstances; but he who is simply waiting for favorable circumstances will not create such circumstances.

To proceed to do now what we can do now, what we ought to do now, or what is possible now, is to place in action our most powerful energies; and it is the energies we place in action in the present that create those circumstances in which we shall shortly find ourselves. All things work together for greater and greater good to him who is making the best and the fullest use of what he may possess now. He who turns everything in the present to good account is turning everything in himself to good account; he is therefore daily becoming a greater and a greater power in his own world.

The man who waits until he can do better is retarding the development of that power within himself that can do better; while he who does his best now is steadily gaining in that power and will shortly be competent to do whatever he may desire to do. There is no end to the possibility of human nature. It is only a matter of gaining sufficient knowledge and sufficient power to enable a man to attain or accomplish whatever he may have in mind, and he who is steadily gaining in knowledge and power will shortly secure the desired amount. To gain steadily in knowledge and power,

Practical Self-Help

the principal secret is to make the fullest possible use in the present of all knowledge and power that may be at hand in the present. However, to neglect to do now what is possible now is to cause much time and energy to be wasted. All the knowledge and power at hand will not be used. Therefore, no gain of any account will be noted.

Never say you expect to succeed. Such thought will put present possibility off into the future. Be determined to succeed now. Every person can succeed now; and he who places in action now all the powers of success that he may possess now will steadily advance into greater and greater success. Do now what you feel convinced that you can do now. Then work in the faith that you can carry it through, and you will.

To avoid premature action live so absolutely for the present that your understanding of the present is practically perfect. Those who do not know what is best for the present, or what course of action may be successfully pursued in the present, do not clearly understand the true conditions of the present; and the reason why they are deficient in this understanding is because the forces of their intelligence are scattered over vast areas, extending from the remotest past to the most distant future. In order to understand the needs, the possibilities and the conditions of the present moment all the forces of intelligence must be concentrated upon the present moment; but he who would do this must live absolutely for the now.

The more intelligence that we concentrate upon a certain subject the more clearly can the mind understand that subject. The same is true of the greatest of all subjects — the life of the great eternal now. It is therefore evident that when the entire intellect is concentrated upon the present moment the mind can understand the present moment so perfectly that no mistakes will be made with regard to what course of action should be pursued. When the rays of a certain light are scattered in every direction no one place is properly illumined; but a vast difference is noted when all the rays of that light are focalized upon one particular point.

The only period of time that we can live for or act upon is the now. We can do nothing for the past, and we cannot act upon that which has not yet arrived. Therefore, to scatter thought and attention over past time or future time is to waste the power of thought and every thought is wasted retards the progress of life. Everything that is to be done must be done now and everything that can be done now should be done now. But he alone can know what can be done now who focalizes all the light of his intelligence upon the present moment.

It is permissible to plan for the future when such plans are necessary to the promotion of present action, but otherwise all planning for the future or thinking of the future is a waste of present energy. However, while the individual is making those necessary plans for the future he should live absolutely in the present. To live in the present tense is to formulate all thought and expression in the present tense and, therefore, to utilize the whole of consciousness in the discernment of the now. The term "after a while" is eliminated from thought and speech; we are concerned only with that "while" that we are conscious of now, and we do not wait to do what we expect to do, but instead proceed to do that thing now.

We should not. wait for the opportune moment to produce a change in our nature, but we should change now as far as we possibly can and thus fit ourselves for the highest and fullest expression when we have formed those opportunities that we ourselves ate creating. The average person declares that he will change in this or that respect when the greater opportunity arrives; but the fact is that he who produces in himself a desirable change now will shortly meet the greater opportunity. He will not have to wait for the call to come up in front. He will be wanted up in front the very moment he has produced the desired change in himself. This being true, and the fact that any person can produce in himself the change desired now, proves conclusively that he who lives absolutely in the present has the future completely in his hands.

The man who gives all his intelligence and power to the actions of the now will make those actions great; and every great action is invariably followed by a still greater action; that is, when the greatness of the cause is given absolutely to the creation of the effect. Much gathers more so long as much is used exclusively for the purpose of gathering more. That which grows great grows greater; but it is only the action of the now that can cause anything to grow, develop or advance. No action avails but the action of the present. Therefore, he who would begin to grow great must give all his power to the present. He must act in the present and give all the life, all the energy and all the ability there is in him now to the purpose of that action.

Chapter 25

Actions That Produce Response

Those actions that produce response are the only actions that produce results. Therefore, in promoting effective expression, as well as securing something of worth from every effort applied in work, it is highly important that we learn to discriminate between actions that produce response and those that do not.

To act upon anything, physically or mentally, that has actual existence is to secure response according to the nature of the action, while to act upon that which has no actual existence within our sphere of action is to waste our energy and receive no response whatever.

To try to act upon something that cannot react is not only to waste time and energy, but also to produce a most unfavorable condition in ourselves, a condition similar to that experienced when striking at empty space. The law that governs this phase of action and reaction is one of the most important of all laws in the human system; and there are few laws that are violated as frequently as this, due to the fact that most of us have the habit of acting upon nothing the greater part of the time.

One of the most usual of these violations is that of talking mentally to imaginary people, or to the mental pictures of people we know. This practice is very common and invariably tends to weaken both the mind in general and some of its principal faculties, which is natural, as all such mental actions are simply efforts to act upon something that has no existence within our sphere of action. When we have something to say to anyone we should always wait until we meet that someone in person. When we are tempted to talk to him mentally, or at a distance so to speak, we should positively refuse. We should instead think of something else, something upon which the mind can act effectually in the present. It is permissible, however, to study out what you intend to say, but you should never say it until you meet the person to whom you wish to speak. While you are thinking over what you expect to say, dwell on your subject only, as your subject is at hand and can be acted upon; but do not think of the person nor direct your attention towards him while thinking over your subject. The person to whom you are to speak cannot be told until you meet him, therefore all mental talk to that person in your imagination is not only a waste of time and energy, but a most serious misuse of the imagination. You know what a jar your body receives when you strike at empty space; but when the mind acts upon nothing a far more serious jar takes place. You may not always feel the jar itself at the time, because the action is usually gradual and prolonged. It is not as sudden as the striking at empty space with your fist, but the effect never fails to come, and it is so detrimental that you cannot possibly afford to permit it again.

When we encounter troubles, misfortune and other things we do not want, we usually blame all sorts of external causes; but as a rule, the cause of nearly all of those things can be found in the misuse of our own minds. The mind is so closely related to all other things in life that when any of its numerous laws or functions are misapplied there will be trouble in many unexpected places; and to try to act upon something that cannot produce response under the circumstances is a most serious misuse of the mind. For this reason we should always remember that whenever the mind acts it should be caused to act upon something — something that is at hand and that can actually respond.

Practical Self-Help

A great many people have the mental scolding habit, and frequently wear themselves out laying down the law, so to speak, to persons that are miles away. Others have imaginary foes, or imagine that certain persons they know are their foes; and accordingly resist and antagonize those foes in their imagination a great deal of the time. But all such practices are simply the mind acting upon nothing, striking at empty space, and not only throwing away precious energy, but producing most detrimental jars both to the mind and to the nervous system. All such habits, therefore, should be eliminated completely, and the simplest way to remove them is to train yourself to act only upon such things, whether physical or mental, as are present and ready to respond to your actions.

An illusion that has been very prevalent in recent years is the belief that we can be influenced at a distance by people who bear enmity toward us; but hundreds of such cases have been thoroughly investigated, and it was a case of illusion in every single instance. Not one genuine case has ever been found to prove that this uncanny belief has the least foundation. We may, therefore, conclude that all those who believe that they are influenced in such a manner are simply deluded. His influence, however, seems very real to the person who entertains that belief, and the cause is found in the fact that the belief that you are influenced by something or somebody will produce such an influence in your own mind. You yourself, therefore, are your own enemy, and no one else. Strictly speaking, no one can influence us but ourselves. People at a distance cannot influence us adversely in any shape or manner. People who are with us can influence us only when we permit it. If we refuse to accept their suggestion or advice, their words will have no effect upon us whatever. So therefore, in the last analysis we are absolutely our own masters, and should consider it a

Practical Self-Help

privilege to exercise that mastership to its highest degree at all times.

To dwell mentally upon foundationless beliefs is another habit violating the same law. It is an action that cannot produce reaction. It is throwing your mind away and getting absolutely nothing in return. Whenever we accept something as true without giving the matter the least analysis or individual thought, we are liable to center our minds upon nothing; and most of the doctrines taught by the old school of philosophy are of this kind. They are mere beliefs, and the only fruit they are capable of producing is nothingness. The human mind, however, was not made to deal with the absence of things, but with things present.

Whenever we live in the past we are acting upon nothing. The past is no more; therefore, to turn attention in that direction is to strike at empty space; it is to give life to oblivion and receive nothing in return but consciousness of weakness and waste. The habit of living in the future, however, is no better. What is to be has not as yet been created; or if it has been created, it is not at hand, so that it cannot be acted upon; and if it cannot be acted upon it cannot react. Therefore, it can give you nothing in return for the life and thought you are sending in that direction. All your thought and all your energy can be wisely employed only upon the tangible things that are now at hand; and it is such use alone that brings results.

To resist imaginary wrongs and mentally com-plain about grievances that have no actual existence is another source of much mental and physical disorder, and it is a habit that is very common; as the majority seem to think that they are being wronged by somebody or something, and are daily fighting those fanciful wrongs in their own imagination. If those wrongs actually exist, they can be removed only by going to the cause, and by acting directly upon that cause; but when we try to remove any particular cause we do not give the condition in question a single antagonizing thought. In fact, we do not think about that condition at all. There is no value in mentally fighting a weed while we are trying to pull it out. In fact, the more calm and serene the mind continues at the time, the more strength we shall have with which to remove all the weeds that may be at hand.

Study out plans of procedure by which you can get at the cause of those wrongs in your life that actually do exist, but do not mentally antagonize the wrong itself, as your energy is needed for the other side of the work. Most of our wrongs, however, are imaginary or self-inflicted, and they will therefore disappear of themselves when we forget all about wrong and give our whole attention to the building up of the right and the good. If we would, in this connection, make it a point to live and act so that we are constantly becoming stronger, more capable and more useful, and thereby continue steadily on the upward, onward path of life, we shall find ourselves realizing complete emancipation from every adverse condition that may exist in our world.

Never give any attention to desires that cannot be gratified now. To think about the object of such desires is to act upon nothing. That object is not within reach, therefore cannot be acted upon; and to attempt such action in imagination is to strike at empty space. When a desire is felt that cannot be realized at the present time, the energy moving in that direction should be transmuted and turned into channels where it can be employed now. Such a practice will be found to be exceedingly beneficial and of exceptional value in a number of ways.

Practical Self-Help

Ambitions that are premature should be dealt with in a similar manner. The great things in the future can be accomplished only by doing properly what is at hand now. Instead of dreaming about future attainments and longing for things that are not within reach, we should use time and attention, in the present, in working ourselves up to where those things actually can be reached and attained. True, we should aim high and have the most remarkable goals in view, but thought and life should be centered upon the present as we are moving towards those lofty goals. You can aim high and move in that direction at the same time; but to move in that direction you must act upon the present mode of motion. You may aim high for ages, but you will never reach your goal if all your present attention is centered upon those high places of the future, and none of it given to the moving process of the present.

Too many idealists think only of the marvels that are to be, and give no effort to the practical work that will finally make those marvels possible. Too many young people dream and dream, wishing and wishing that they might someday reach the goal of their ambitions, but those goals have not as yet been created. They are possibilities, and the pattern has been seen in the minds of interior vision, but the thing itself has not been produced. To give one's whole attention, therefore, to those future possibilities in that manner is again to act upon nothing. Instead of using the material at hand to build a tower that will reach the heights, such people arc wasting all their time wishing they were on the heights; but they are not only wasting time, they are also getting into the habit of giving energy to such things as do not exist; and anyone who gets into that habit will soon become incapable of using energy wisely for any purpose.

To give your energy where it can be used now, so that it will bring returns to you in the present, you simply must have returns from your actions. If you do not get them you will soon enter the negative state of life, and thus become a leaf in the whirlwind. It is the returns or reactions you receive from your actions that make you strong; and the more reactions you receive in life the stronger you become. Therefore, you should permit only such actions as produce favorable reactions, for this is a matter of vital importance.

Tendencies that move toward the empty things in life should be reversed, because they are sending forces into states of nothingness. The average mind, however, is frequently filled with just such tendencies. All aimless thinking is the result of such tendencies; it is thought moving toward emptiness, and therefore gives the mind the habit to act upon nothing. To correct this habit, every tendency of the mind should be trained to act with the process of construction, and should be prompted to deal exclusively with the elements of quality and worth.

To worry about failures that have not appeared, and are not liable to appear, is a violation of the same law, and is a habit that is almost universal. It is found on every hand, with countless effects, all detrimental. To worry about anything is a mistake, but to worry about nothing is a habit that we have not adjectives to describe. Since the failure has not appeared, it does not exist. Therefore, to permit the mind to act upon its imaginary existence is again to strike at empty space. There may be indications that seem to point to such a failure, but indications never constitute evidence, and as the failure has not taken place, we cannot give it a single thought if we are to be true to the laws of mind. When we see adverse causes at work in life we should proceed at once to change those causes; but our power to change causes is largely lost when we permit ourselves to worry about effects that have not arrived. To proceed at such times, act so thoroughly and so scientifically upon yourself that you completely change yourself for the better. When you change, you cause everything in your life to change in the same manner.

You are the prime cause in your own sphere of existence, and as you go everything in your life will go. Give no thought or attention, therefore, to anything but that which you wish to build up and perfect in the present. It is in the present that we must act to secure results either for the present or for the future. We must sow now to reap in days to come; but how well we are to reap will depend entirely upon the seeds we select now, and the way we cultivate the soil now. Select the best seeds in the present, cultivate the soil according to the best science in the present, and you need never be disturbed about the future. All your life and all your power will be wisely applied at every step of the way. You will gain response and results from everything you do; and you will not only grow in strength, ability, worth and usefulness, but your possessions all along the line will increase in proportion. Briefly, make it a point to act upon the real, and act well. That is one of the greatest secrets in life, no matter what your purpose or goal may be.

Chapter 26

Directing the Forces of Life

The forces of individual life are either ascending or descending, depending upon the attitude of the mind. When these forces are descending they lead to sickness, trouble and failure. When they are ascending they lead to health, happiness, harmony, power, attainment and achievement. The forces of life are all creative; and the ascending forces invariably create the larger, the greater, the superior and the ideal. Therefore, the individual who will continue to direct the forces of his life in the ascending scale will steadily create for himself a more beautiful life, a larger future and a greater destiny.

To direct the forces of life in the ascending scale, only those mental attitudes should be permitted in mind that have an upward and an onward tendency, because all the forces in life move through mental attitudes, and are determined in their actions by the position of those attitudes. The most detrimental of those attitudes that cause the force of life to descend is worry; while faith is the most beneficial of those attitudes that cause the forces of life to ascend. For this reason whenever you think you have occasion to worry proceed to have faith instead. When adverse circumstances are at hand the practice of worry invariably leads from bad to worse, because to worry is to weaken both mind and body, thus making the individual less capable to cope with the adversity that may be at hand. The worried mind is always confused and makes far more mistakes than the normal mind. To avoid worry absolutely, therefore, is most surely the height of wisdom.

When adverse circumstances are at hand the practice of faith invariably leads to victory and emancipation. Faith is inspiring, upbuilding, constructive, strengthening and ascending; and in consequence gives you that greater power and that finer intelligence with which you will be able to work out the trouble that may be at hand.

When all is well we may produce real trouble if we worry over imaginary trouble; and three-fourths of the real troubles we meet come originally from the habit of fostering imaginary troubles. But when all the forces of any individual life are caused to move in the ascending scale, the troubles that may have existed in that life will be largely reduced; in fact, reduced to a minimum and finally removed completely.

To enter into any mental state or attitude that will cause the forces of life to descend is to change health into disease, harmony into discord, success into failure and joy into gloom and depression. And the reason why is found in the fact that the descending forces in human life invariably produce detrimental conditions. The ascending forces, however, never fail to produce wholesome, beneficial conditions; and if continued in the ascending scale will finally produce every desirable condition that mind can possibly imagine.

To train the mind to live only in those attitudes that cause the forces of life to move in the ascending scale is therefore of the highest importance, and such training may be promoted by keeping the mental eye single upon the greater goal in view. Think only of greater things. Desire only greater things and constantly expect the realization of greater things. When the lesser seems near, be more determined than ever before to enter the world of the greater; and inspire every atom in your being with that same irresistible determination. To give added force to this determination avoid absolutely all depressed states of mind such as worry, fear, discontent, grief, regret, discouragement, pessimism and the like, and cultivate faith, aspiration, ambition, high resolve, idealism and every state of mind that tends to elevate thought to the highest state of quality, worth and superiority.

To direct attention upon the limitless possibilities of human life, and to hold attention constantly in that attitude, is to cause all the forces of life to enter the vast domain of those possibilities. Those forces will consequently become ascending and will begin to develop those possibilities in the life of the individual. To promote this development, everything that is met in life should be met in the ascending attitude of mind; that is, the mind should look for the better, the larger and the superior in all things, and should aim to enter more and more deeply into the realization of the better, the larger and the superior in all things.

The action of the mind at all times should move toward the heights of human existence, and should never take cognizance for a moment of those conditions that are inferior to what the mind aspires to be. To follow the ascending scale should be the ruling desire of every feeling and every thought; but this desire should not be confined to any limited conception of life or its possibilities, because to follow the ascending scale is mentally to face the limitless at all times and in every circumstance. To train all the forces of mind to move in the ascending scale is to cause everything that is undesirable in the life of the individual to be outgrown, the reason being that all ascending forces create the better; and to create the better is to eliminate that which is not desired. When all the forces of life follow the ascending scale the life of the individual will steadily change, and every change will be for the better. To continue this process of change for a time is to place the individual in a world of his own creation, a world that will be the exact likeness of his own ideal world.

Chapter 27

The Right Use of Life

We frequently wonder why the worst sometimes comes to those who seem to deserve the best; why we sometimes get what we do not want; why many suffer who have not willfully caused suffering; why we frequently meet troubles and ills that we have not knowingly produced; why sickness, want and adversity in so many instances come to those who are living good lives and who are trying to do their best for everybody. And we also wonder in the face of these things if we actually produce our own troubles and if so, how; but if not, what the cause of our trouble might be. These are great questions, but the answer is simpler than one would suppose. Whether those who seem to deserve the best actually do deserve the best depends altogether upon how much of the real in their nature is in full accord with the seeming. In other words, are their invisible actions just as good as their visible actions seem to be? The visible actions are few compared with those that are not visible, and since it is the invisible actions of mind, thought, feeling, character and life that determine the real nature and the real destiny of man, we cannot accept as final any judgment of the case that is based solely upon appearance.

Like attracts like, and therefore what man is in the sum total of his nature will determine what is to come into his life and his sphere of existence. He therefore does not deserve the best unless he constantly is his best in every phase of his being. There are great numbers who seem to do their best on the surface, but who are the very opposite in the deeper realms of feeling, thought and subconscious action. Not that they do not mean well; the majority do mean well, but good intentions are not sufficient. Neither is it sufficient to be right in a moral sense. Those who live good moral lives, however, do not always live good mental lives, and the one is as necessary as the other.

The violation of moral laws will invariably produce disaster of some kind either in mind or body, though the same is true of anger, fear or worry. A dissipated life is no more detrimental to the human system than a worried life. In fact, it is the latter that is the most detrimental, because where a thousand die of dissipation ten thousand die of worry. The reason for this is found in the fact that worry is considered respectable, so that a greater number naturally indulge in worry than in physical dissipation. The tide of thought in this respect, however, is changing so that in the future the man who worries will not be considered any better than the one who dissipates. Some people drown their troubles in drink; others try to drown them in worry; but one is no better than the other; while both are equally ineffective in removing the trouble. The man who takes to drink when overwhelmed with trouble is weak, but the man who takes to worry under similar circumstances is not any stronger in the least. Both lack faith in their own powers. Both ignore the fact that the power of man when aroused is greater by far than all the troubles in the world.

The majority live in the belief that kindness and charity should bring blessings and abundance to all who practice those virtues. Their belief is, "I AM good to everybody, therefore everybody ought to be good to me"; and this belief is sound doctrine as far as it goes. But kindness and charity cannot counteract the ill effects of anger and worry. Neither can goodness to mankind remove all the detrimental results that come from fear, mental depression and other destructive states of mind. Those who are good and kind to the world have as a rule just as much sickness and trouble as those who live principally for self. And the reason why is that the good results that should naturally come from good deeds are neutralized or destroyed through the practice of habitual wrong thinking. Such people seem to deserve the best, but they do not receive the best because they daily violate nearly all the laws of mind.

The good things of life come from the right use of life; while those things that are not good come from the wrong use of life. And it is the one that happens to be in the majority that determines whether the nature of the individual is to attract and produce that which is good or that which is otherwise. The wrong use of life comes from wrong thought. The right use of life comes from right thought. The thinking of wrong and the living of unnatural mental states constitute wrong thought. The thinking of the truth and the living in ideal mental states constitute right thought. It is therefore evident that so long as wrong thinking predominates in any individual life the worst will naturally come to that life even though many good deeds on the surface should indicate that something better was deserved. To secure the best at all times, the best expression of the whole of life must take place at all times. It is not sufficient to be good and kind along the lines of personal actions. The whole interior mental life must be right, exact and scientific.

The violation of one leading mental law may counteract all the good results that would naturally come from the many good things that the average person is usually capable of placing in action. For this reason exact scientific thinking along all lines becomes indispensable. There is many a person who thinks he deserves a great deal more than he has received, and usually bases his conclusions upon the fact that others not as good as he, or as able as he, have received more. But have those others worried as much? Have they lived in the same constant fear? Have they kept their minds constantly in antagonistic attitudes? Have they mixed their best efforts with resistance, bitter feelings, critical thoughts, wavering desires, restless mentalities, abnormal states of mind and periods of disgust, discouragement, gloom or despair? That is the question.

A small mind that properly applies the present power in its possession, and that does not counteract results through the misuse of mind, will accomplish far more than the great mind that is constantly doing something to spoil things just as results are about to be gained. There are thousands of fine minds that constantly or periodically violate one or more of the mental laws, and there are thousands of splendid characters who are getting the worst of nearly everything for the same reason. They are excellent in some respects, but in other respects they are wrong, perverted or inferior; and no matter how great or good a person may be in some respects, if the larger part of his life is misdirected he will not accomplish any more than if he were a small and ordinary mind.

Therefore, if you would receive everything that you justly deserve, think scientifically; be your best at all times; and in all things seek constantly to improve everything in your being; combine unlimited faith with all the ability you possess and all the work you can normally promote, and train all the forces of your being to work together for the goal you have in view.

So long as a single inferior quality is permitted to express itself in the nature of man, and so long as a single law of life is persistently violated, the worst in one or more of its forms may appear at any time, though this fact should not cause anyone to fear the probable consequence of past mistakes. In the first place, fear is a violation of mental law and must not be permitted at any time; and in the second place those adverse conditions that may now be brewing in the human system, the results of past mistakes, may be eliminated completely before they succeed in producing tangible results. This, however, can only be brought about through scientific thinking; and when scientific thinking begins, the violation of law will cease. Henceforth the individual will receive what he deserves. His own will come to him without fail, and only that which is desired will come into his sphere of existence.

One of the principal reasons why we so frequently get what we do not want is found in the practice of giving what is not wanted; that is, giving less than we can give, because the world wants all that any individual can give and the best that he can give. When we give less than we are capable of giving we will receive less than what we might have received. When we are less than what we can be, we will attract that which is less than we might attract; and when we are able to appreciate the greater we can never be satisfied with the lesser. When we give to the world the best we have we will receive the best that the world may have; and the best always satisfies. But when we fail to be our best, do our best, or give our best, we will fail to receive the best. Accordingly, we may receive what we do not want. Then we must also remember that we frequently get what we do not want, because we accepted it when our real judgment was set aside by abnormal sympathy or by other abnormal states of mind.

When we keep our best qualities in reserve we appear to be less than we are. We consequently attract the lesser and receive what we do not want. We also accomplish less than what we have the power to accomplish, thereby failing to secure our own. The same is true when we permit mental states that tend to misdirect. The critical attitude, the resisting attitude, the antagonistic attitude — all such mental states have the tendency to cause the person to be misdirected or sidetracked, so to speak, where he will be in a false position. Accordingly, he will not get what is really his own, but will get what he does not want. But no person who does his best at all times and under all circumstances will ever be placed in such a false position. He will always be in the right position; and whatsoever he may desire or wish for, the same will be received the very moment it has been earned.

Every person produces his own troubles, and the sooner he accepts that fact, and ceases to create more trouble, the sooner will trouble, trouble him no more. Some troubles are produced directly, others indirectly, though the person is in each case responsible. We produce our own troubles directly by creating trouble; and we produce them indirectly by willfully or ignorantly going into troubles that others have produced. There are a number of people who suffer from ills they have not produced, but they themselves have gone into those ills; therefore, none others are responsible, not even when those who created the ills are close relations, because we do not have to enter into the troubles of anyone. And what is highly important to know is that we can help those who are in trouble far better when we refuse to be troubled. The mind that becomes troubled becomes weak; but to help others out of trouble we must remain strong; and we can remain strong no matter what the circumstances may be.

When we violate the laws of life we create trouble; and the reason why so many good people have troubles is because they constantly violate the laws of mind, not knowing that the mental laws are just as important as the moral laws, and must therefore be applied with the same rigid exactness. And here it is well to understand that the violation of mental laws takes place principally through fear, anger, worry, resistance, depression, the critical attitude, the antagonistic attitude, the materialistic attitude and the attitude of misdirected desire. The laws of mind are also violated when we form false conceptions or inferior conceptions of anything of which we may be thinking. All this, however, may be prevented through scientific thinking.

The two principal reasons why we enter into the troubles that others have produced are found in morbid sympathy and in lack of judgment. But scientific mental development will remove the latter, while the former will disappear when we understand that to enter into sympathy with trouble is to create more trouble; and that before we can help others out of trouble we must absolutely refuse to enter into those troubles ourselves. In fact, to help ourselves out of wrong or adversity we must rise superior to those conditions from which emancipation is desired.

The mind that is worried makes mistakes; and mistakes cause trouble. The troubled mind creates trouble; therefore the less we are troubled about troubles the less we shall be troubled by trouble. When we are troubled about trouble we multiply those troubles; in addition, we give them more power, and thus prolong their existence. To worry over present trouble is to increase the trouble of the future. To cease to worry about any trouble will soon bring all troubles to an end. It is a fact that those who worry most about trouble always have the most trouble, while those who never worry about anything have seldom anything serious to worry about. Those troubles that we usually meet would not last long if we refused to be troubled; and they would disappear instantly if we would arouse and apply that power within us that is greater than all the troubles in the world.

Chapter 28

The Most Helpful Principle Known Today

The knowledge we possess today is so vast and so varied that we all should be able to say that we know exactly what to do, and how, under every circumstance; but the majority of the principles involved in modern knowledge are applicable to certain fields of action only; and as it is only the few who have sufficient range of mind to comprehend all fields of action, we understand why the many secure merely a fraction of the helpfulness that the great learning of the world could give.

There are certain scientific principles that only the expert scientist can apply; there are certain psychological principles that can be made practical only where the mind is trained for constructive thinking; and there are certain metaphysical and spiritual principles that can be appreciated by certain types of mind only. And therefore, the larger number of the principles we understand today do not, as yet, have universal application.

There is one principle, however, that all types of mind can apply at all times and under all circumstances — a principle that the uneducated mind can apply on a small scale, and with decided success, and that the highly developed mind can apply on a wonderful scale. And this principle may be defined as "**The Power of the Inner Life to Respond Absolutely to Every Need, Desire or Demand of the Outer Life."**

At first thought such a statement may seem to be extreme exaggeration; but modern psychology is proving the fact, through varied and numerous experiments, that there are vast reservoirs of unused energy back of and beneath our ordinary, waking consciousness; and, literally, these reservoirs can be tapped, at any time, for any amount of energy desired.

There are a great many striking illustrations from everyday experience that fully substantiate such a possibility; that is, where certain individuals have suddenly become possessed of enormous energy and working capacity; and where the mind has been positively charged with forces and ideas in a most extraordinary manner.

You have frequently realized in your own experience that when you simply had to have twice as much energy and endurance to get through a certain ordeal — and when you were determined to have it, refusing absolutely to give up — you always did secure the added measure called for.

We frequently hear this statement: "How I got through is a mystery to me; but I knew that I simply had to do it somehow; and before I was aware some enormous power took possession of me." Although such incidents have been variously explained, we now know that this "enormous power" came forth from those vast reservoirs of energy that are submerged in the depths of every mind; and that such a power came forth because the individual had to have it. The inner life always responds when we "have to have it" — a fact of striking significance that we all should remember.

Another fact that we all should remember is this, that the inner life responds remarkably and instantly to every deeply felt and tremendous demand, whether the individual understands the exact workings of the mind or not. Therefore, any mind, however simple or undeveloped, can use this principle to a marked degree.

True, we always secure more varied and more valuable results when we apply the laws and principles of life with increased knowledge; but if we do not have the knowledge, we need not wait; we can make a beginning — a small beginning, and even a large beginning; this particular principle will respond according to how deeply and earnestly we feel that we "have to have it."

Here then is information that should be proclaimed from the housetops — that should be given out broadcast all over the world. It is one of those great and startling facts of life, the helpfulness of which is beyond computation, and the principle of which all can apply regardless of beliefs, conditions or training.

However, we shall find a great many other possibilities, equally wonderful, when we search for the deeper and larger resources of the mind; and among them, greater possibilities for positive mental action, thinking capacity and mental range; greater possibilities for discernment, penetration and mental keenness; greater possibilities for creative thinking and actual genius; and in brief, greater possibilities in every phase or field of thought and action.

And again, all such statements are fully substantiated by the experiments of modern psychology and by striking incidents everywhere. In fact, we can find any amount of evidence to prove that we have, as a race, merely touched the outermost surface of the mind; and that farther back and deeper down in mentality there are resources of every description that are simply marvelous.

Therefore, we may have unbounded faith in the statement that the inner life can respond, and respond absolutely, to every need, desire or demand of the outer life.

Practical Self-Help

In your own personal experience, there have been moments when your mind became far more brilliant, and your intellect wonderfully keen. At other times, your thinking power seemed ten times greater than usual, and your mental range a hundred times greater than that of average experience.

Then you have produced ideas, during exceptional moments, that were positively the creations of rare genius; and, upon many occasions, your mind has gone far beyond itself along one line or along several lines, all of which proves that the mind can do vastly more than what it is usually called upon to do. But we have not taken full advantage of this great truth; we have not had the courage or the faith to demand more from the inner life; we have not gone to work in positive earnestness to develop the larger and richer resources of the mental world. This, however, we must do; and because we can.

Illustrations and incidents from everyday life could be recounted, almost without number, evincing the fact that the mind can, upon special occasions, outdo itself, and to a remarkable degree; that we can, by making a tremendous demand upon the inner life, cause the mind to draw enormously upon its vast interior resources; then why should we not do so whenever the need is great, and do so on the largest scale conceivable.

When we examine this principle along its various lines of effectiveness, we find, first, that whatever we may require for any purpose or occasion — the mind can find a way. If we make the proper demand, in full faith, and in the deepest depths of earnestness and determination — if we proceed with the feeling that we simply "have to have it" — we will surely get it, and very soon.

Your own mind can find a way out of any circumstance or condition; or find the means to a new life, to a new work, to a new world. And why not? You have, thus far, used only a small fraction of that power in the mind that produces ideas. If you would use all of that power, you could produce ideas so brilliant that your every problem would be solved.

We find, further, that we can, through this principle, secure more life, more power, greater endurance and capacity, and the best of health; for, indeed, the inner life is teeming with energies and life forces; and good health is largely the result of an abundance of vital energy acting in order and harmony.

The mind is creative; therefore, conditions of perfect harmony, together with positive states of expression, can be produced and given full action in every part of the physical system. And here we have the simple secrets of life, health and power in great abundance.

The mind can find a way to do what we want done, and also provide the method and the power. And another reason for this fact is realized when we learn how the mind can increase remarkably the range of consciousness, and bring intellect up to a marvelous point of keenness and brilliancy, thus, for the time being, discerning things and knowing things that are heights and heights be-yond the usual field of thought.

These things the mind can do, and will do, if we so demand and desire — if we are tremendously in earnest — if we feel that we simply "have to have it" — if we apply this principle as if our very existence depended upon unquestioned results.

And we perceive that the possibilities of this principle are so vast and so remarkable that words can neither define nor describe. It is a principle of universal application, and can be used successfully at any time by any type of mind, and for any need or purpose.

To you who understand this principle, there is no place in life where all is gone; where hope is lost; where there is nothing more to live for; where we find the end of ideals, or dreams, or cherished desires. No indeed; positively not; for at any time, you can take your life into your own hands, remake yourself, rebuild life, create a new future and a new world according to your greatest desires and highest ideals.

To you who understand this principle, there are no problems that cannot be solved; no difficulties that cannot be met successfully; no obstacles that cannot be removed. You know that your mind can find a way. You know that your mind can work out the right plan and provide the necessary power.

You are ready for anything that life may demand of you, or that your work or position may require. You are equal to it all. The personal man may not seem equal; but the inner life will respond to every need or desire, provided you believe in the absolute and limitless responsiveness of the inner life, and act with full faith and power — as with a soul on fire.

If you have not gone very far in your study of life, and are only in the first stages of wisdom and development, use this principle as far as you understand it, and with all the faith and earnestness that you can possibly arouse. You will have results; and as you advance in faith and wisdom, those results will become remarkable.

If you have given much study to the great laws and principles of life, and feel that your understanding is among the best, then remember that there are greater and ever greater heights for you to attain and master; and the vastness of the inner life can provide your every need for this larger and more wonderful undertaking.

You should use this principle upon the largest conceivable scale, and proceed in the dearness of your own highly developed consciousness. But you should not confine yourself to your own personal attainment. Here is a principle that each and every mind can apply according to need or development. You should make that truth known everywhere. You should present that truth in its simplest form to those who are still at the first stages of understanding; you should present it with all its marvels to those who have gone far up the way.

"The Power of the Inner Life to Respond Absolutely to Every Need, Desire or Demand of the Outer Life" — this is a principle that should be made known to every human being; here is information that should be proclaimed from the housetops — that should be given out broadcast all over the world.

The Scientific Training of Children

The Scientific Training of Children

IT IS the truth, and a most important truth, that a genius does exist in the subconscious of every mind. Every child is born with that interior something which when developed can produce remarkable ability, extraordinary talent and rare genius. It is therefore of the highest importance that the young mind be so trained that all of its latent power and capacity be developed, because everybody should be given the opportunity to become as much as possible.

In the past we believed that if any child was not born with remarkable ability no system of training could give him such ability. We believed there was very little in him because we did not see any signs of talent on the surface. We therefore concluded that he would have to live his life as an ordinary mortal. But now we know that every child is born with something of exceptional possibility in him, whether it shows on the surface or not. And we also know that that something can be brought to the surface by the proper system of training This being the truth no child should be neglected simply because he does not manifest exceptional brilliancy in the beginning.

There is just as much talent and genius in the dull child as in the bright child, the only difference being that in the latter genius has become active, while in the former it is as yet inactive. But it can be made active in every mind to its fullest capacity and power. In the scientific training of children the first principle to be recognized and applied is, that remarkable ability, extraordinary talent and rare genius does exist in the deeper mentality of every child. And that whatever exists in the deeper mentality can be developed and brought out into tangible expression for practical use. It is only a matter of knowing how.

The Scientific Training of Children

The belief that child training should be deferred until the ages of six, eight or ten is not consistent with the natural law of development. Such is simply a belief that has originated from the fact that the modern system of training is in so many instances detrimental to the best mental welfare of the child, the reason being that it tends entirely too much to cram the surface of the mind, thus overworking and stupefying in many instances what intellect there may be in action on the surface. As a system it does not bring out the greater mentality of the mind, not knowing that that greater capacity has existence.

The fact is that the proper development of the child cannot begin too soon, for when the development is proper, every day will add to the strength and power of the child's nature, both physically and metaphysically. What can be done now should be done now, for if it is not done now it will have to be done later. But no time should be lost, and no energy wasted. Everything should be made to count because what is not for a person is invariably against him.

Every child has the latent capacity to become much and achieve much. The child that remains ordinary remains ordinary because it is neglected. It is not being taught to bring out the power, the talent and the greatness that exists within. But if we wish to promote the welfare of the individual as well as the race, and we all do, we cannot afford to neglect a single child.

After having recognized the principle that every child is born with capacity for greatness, the next step is to so train the child, both in thought and action, that everything he may do will tend to bring out the talent and the genius that does exist within him. In other words, he should be trained to so live that all things in his life will work together for the promotion of the one great purpose — the bringing out into practical use every spark of greatness that he may inherently possess. And every child does possess the capacity for greatness, superiority and high worth. This capacity we all have inherited from our one Supreme Source — a fact which modern psychology has demonstrated conclusively. Therefore we should act accordingly, making it possible for every person to be all that is in him to be.

To train the child to develop and bring forth the best that is in him, we must first train him to make true use and full use of those elements, forces and faculties that are already active in his life. This will not only turn all active forces to good account now, but will also make the outer mind a more perfect channel through which the genius from within may be expressed when we proceed to develop that genius.

In this connection the first essential is to give proper direction to the energy that is generated in the system of every child. The average child generates an enormous amount of energy, and not being taught how to use this energy burns it up recklessly, mischievously, barbarously, and too often abusively both to self and others. He is constantly scolded and frequently punished for doing what he simply has to do. The energy is there and he is positively unable to rest until he has disposed of it in some way. For the fact is, so long as he is not taught how to use this energy orderly and constructively, he will follow primitive tendencies and use it disorderly and destructively.

Here we should remember that no child was ever punished justly. So long as parents do not teach a child how to dispose of surplus energy to good account the child cannot be blamed for using that energy recklessly, which usually means destructively. And practically all mischief among children can be traced to one cause; that is, a superabundance of energy with no knowledge as to its wholesome use. Therefore what the mischievous child needs is not a switch, but a little more practical instruction. The rod never conveyed any knowledge and never will. And no one can expect to avoid the wrong until he knows the right.

Punishment may suppress evil tendencies, but it does not produce the better tendencies. And what is very important, no form of suppression ever produced a permanent good. The good, the true, and the worthy comes not from suppression, but from proper direction. The surplus energy of the child should never be suppressed, for suppressed energy is wasted energy, and power is too valuable to be thrown away.

We cannot have too much power when we know how to apply it in the building of a great life. And this is what every child should be taught just as soon as he can understand simple words. The child should not be permitted to waste his surplus energy in wild conduct and harum-scarum living simply because a false conception of human nature has taught us to believe that "boys must be boys." The fact is, boys do not have to be boys in the barbarous sense, and they do not have to be mischievous in order to prove there is something in them. We do not have to be savages in boyhood in order to amount to something in manhood.

Such a view of life is simply the result of deep-dyed ignorance of child psychology. And because we have been ignorant along this line so long, it has become a habit to believe such absurdities. However, these beliefs must be eliminated completely if we wish to train our children to become all that they have the power to become. Though we must not go to the opposite extreme and believe as some pseudo-pious, undeveloped minds believe, that the child must remain in the "seen, but not heard" attitude in order to be good.

The Scientific Training of Children

It is not inactivity or lifeless peacefulness that produces goodness, but an extraordinary amount of life and action applied in a wholesome, constructive manner. The child that is alive will necessarily be noisy, though the same is true of the mechanics who are building a skyscraper But noisy children will not disturb us when we know that noise is to some extent a necessary part of the making of things.

It is not noise among children that should be eliminated, but the reckless and destructive use of energy. Parents who have a habit of compelling their children to be absolutely quiet are actually placing a serious obstacle in the way of the future welfare of those children; because to suppress energy is not only to waste energy — it is worse than that, for continued suppression will after a while decrease the amount of energy generated; and the less energy you generate in your system the less you can accomplish.

The Scientific Training of Children

TO train the child to make profitable use of surplus energy there are several methods that may be employed to advantage. The first of these is to find the natural talents of the child and then give him work to do at frequent intervals that will bring those talents into play. This will develop those talents and at the same time turn the mind away more and more from the tendency to be wild, reckless or mischievous.

There are parents, however, that do not care to have their children develop such talents as may appear in childhood unless those talents are considered wholly respectable. But to secure the best results every child should be developed along the line of natural aptitude, and should not be forced to do something different simply to please the high-toned notions of parents or near relations. We must remember that a genius is a genius, no matter what his occupation may be. And in the long run it is not a certain kind of work, but good work, that brings honor, happiness and due reward. There are times, however, when it is advisable to develop the child mind along lines that are entirely different from the talents that are indicated in the beginning, though this is a subject that will be discussed later on.

The belief that children should never work, but only play, is also a mistake. A certain amount of work is necessary to the best result in the development of the child, because all energy that is applied in work is turned into constructive channels, and will produce the tendency of construction in the system. The stronger this tendency is in the system the more rapidly will the various faculties and talents develop, provided, of course, such development is desired. And those tendencies that are established in childhood are always the strongest.

The Scientific Training of Children

Therefore, to train the young mind to do something constructive, that is, to be engaged more or less in work, is highly important. This is especially true when the child is given work that he likes. Though in this connection we must remember that when the child is compelled to do too much, even of that which he likes, the work becomes drudgery and has a detrimental effect. The child should be permitted to choose his work and the amount of time to be given to such work; and he will do it wisely and faithfully if well instructed as well as thoroughly trusted by the parent.

Remember here to have faith in your children Live constantly in the faith that they can and will apply your instructions properly, and they will seldom, if ever, fail to do so.

That young minds despise work is not the truth. There is scarcely a boy who does not long to do something useful, provided he is permitted to choose his work and is not driven. While the average lady of four would be more than delighted to help mother in many ways if she were only permitted; and she ought to be permitted, even if all her work had to be done over. For if she were gradually instructed and made to feel that her efforts were truly appreciated, she would soon become a most valuable assistant, and at the same time she would develop the constructive tendency in her mind.

The idea of giving children something useful to do at frequent intervals is first, to turn more and more energy into the process of construction; and second, to cultivate the art of doing things. It is practical results that count, and when the art of doing things is developed early in life it will come easy later on to turn all things to practical use. The importance of this becomes very evident when we know how many bright minds accomplish little more than nothing

The Scientific Training of Children

because they do not have the knack of making themselves practical.

However, the idea of putting children to work at anything and everything, simply because we need their assistance, is a mistake. Such a course will not produce good results, but will in the majority of instances prove detrimental to the child. The child should be given work for which there is natural aptitude. Help him to select that work and direct him in turning his best talents into his efforts. He will thereby not only promote his development along natural lines, but a great deal of energy that was previously wasted will be turned to good account; that is, his energy will have become a building power in his mind and personality.

The modern tendency to combine industrial training with intellectual training in the public schools is a move in the right direction, though it will not fulfill its purpose completely until each child is given practical training along the lines for which he is naturally fitted. We must adapt the educational system to the needs of the child, and not compel the child to become simply a cog in the machinery of that system.

Another method through which the child may dispose more properly of a great deal of surplus energy is to have him engage in play that requires just as much thought as action. This will reduce the action somewhat so that there will be less noise and more order; the interest will be deeper, the pleasure much greater, and considerable energy will be drawn into the mind, thus increasing the capacity and the power of mentality.

However, we must not try to feed the mind with extra energy at the expense of the body. We cannot afford to do this because a strong mind requires a strong, vigorous body.

But all that energy that is not required in the body of the average child, and there is a great deal, should be turned into the mind. It should not be wasted, and the simplest method for turning it into the mind is to encourage children to engage to some extent in play where considerable thought is required. Such play always gives the greatest pleasure. It will therefore be an easy matter to get children to make such plays a permanent part of their daily enjoyment.

In this connection we should remember that the child must play, and that pleasure is just as necessary to the growing minds as sunshine is to the flowers of the field, though this is true of all minds in a measure, whether they are under ten or over ninety, or anywhere between. No mind can develop or remain healthy unless it receives a certain amount of enjoyment every day. All young people should have a good time and they should continue young as long as they live, but they should not be taught to believe that reckless living between the ages of twelve and twenty constitutes real pleasure.

We are too well aware of the fact that the good time that the average person takes usually lasts until twenty or twenty-two only, when it is followed by a decrease in personal power and mental activity, and not infrequently by some chronic ailment that lasts all through life. We do not have to violate natural laws in order to enjoy ourselves; this, however, too many young people do as we all know. But such is not pleasure. It is mental intoxication. And the result is that girls frequently lose the bloom of youth and the boys their brilliancy, their vigor and their ambition, while the majority of both sexes lose more or less of their health, working capacity and virility.

But we cannot blame the young people. They have surplus energy that they simply must dispose of. And they have not been taught how to use their energy in such a way that pleasure may be secured in connection with a constant development of greater ability and power. It is therefore highly important that the child be trained early to seek pleasures that give mental enjoyment as well as physical. The happy blending of both, enjoyed in perfect harmony with the laws of life, will bring the best results, and such a mode of enjoyment will be all gain, with absolutely no loss.

After the child has passed the sixth or seventh year it should be taught to conserve its energies consciously within its own system by concentrating attention for a few minutes every day upon the various nerve centers, while during the time of concentration gently desiring the energies of the system to accumulate in those nerve centers, including the various parts of the brain. It is just as important to teach this to the child as to teach him the alphabet, and he will learn the one as readily as the other. The child that is taught to practice the conscious conservation and transmutation of energy will increase the capacity and power of his mind and body to a remarkable degree, and will also develop a strong, fine personality which is a matter of extreme value in the worlds of attainment and achievement.

This practice will also save the child from the misuse of that phase of creative energy that is expressed through the sex function, and there is nothing more important than this. The misuse of this energy has spoiled the brilliancy of thousands of young minds. And it is a fact, that if all had been taught in childhood how to control and conserve these vital energies of the system for constructive use, we should have many times as many great men and women as we have m the world today.

Every child should be taught as early as possible the practice of poise so that all nervous actions, inharmonious

The Scientific Training of Children

actions and wasteful actions may be entirely avoided. The average child generates an enormous amount of energy; in fact, enough energy to develop exceptional ability and power in anyone if properly directed and employed. To know how to train the child to use this energy in building up his mind, his body and his personality to the highest degree, and at the same time enjoy the days of childhood just as much as the happiest child that ever lived, becomes therefore a matter that is second to nothing in value and importance. And in this connection, the methods just presented, if wisely employed, will produce most gratifying results.

The Scientific Training of Children

THERE is no mental faculty that is more important than that of the imagination. Without an exceptional imagination high attainments and great achievements are not possible. This being true, and the fact that the average child has an exceptional imagination, one of our leading problems will naturally be how to so train the young mind that the original imaginative powers will not only be retained, but constructively developed. The function of the imagination is to receive the many impressions that enter the mind through the physical senses, through the finer perceptions or through original thought, and then to combine those impressions into new ideas, new mental concepts, new mental states, new thoughts or new lines of mental action.

The new ideas thus formed will enable the mind to make a new and better application of such things as it may possess at present. The new concepts will enlarge and develop the mind. The new mental states will change and improve the entire mentality and will produce many similar changes in the personality. The new thoughts will bring new life which will develop in the subconscious the new man; that is, the superman. And the new mental actions will lead the mind into new realms which will result in new discoveries of many kinds.

The function of the imagination therefore is extremely important, but it is a function that few employ properly, the reason being that they have not been trained from childhood how to imagine the wholesome, the constructive, the true, the greater and the ideal. The average adult has very little imagination. It was educated out of him when he was young. He has therefore little or no originality, and in most instances is unable to rise above the level of the ordinary. He can, however, regain his imagination through the proper mental development.

The Scientific Training of Children

All great men and women of modern times are great largely because their imaginative faculties were too strong in childhood to be downed by the educational systems in vogue, although it would be interesting to know to what heights these same men and women would have risen if their early education had been applied in the development of imagination instead of in partly destroying it. However, we can imagine what the children of today can become if they are properly trained in this respect.

But we must not infer that the imagination is the only faculty necessary to greatness. It is only one among the many that are required, but among these many it occupies such an important position that no one can ever attain real greatness or make the best of himself unless he has an exceptional imagination. We realize therefore the importance of giving the child the proper training in this regard.

To train the child in the proper development of this faculty it should not be permitted or encouraged to form mental pictures of anything that is not thoroughly wholesome. The child should never be taught or led to imagine monstrosities or anything of any nature that might excite fear. No evil personage of any description should ever be mentioned to the young mind. Neither should the terrors of the dark be suggested under any circumstance.

One of the greatest obstacles to the highest welfare of the race is the tendency to fear. Every method, therefore, through which fear may be eliminated should be employed. And the best among such methods is the proper training of the young imagination, because fear depends entirely upon the imagination for its existence. When the mind pictures the monstrous or the evil, the imaging faculty itself is misused, while thinking n general is given all sorts of false and disagreeable patterns. As a result, thinking will become

The Scientific Training of Children

wrong and detrimental in many ways, the effects of which will appear both in mind and body later on.

To use a faculty in dealing with the unwholesome is to cause that faculty to deteriorate. For this reason those children that are constantly being scared and threatened with invisible demons and the like grow up with a diseased imagination. Although they are scared in this way in order that they may be kept good, still it is quite evident that no mind can be good that has a diseased imagination. Neither can any person be good in the best sense of the term who is kept straight through fear.

The man who is really good is good not because he fears punishment, but because the good qualities in his nature constitute the ruling majority in the world of his thought and conduct. To be good because you want to be is quite different from being good because you have to be. In the former sense you have character while in the latter sense you are a mere puppet to the force of circumstance. And those men or women in authority who keep their subjects in the puppet stage are surely among the most serious obstacles to the welfare of the race that we can have in our midst.

The greatest thing that you can do for a man is to teach him to become every inch a man — a man that can stand upon his own feet, not having to depend upon any mortal mind in existence, having found that strength of character and worth that makes him a master over his own life instead of being subject to fear, habit or the authority of self-styled superiors. In this connection it is highly important to remember that any system of thought that gives one human mind the authority to dictate to another mind what he shall do and what he shall not do, tends directly to keep the adherents of that system in the puppet stage; and to keep

The Scientific Training of Children

any man in that stage is criminal — a wrong not only against the individual, but against the whole race.

If you wish to train a person to be good because he wants to be good his mind must be made clean, strong and wholesome. But no mind can be clean nor strong that is constantly living in the fear of imaginary demons or monsters of the dark. To imagine the evil is to impress the evil upon the mind, and the mind that is filled with all sorts of evil impressions cannot be good. Muddy water is not pure water even though it does at times flow peacefully in its own channel. The impressions that are formed in the mind lead to thoughts, and thoughts lead to tendencies; therefore the more evil the mind imagines, the stronger becomes the tendency to do evil, and the harder it will become for that person to remain in the path of the right.

When we train the mind to imagine the good, the true and the wholesome, both the tendency and the desire to do right will become stronger and stronger, and in time will become so strong that any temptation can be resisted and overcome without difficulty. It is therefore evident that to teach the young mind to imagine evil personages, invisible demons and the like, and to cause such minds to fear punishment from these demons, is not only to cause the imaging faculty to weaken and deteriorate, thus practically compelling that child to remain an ordinary creature all through life, but this practice will also increase in the mind of that child the tendency and the desire to go wrong which will make him a constant victim of temptation. This being true we readily understand why the average person finds it so easy to go down, and why the majority find it is so difficult to accomplish anything of real worth.

All of this can be changed, however, by training the imagination to picture the good, the right, the true and the

The Scientific Training of Children

wholesome at all times and under every circumstance. We might state it as a general rule, therefore, that the imagination should never be permitted to personify evil in any shape or form, though the personification of the good, the true, the great and the worthy should be encouraged as far as possible.

Every once in a while the idea is brought up that it is wrong for the child to be permitted to imagine the existence of that kindly personage usually called Santa Claus, but there is another side to the question. It cannot be proven that any child has ever been harmed by giving this good man a place in its imagination, but it can be proven that it is highly beneficial for the young mind to picture in mind the personifications of goodness, gentleness, kindness and generosity. That the child is deceived when taught to believe in Santa Claus is not true, because this good man really does exist as a personification of generosity. And the same is true of kind fairies, ministering angels and the like. In a certain sense all of these do exist just the same as the characters of a novel do exist. Though they do not have flesh and bones they are real in their own world, and we must remember that flesh and bones are not the only things that we are living for.

It is the truth that there actually is truth in fiction. In fact, all fiction is truth in a certain sense, and it is just as important to be true in one sense as it is in another. The problem is to select fiction that tends to arouse and enlarge the imagination along constructive lines. And though the basis of all fiction is truth, still the truth in most fiction is not presented in such a way as to cause the imagination to act toward the new and the greater. For this reason wise selection is required in all matter of a fictitious nature.

To permit the child to imagine the existence of personifications is most desirable, provided those

The Scientific Training of Children

personifications tend to develop the same good qualities in the child; and in addition, this practice will produce a tendency of the mind to search the unknown which will invariably result in discoveries later on. The progressive mind, the inventive mind, the original mind, the growing mind, the mind that improves things, the mind that does better things and greater things — all such minds have a strong tendency to search the larger realms of life; they want to know what is not known, and to find what has not been found. Every invention, every discovery and every improvement that any age has produced has been the result of a strong development of the tendency to search the unknown. It should therefore be strongly encouraged in the imagination of every young mind.

To teach the child to imagine a superior and the ideal is of extreme importance because that form of imagination will invariably cause the child to hitch his wagon to a star; and the earlier a child is taught to aim high the better.

The young mind should be supplied with an abundance of fiction that tends to arouse, animate, expand and develop the imagination. And this method will be found to be the simplest, the most direct of all methods, though it is by no means the only method that should be employed. In fact every method should be used that is available, and especially that of the mature mind inspiring the imagination of the young mind through illustrations taken from life.

To find an abundance of the right kind of fiction may be a problem because fairy tales and stories for children have not as a rule been written with this greater object in view. There is considerable fiction to be secured, however, that will serve this purpose fairly well, and increased demand will produce the necessary supply.

The Scientific Training of Children

Those who know good opportunities when they see them will here discover a new and a very rich field for the writer of fiction. To write stories for children that are not only fascinating and interesting, but that also contain the power to appeal to the young imagination in such a way as to make that imagination more vivid than ever, and at the same time give expression to all the greater possibilities of the mind in the most orderly and constructive fashion — this would be a work the value of which can hardly be estimated. And it is a work that is open to a large percentage of those who have the faculty of writing fiction.

In the average young mind there is a strong tendency to imagine the unreal, or to form mental pictures or combinations of pictures that may very appropriately be termed mental rubbish. But to tell the child not to think of such things, or to ridicule the matter is a mistake. The imagination that is laughed out of court is very liable to stay out, and when the imagination is gone the principal secret to a greater and a richer life is also gone. We should never ridicule the first efforts of the young imagination, but instead should try to lead the child away from the unreal or the absurd by calling attention to the marvelousness of the real and the splendor and beauty of the ideal. The child will soon see the difference without being told and will unconsciously select the wonderful fields of reality in which to give its imagination full play.

In this connection we must remember that the imagination must be exercised if it is to live and grow. Therefore, while we are leading the young mind away from the absurd we must give it something better and something more wonderful upon which to apply the imaging faculty. And while we are trying to lead the young imagination into the more wonderful we shall find our own imagination being developed at the same time so that it will be time and effort most profitably applied to everybody concerned.

To distinguish between the real and the unreal is another problem because in the field of the imagination we find that what at first appeared to be most unreal later proves itself to be the most real and the most practical. This problem, therefore, cannot be solved by judging from the viewpoint of mere superficial appearance. On the contrary, it is the tendency of mental action that will determine what we wish to know in this respect, because it is not what the mind may imagine that concerns us — it is the results that follow what the mind imagines.

To illustrate, every exercise of the imagination that tends to make the imagination more vivid gives action to the wholesome and the constructive, and deals with a certain phase of the real, even though the description of the mental pictures formed may indicate the contrary. In like manner, every exercise of the imagination that expands and enlarges the mind, and that tends to increase the desire to attain the greater, and even what may seem to be the impossible, is also constructive and deals with the world of the real. In other words, it is not what we imagine, but how that imagination affects the mind that must be our guide in this respect. We conclude therefore that the imagination that draws the mind into the true, the great, the beautiful, the ideal, the wonderful, the marvelous, is the kind of imagination to encourage in the child, because the effect will not only be wholesome and elevating to every faculty in the young mind, but will also inspire all the efforts of that mind to work for the greater, the richer and the superior in human life.

In this way the exceptional imagination that is possessed by the average child will be made even more remarkable, and all the elements of the imaging faculty will become creative. This means that the child has been taken directly into the path that leads to a life of greater attainment and greater achievement, because the creative mind invariably becomes a great mind.

The Scientific Training of Children

AN exceptional amount of energy is generated in the personality of nearly every child. The imagination is vivid and the finer perceptions are highly active. And since the future of the child depends so much on these three factors the first steps in the scientific training of children will naturally be to promote the constructive use of this energy, to direct the imagination along lines of originality and mental growth, and to train the finer perceptions to deal with the practical side of the greater things in life.

Having considered the proper use of the energy and the imagination of the child, we may now proceed to consider the right use of the finer perceptions. That nearly every child is in possession of perceptions that are higher and finer than ordinary objective intelligence we all know. But we all do not know the purpose and function of those perceptions, therefore the power which they possess is seldom taken advantage of.

The fact is that no person has ever achieved greatness who did not possess those finer perceptions. And no person ever can achieve greatness unless he has or develops those finer perceptions. It is therefore of the highest importance that those perceptions be properly developed and directed in the child, and not suppressed, as is usually the case when the average parent or teacher discovers that the child is living more or less upon the mountain top of existence, or seems to touch the realms of the great unknown. As a rule, immediate means are sought through which the child may be brought down to earth and made more sensible and practical. Sometimes these means are both strenuous and cruel, but they generally accomplish the intended purpose. In fact, they usually accomplish more. They not only bring the child down to earth, sometimes the most ordinary of the earth earthy, but they also quench that little flame of higher

The Scientific Training of Children

intellect in the child which if permitted to live and develop would become a great and brilliant light in the world.

It is the truth that nine children out of ten have this flame already burning in their mentalities; that is, they have that something that can produce mental brilliancy of the highest order if properly directed and developed. But it is neither directed nor developed by modern systems of training. On the contrary, it is usually looked upon as an enemy to practical endeavor and is therefore suppressed.

In this connection, however, we should remember that practical endeavor does not consist of dealing with ordinary things exclusively, for the most practical of men are invariably those who have the insight, the understanding and the intelligence to take the highest and the finest dreams that the age can produce and cause those dreams to come true in real life.

Occasionally these finer perceptions that appear in the child are not suppressed, but are left to themselves; that is, to act as prompted by circumstances, or to remain dormant when there is nothing to call them into action. The result is that this faculty which could, if directed, discern the very highest forms of truth, and originate the most valuable of ideas, is left to drift or act solely in the world of illusion.

Every faculty that is prompted to act indiscriminately and without definite guidance will be misdirected, and will in consequence produce false ideas which in turn will lead to all sorts of mistakes and troubles. When these finer perceptions are not wisely directed they will mislead every phase of judgment and intelligence, and will give the mind a false conception of things. But when these perceptions are wisely directed and applied understandingly they will increase the brilliancy of every phase of intelligence and give the mind a

The Scientific Training of Children

larger, a truer and a more comprehensive understanding of everything.

It is the finer perceptions that discern the greater things It is these perceptions that lead the mind out on the verge of the more wonderful and thus reveal the remarkable possibilities that are latent everywhere. And it is these perceptions that cause the mind to penetrate to the very soul of things, thus giving the mind the power to see through all things.

When these perceptions are not in action the mind is more or less in the dark, and generally gropes blindly. But when these perceptions are in action the mind is in the light. Accordingly it knows what it is, where it is going, what it wants and where to go to get what it wants.

To possess these finer perceptions is to have that interior insight that knows instinctively the false from the true, that can distinguish the worthy from that which has no worth, and that knows intuitively where to act in order to secure the results desired. It is this insight that enables the successful to do the right thing at the right time, to take advantage of genuine opportunities during the psychological moment, and to carry the most extensive enterprises through to a successful termination regardless of obstacles, adversities, difficulties or threatening failures. The fact is man can accomplish almost anything when he can see how to make each important move, and it is these finer perceptions that give him this insight.

The majority, however, do not have it because it was ridiculed out of them or completely suppressed in their minds at childhood. In consequence they do not accomplish nearly as much as they originally had the power to accomplish. When they were children they were soaring on

The Scientific Training of Children

the heights, they were in touch with great things, they felt the power that can do great things, and they dreamed of the day when they should be doing great things. But their practical parents, in their ignorance, brought those children down to earth. And there they continued to remain, never becoming or achieving more than the usual.

To the inventor, the writer, the artist, the composer and the teacher these finer perceptions are indispensable, although they are almost of equal importance in almost every other vocation. No man in the business world can expect to rise above the ordinary unless he has, or develops these perceptions, because in order to rise above the ordinary the mind must be led on by that which discerns the extraordinary; and this is the exact function of the finer perceptions — to discern the extraordinary.

Most people imagine that these finer perceptions deal exclusively with the uncertainties of some other sphere of existence, but such is not the case. It is the greater things that exist in this sphere, and the finer things that exist in this present life, that reveal themselves to the finer perceptions. And it is the function of these perceptions to give the mind the insight to see and understand the larger, the greater, the better, the extraordinary and the ideal in all things. When these perceptions seem to try to penetrate the unknown of other spheres they are simply expanding consciousness into a realization of the greater mental life that we may employ now, and it is in this greater mental life that we find the greater ideas — ideas from which may be evolved superior plans, methods, attainment;. and achievements.

It is therefore perfectly safe to permit the finer perceptions to penetrate the seemingly unknown, and especially so when our predominant desire is to make practical use of what those perceptions may reveal. However, to permit the mind to simply speculate or theorize about such ideas or experiences is to encourage the formation of illusions. In the training of the child, therefore, along these lines, the leading purpose should always be to direct the finer perceptions to search for the practical side of all such greater things as may be revealed.

When the child discerns the extraordinary the question should be what use can be made here and now in everyday life of that which has been discerned. Such a question will turn the child mind to the practical side, and when the power of finer perception is combined with the power of practical application we have the beginning of a great mind, a mind that will do great things — things that are thoroughly worthwhile.

Among the majority of children the finer perceptions do not need development, but they do need orderly direction, and this direction should have two objects in view. First, to keep these perceptions in the highest form of activity; and second, to turn to practical use all such ideas as may be gained through that finer source.

To promote the first object we should make a special effort as frequently as possible to call the child's attention to the finer things in life, to the superior side of everything and to the greater possibilities that are latent everywhere. In other words, the child should be encouraged to think a great deal about that which is above and beyond the ordinary. This can readily be done through the medium of conversation, and when made very interesting, as is always possible, will produce a deep and favorable impression upon the young mind. The matter, however, should not be carried to an extreme, or overdone, especially at first; but ere long the child's curiosity in this respect will be so aroused that you

The Scientific Training of Children

can scarcely ever give the subject so much attention as to produce weariness or indifference. However, it will be found advisable under any circumstances to proceed slowly and gradually.

A number of children have strange visions and day dreams, but these should not be ridiculed or ignored for they may contain the very ideas that will finally carry the mind to the highest conceivable attainment. These visions should be encouraged along wholesome lines, and we should impress the fact upon the young mind that there is something in them all. In addition we should always impress upon his mind the fact that he should and can find that something himself. Also that that something when found will prove to be a great discovery. To call his attention to the something real that may be back of and within his exceptional experiences or visions will cause his mind to work towards that something, and in many instances valuable ideas will be found.

Here we should remember the great law that whenever attention is called to the finer things the greater things or the extraordinary, we cause the actions of the mind to move toward the finer and the greater because the actions of the mind always follow wherever attention may be directed. This will actually cause the mind to enter into the finer and the greater, in a certain sense at least, and will thereby awaken and develop to some extent the finer perceptions and the greater faculties that we possess.

Where these perceptions are already in a high state of activity, that activity can be perpetuated by frequently calling attention to the finer and the greater things in life, and this is the simplest secret of keeping the finer perceptions of the child in full continuous action. The fact is that by directing the child's attention you can perpetuate any belief, any tendency or any state of activity that you like. You can also awaken any new tendency, faculty or state of action that you like.

To direct the child's attention the secret is interest and perseverance. Present things in such a way as to arouse his interest. Repeat the process at frequent intervals until you have results. It is through this law that certain religious organizations succeed in holding within the fold nearly all the children that are trained in their own institutions. They do this through the systematic direction of attention. For where the attention is constantly directed, there all the actions of the mind will go, and the child will naturally think and believe what corresponds with those particular lines of action.

Continue to direct attention constantly upon certain ideas or beliefs and all actions of the mind will tend to reproduce those beliefs; that is, reimpressing them upon consciousness and feeling whether they be true or not. In consequence all other lines of thought will be more or less ignored because the whole of the mind has been trained to focus itself upon the one belief. This, however, is a misuse of the law of attention, and no child should ever be subjected to such a process.

Although it accounts for narrow mindedness, sectarianism and bigotry in all of its forms, it also explains why people think what they think on subjects to which they have given no original thought.

Continue to direct attention upon the finer and the greater and all actions of the mind will begin to move into the finer and the greater, and will accordingly reproduce those finer and greater things with which consciousness may come in contact. This process, however, instead of causing the mind to move in a groove will expand consciousness constantly, thereby producing original thought, freedom of thought and greater thought.

To those who understand the law of attention it is therefore evident, that to turn the child's attention upon the beliefs of a fixed system is thoroughly wrong because the mind will be trained to move in a groove. And it is great minds that we want, not minds that will float with every stream in which they may be placed. Every child has the right, not only to be born great, but to be so trained that all its greater possibilities will constantly develop for actual and practical use. And one of the principal secrets through which this may be promoted is the right use of the law of attention. We should make it a point therefore to direct the attention of every child upon the finer, the greater and the extraordinary, and to persevere under every circumstance. The results in every case will be most gratifying, and in many cases will be even remarkable.

The Scientific Training of Children

THE child naturally imitates, so that its strongest tendency is to do, not what it is told to do, but what it habitually may sees others doing. For this reason those who associate the most with the child should try to be in character, disposition and action those very things that they desire the child to be.

It is almost impossible to find a child that will not respond in a short time to the influence of superior association. And in the scientific training of the child it is necessary that everything with which the child may come in contact be of a superior nature. The importance of this fact will emphasize itself in our minds when we realize that everything with which we come in contact has a tendency to impress itself upon our consciousness, thereby affecting every phase of our nature. This is the reason why it is so highly desirable to secure the best possible environment of every growing mind.

Every phase of environment will produce an impression upon the mind, and every impression made upon the young mind will count. If not sooner, it positively will later. Accordingly we should impress the young mind with that which we desire to see developed in that mind. And we should impress in this manner everything that we do wish to see developed. Nor need we hesitate in producing as many desirable impressions as possible, because so long as the child is interested there will be no danger whatever of cramming the mind.

The mind is crammed only when we try to force into the mind a great deal of material that does not interest the mind. The human mind has unlimited capacity for appropriating, retaining and assimilating that which is received with interest. Therefore by cultivating a continuous wide-awake interest the mind may be expressed most extensively and educated upon the largest possible scale without being crammed or wearied in the least.

To keep the young mind interested find that point of view that is naturally interesting to the young mind. Everything is interesting to everybody from certain points of view. And these points of view can be found by anybody who will look for them.

While conversing with the child emphasize only the strong and the positive qualities. Weak conditions should be ignored as far as possible, and when they are mentioned out of necessity, the idea should always be conveyed that the matter lacks importance. All conversation with the child should be made interesting though no one side of the child's nature should be given the sole attention. The one idea system of training will spoil any mind.

Keep high ideals before the young mind along as many lines as possible, but do not preach. Aim rather to instruct and influence by noble example. Never under any circumstances make it a practice to scold a child. To scold a child for any wrong act is to reimpress its mind with the very thought that originally produced that wrong act, and the tendency to go and do it again will become stronger than before.

This tendency may be counteracted to a degree by fear of punishment, but no mind can be its best that is made a battlefield where tendencies to do wrong are constantly warring with feelings of fear and dread. Such conditions not only waste mental energy to a very great degree, but are also destructive and deteriorating to all that is worthy and true in the nature of man.

The Scientific Training of Children

When the child is headstrong, or contrary, reason and logic should be the methods employed, and we should give just as much consideration to his arguments as we do to those of mature minds, and in fact just as much as we receive from our own. Reason with a child as your equal, and if you are in the right he will soon be convinced. Few parents reason with their children. They simply try to force the child to accept those conclusions that are supposed to be compatible with mature experience but they give a child no reason why he should accept those conclusions.

The practice of reasoning with a child will have the tendency to develop clear thinking and greater mental lucidity in that child. Therefore when scolding is abandoned and reason adopted in its stead a most important mental faculty will be developed in the child, while peace in the family will be permanently established.

Every child should be given freedom to express himself in his own way, but he should be trained to avoid misdirection both of thought and energy. He should not be taught to believe that he may do as he pleases, neither should he be forced at every turn to do otherwise. Proceed by making the child interested in what you wish to have him do.

In the training of children positive commands are entirely out of place. The child should never be commanded, but should be requested, and requested with kindness and in gentle tones. This will place him on an equality with yourself, where he belongs. And when he is made to feel that he is your equal, sharing your responsibilities as well as sharing his own with you, he will take an equal interest with you in what you wish to have done. Should the child refuse to do as requested give him sound reasons why. He will soon respond, and in trying to find those reasons you will stir up a

The Scientific Training of Children

number of dormant cells in your own brain which is by no means unimportant.

When the child holds the best end of the argument, which is frequently the case, adults will find it to their advantage to benefit by such a situation and proceed to develop further originality and independent thinking.

In every effort that is made with the child the central purpose should be the attainment of superiority. All secondary aims should be focused upon this one principal aim, and accord ugly all such aims will be promoted. This means advancement along all lines, and the advancing mind will add power and efficiency to every faculty, which means the constant promotion of every worthy object in view.

No child, however, should be directed to work for objects in view that are not indicated at present in its natural tendencies. All training must work in harmony with those constructive tendencies that are in evidence at present. Encourage greatness and greater worth in every present indication towards attainment and the mind will gradually outgrow everything that may tend towards the ordinary or the inferior. In this way the simpler ambitions that were at first the only objects in view will be superseded by the more difficult and the more important in the world of achievement. No advancing mind will be content with early ambitions if those ambitions are inferior. But if the mind is to advance at all it must begin with those ambitions, desires and tendencies that are in action now.

In the development of the young mind for the vocation that is indicated, thorough attention must be given to the brain as well as to special faculties. The brain is the instrument of the mind and therefore must be highly developed both in quality and capacity if the expression of the faculties and talents is to be complete. By controlling and directing the attention of the child any part of his brain may be developed in a natural and orderly fashion, because mental energy tends to accumulate wherever attention is directed, and thereby build up or develop in that region. When attention is directed to certain qualities in such a way that a deep interest is felt, the mind will invariably concentrate upon that part of the brain through which those qualities find expression. In this way any part of the brain may be developed even to a remarkable degree through methods that are purely mental.

If mechanics is made deeply interesting to a boy's mind every day, the larger part of the energy of his mind will make itself active in the mechanical brain as well as in the mechanical faculties, so that both the brain and the faculties will in this way receive steady and orderly development. The same results may be secured by interesting the young mind in any other subject, object, undertaking or vocation, the principle being, to direct attention upon those faculties and qualities wherein development is desired.

In connection with general education the young mind should be taught not simply to remember, but also to think. The mind that can think clearly usually remembers everything that may be necessary to retain. While a poor memory comes as a rule from a lack of clearness in thought. Learn to think clearly, consecutively and constructively and you will have the power to recall almost anything at any time. Therefore the usual methods of education, which aim principally to develop memory at the expense of mental clearness, are moving in the wrong direction.

To develop the power of clear thinking the young mind should be encouraged to form his own mental views on every subject and event. And those views should not be ignored as

The Scientific Training of Children

useless by older minds, but should be wisely considered and thoroughly analyzed the same as if they were the views of some master mind, which they may be. Many a young mind has a revelation, but it is usually ignored because the young mind is not supposed to have the power of discovery or originality. However, most of those revelations are adopted centuries later. In the meantime the world has lost much because it did not adopt them at once as they were produced by the child mind.

To encourage original ideas when they do appear is to increase the power of the mind to secure more ideas of the same kind. Many a young mind that has been on the verge of great discoveries or attainments has fallen back into the world of the ordinary because the burden of ridicule and discouragement was too great. We must therefore aim to avoid such a culmination in the life of every original thinker. And we can by giving scientific training to every child. To recognize worth, no matter how limited it may be or how premature it may be is to open the way to greater worth. And this may in the training of any mind be considered the first law.

The Scientific Training of Children

THE young mind is highly sensitive to every impression that enters consciousness, and what is impressed upon the young mind usually continues all through life unless removed later on by some special effort. Every impression that enters the mind produces a mental tendency and every tendency that originated in childhood is firmly established in the subconscious. Such a tendency becomes second nature, or what may be termed the thought of the heart, and will continue to affect mind and personality for years, or all through life. If this tendency be adverse it will act as an obstacle in that child's life and will interfere more or less with everything he may undertake to do. True, such tendencies can be removed if the child becomes proficient later on in the use of mental laws, but even then considerable time and effort will be required to remove what is not wanted. Therefore such tendencies should be prevented in the beginning.

We are all familiar with the experience that is encountered when we try to eradicate from the subconscious something that has had full sway from childhood; but it is something that has to be done if we are to obtain complete freedom and prepare ourselves for a greater and more useful life. There is no reason, however, why we should impress such tasks upon the new generation if we can help it. And we positively can help it. The child can spend its future years in a far more profitable manner than in overcoming early mistakes that could easily have been avoided.

Good impressions when formed in early years will not only tend to build the mind, but will tend to protect the mind during temptations. Such impressions will constitute a guiding star, so to speak, in difficult undertakings, and will also be instrumental to a great degree in harmonizing the various experiences of everyday life and thus cause all things to work together for good. When we know that wrong

The Scientific Training of Children

impressions entered upon the child mind may finally make that child a burden to society; and when we know that good impressions formed at this early period may be instrumental in giving that child an illustrious future, we shall give the greatest possible attention to the art of impressing the mind of the child.

The young mind is impressed in many ways, but is usually impressed most deeply by what is spoken, and especially by what is spoken by parents or teachers, or others that may have the child's confidence and attention. How to talk to children, therefore, is a great art, in fact an art that needs the most scientific study and the most thorough consideration if we wish to train the child scientifically and build the child mind into something that is worthwhile.

Since all adverse impressions become weeds in mentality, and since weeds always choke the most desirable plants, we can readily understand how many a brilliant mind has been spoiled in childhood simply because it was not properly impressed. Some may overcome these detrimental conditions later on, but the majority do not to any great extent.

Every day we meet men and women living commonplace lives, almost useless lives in many instances, who could have achieved greatness and rendered a high service to the human race if the early flowers of greatness had not been choked out of existence by the weeds of undesirable mental impressions. Those who have mastered the science of practical idealism can overcome these things and finally secure their birthright, but there is no reason why anyone should be compelled to spend time or effort in overcoming the useless or the adverse when all such time can be used so profitably in attaining still higher states of mind and soul.

The Scientific Training of Children

The demand for great men and women is becoming larger and stronger every day. Therefore everybody should be given the fullest opportunity to supply this demand, and no obstacle whatever should be placed in the way. Every child coming into the world has the right to become as much and achieve as much as the very best opportunities will permit. To be just to every child therefore this subject of impressing and building the mind in the proper manner should be well considered.

The proper training of a child is a very large study, but its basis may be found in a few fundamental principles. And the scientific application of those principles in daily conversation with children will bring about most excellent results. One of the first essentials is to surround the child with intelligence, and the ideal expression of that intelligence in all conversation. No child should ever be placed in the care of an ignorant or uncultured nurse. The future of the child is entirely too important to have its mind impressed by such associations.

The mind of a child is very much like a clean slate. Anything can be written thereon, but no one should have the opportunity to write who does not have the intellect to write what is true and beneficial. The average child is quite receptive to everything with which it may come in contact, and is influenced extensively by its environment and by those people with whom it associates the most. Such associations therefore should have a tendency to impress the child mind with the very best along all lines.

However, to expect the mother to have all the care of her children is not the idea. But before children are brought into the world provision should be made for their proper training. Otherwise we are not dealing justly with those children in any sense of the term. In this connection we should

The Scientific Training of Children

remember that where there is a will there is always a way, and those who really wish to give their children superior advantages and scientific training from the very beginning of the life of those children will positively find the way.

To be strictly correct in conversation with the child every sentence should be studied before it is uttered, not only in answering their strange questions, but also in correcting their tendencies to do what is not conducive to their welfare.

In correcting a child it is not necessary to think of that child as something inferior that has to be literally driven at every turn. On the contrary, the mind of the child is in many instances just as brilliant as that of the parent, and frequently more so; the principal difference being that the adult mind is full of fears and wrong thoughts, with a few experiences with doubtful value, while the child mind is practically clean. The fine intuition of the child is in many instances far superior to the judgment of the adult, but the child is seldom permitted to use it, and therefore one of the finest faculties of the human mind is retarded in its development.

We may talk to a child in about the same way that we would talk in a scientific or ideal manner to another adult only using more simplicity in our language. The average child can understand almost anything if spoken to in a language with which it is familiar, as its fine imagination gives its mind the power to see through things very readily. In fact we may discuss some of the greatest things in life with the child and receive intelligent appreciation.

All of us, when we look back to the time when we were six or seven and remember the beautiful thoughts we had about life, about the Infinite, and about the high, the worthy and the ideal in general, realize that most of those same thoughts constitute our very highest thoughts today. They were so lofty and so beautiful that we have never succeeded in improving upon them to any extent in later years, unless it should b? that we have gained a better understanding of the principles upon which those thoughts were based.

When the child wants to know anything about the mysteries of existence we should not tell him that he cannot understand those mysteries. When we tell him that his understanding is too limited we impress limitations upon his mind; thus he will think that he is incapable, and will then and there form a tendency that will act as an obstacle in every attempt he may make to develop his mind. Here we should remember that if we form the habit of thinking that our minds are small, incapable or limited we shall find it very difficult to develop our minds beyond those limitations. "He can who thinks he can," but he who does not think he can is usually limited in his power or mental capacity according to the limitations he has thereby placed upon himself.

The fact is the child positively can understand those wonderful things he is asking about and he knows that he can; and when told that he cannot his sensitive mind is shocked, and even crippled to an extent that is far greater than we have ever imagined. When he is told that he cannot understand the answers to his questions you impress his mind with the belief that he is inferior.

And whoever thinks habitually that he is inferior creates a mental tendency that will produce inferiority in many ways. This is a fact of extreme importance; therefore we should never impress inferiority upon the mind of any child, for of all impressions this is to be avoided with the greatest of care.

Tell the child in the most positive manner that he can understand the answers to all his questions. Tell him that he can become what he may aspire to become, and tell him why. Explain to him the greater possibilities that exist within him. He will appreciate the fact. Give him something to think about on the great subject of possibility. Encourage him to think more and more about the wonders of his own life. Encourage him to ask about anything that may arise in his thoughts. And let him know what he really is in the larger and richer individuality of his true being. Teach the child as early as possible that the power to accomplish anything he may aspire to attain or achieve, has been placed within him by the Creator.

And help him to develop unbounded faith in that higher power within. This will not make him egotistical nor will it fill his mind with pride. Pride is a trait of the shallow minded only, the mind that has never been touched by the sublimity of those higher thoughts that arise within us when we begin to understand the wonders and possibilities that have been implanted within us by creative powers divine.

When the mind begins to realize, and to actually feel, that there is unbounded power within him, and that real greatness does not exist on the surface of his being but invariably comes from the vastness of the supreme interior life, then all thought of pride, vanity or egotism will disappear completely. When we discern the possibilities of real greatness we discover so much to live for, and work for, that we find it impossible to feel egotistical over those little things that we already may have achieved.

When the mind feels that man is created in the image of the Infinite, and that all souls have the same unbounded possibilities, then the beauty of life, and the loftiness of everything that pertains to life, lifts thought to such a noble state that pride and vanity are forever forgotten. And the mind of the child is more readily impressed with the loftiness and beauty of such thoughts than the more mature mind can possibly be, unless the mature mind has learned to appreciate the eternal youth that is within us all.

The Scientific Training of Children

IN practicing the high art of child training we must overcome and eliminate completely that age long practice of telling children that they are bad. Many a parent is grieving today over wayward sons and daughters simply because the idea of badness was so frequently and so forcibly impressed upon their young minds. Tell a child over and over again, even though it be in play, that he is bad, and he will soon believe it. And when anyone believes that he is bad, the idea of badness becomes second nature to his mind, and will constantly produce detrimental tendencies, desires and thoughts from which will come actions that are evil and wrong. There can be no bad deeds until there are first bad thoughts, and bad thoughts come invariably from that mind that has been taught to believe that he is bad.

To build strength and character in the young mind we must fill that mind constantly with thoughts of virtue, purity, goodness, truth, beauty and aspiration, and we must avoid absolutely everything that may tend to produce adverse impressions. Tell the child that he is bad and you sow weeds in his mind; and it is practically impossible to find a child that has not been burdened in this way nearly every day of his youthful existence. We therefore need not be surprised to find so many weak characters in the world, and so many things that are not as they should be. On the contrary, we may justly feel surprised that we all are as good as we are. Considering the way most of us have been trained in childhood, we are to be congratulated for what virtue or goodness we may possess today. And this fact proves that human nature is inherently good, usually expressing more of the good than the bad, no matter how adverse early training might have been.

Realizing this fact, however, we understand that the remarkable may be accomplished even in most cases where the proper training is given the child in the beginning. The

The Scientific Training of Children

fact is no child is really bad. If its actions are wrong the cause is usually very superficial, due partly to a lack of understanding as to how to use surplus energy; but this cause can readily be removed through proper training.

Every child may have a few adverse tendencies that have been inherited or produced through prenatal influences. But those tendencies should not be made stronger and stronger after birth through a lack of training, or through a wrong system of training. However, whenever you call a child's attention to those adverse tendencies, or tell him that he is bad you make those tendencies stronger. Tell the child that he is bad and you invariably make him worse. You add fuel to those fires which ought not to be there — fires that could easily be quenched if the proper means are taken.

When you impress the child mind with thoughts and ideas that are wholesome you create beneficial tendencies. And these tendencies will frequently become so strong, if encouraged, that all adverse tendencies will be eliminated. You can always drive out darkness with the light; and if you impress upon the mind of the child the fact that every good quality in creation is in him; that he has the power to be good; that he actually is good in reality, you will entirely eradicate in a few years all such undesirable traits that might have come from heredity or prenatal influences.

To scold a child is to shock a sensitive mind, and it will simply make the hardened mind worse than it was before. It is therefore a detrimental practice in either case. If the child mind is sensitive it is evident that there is greatness there. That child has great possibilities and must not be spoiled by being shocked. The hardened child usually has a great deal more worth than he is given credit for, and can, through a few simple methods, be made to come out all right.

The Scientific Training of Children

Tell the child what should be done and why. Never tell a child to do this and so without giving a good, sound, logical reason. And no person should ever be commanded; the child least of all. No permanent good comes from forcing anything or anybody. It is the power of faith and love that leads to the heights. And by using the power of these two superior qualities we can lead anybody to greater and better things.

Tell the child that his whole future will be affected by every thought, word or deed. Then tell him how and why. This will arouse original thought in his mind and original thinking leads to greater things. The average child has exceptional capacity for original thought, and his power in this direction will be steadily developed if you give him a reason for everything that you wish him to do.

Teach the child that his life is a power in the world. Let him feel that there is something exceptional within him that will be of great value, not only to himself, but to the entire race. Let him feel the touch of universal sympathy. And let him realize that he also is here for a great mission. He will soon begin to feel responsibility and will wish to know how best to carry out the purpose of his life.

Make a child feel that you expect him to do certain important things; then have full faith in his ability to do what you expect. This fa.th and confidence in him is of the highest importance, and such a course will bring into action the superior side both of the parent and of the child. The principal idea in all child training is to keep the superior in the foreground, and to forget as far as possible the weak elements in his nature. Help him to overcome his weakness by constantly emphasizing his real strength and his real worth. Tell him what he is in the best sense, and tell him at the earliest possible moment. Tell him what he has the power to do. And so formulate your conversation that everything that you say in his presence will impress his mind with the larger, the better and the superior side of his nature.

However, do not make your conversation so narrow that it becomes a mere repetition of a few ideas about ideals. Cover a wide field and train yourself to make all kinds of conversation conducive to lofty thoughts and sublime ideals. In other words, give an upward tendency to all that you say to the child, and give him an opportunity to enquire into all the vast domains of nature, visible or invisible.

Say nothing that will make him feel that he is inferior or limited, or in any way depraved in character. Impress upon his mind the great fact that all the elements of quality and worth exist in his nature, and that he was created by workmanship divine; then gradually train him to incorporate this great fact in all his thought and speech. Do not force this process of training, however. Give him time, but take advantage of every opportunity that presents itself to carry out the purpose that you have planned for his life.

Have unbounded faith in his responsiveness? to your efforts in this direction, and a higher sympathy will be developed between your mind and his mind which will tend more and more to bring both into the same ascending channel. Then the two of you will in mind and spirit work together; thus he will both consciously and unconsciously carry out your great desires and fulfill those ambitions that you have implanted in his mind. He will become what you wish him to be. He will carry out what you have planned for his career. He will create that future that you can see in your vision when you think of him in days to come.

Thinking for Results

Thinking for Results

THAT man can change himself, improve himself, recreate himself, control his environment and master his own destiny is the conclusion of every mind who is wide-awake to the power of right thought in constructive action. In fact, it is the conviction of all such minds that man can do practically anything within the possibilities of the human domain when he knows how to think, and that he can secure almost any result desired when he learns how to think for results.

Man is as he thinks he is, and what he does is the result of the sum total of his thought. The average person, however, thinks at random and therefore lives at random and does not know from day to day whether good or evil lies in his path What he finds in his path is invariably the result of his own thinking, but as he does not know what results different kinds of thought produce he creates both good and evil daily not knowing that he necessarily does either of these. When he knows what each mental state will produce, however, and has gained the power to think as he likes under all sorts of circumstances, then he will have fate, destiny, environment, physical conditions, mental conditions, attainments, achievements and in fact everything in his own hands.

It is a well known fact that we can produce any effect desired when we understand causes, and can master those causes. And as the process of thinking is the one underlying cause in the life of man we naturally become master over all life when we can understand and master the process of thinking. Each process of thinking produces its own results in mind and body and acts indirectly upon all the actions and efforts of mind and body. Therefore, through adverse thinking almost any undesirable condition may be produced while almost any condition of worth and value can be produced through wholesome thinking. Certain processes of thought will lead to sickness, others to poverty, while processes of thought that are entirely different from these will lead to health, power and prosperity. Through chaotic thinking one can bring about years of trouble and misfortune, while through a properly arranged system of thinking one can determine his own future for years and years in advance.

Everything that happens to a man is the result of something that he has done or fails to do. But since both actions and inactions come from corresponding states of mind he can make almost anything happen that he likes when he learns to regulate his thinking. This may seem to be a very strong statement, but the more perfectly we understand the relation of mental action to physical and personal action the more convinced we become that this statement is absolutely true.

When we study the laws of nature we find that certain results invariably follow certain uses of those laws; and that other results follow the misuse of those laws. We find that a misused law can finally carry you to the lowest depths, and that a law that is perfectly understood and properly applied can carry you to the greatest heights. In the use of natural law, however, we are at liberty to change our mind at any time; that is, when we find ourselves going down we can turn about and go the other way; though the fact remains that if we continue the down grade we will finally reach the lowest depths. The same is true when we find ourselves advancing; we may become negligent and fall back, but the law in question can carry us on higher and higher without end if we choose to go. The laws that govern thinking are just as absolute as the well known laws of nature and will serve man just as faithfully after he has begun to apply them with understanding.

When we understand the laws of thought and think accordingly, we have begun what may properly be termed scientific thinking; that is, we have begun designed thinking; thinking with a purpose in view; thinking in accordance with exact scientific system; and thinking for results. When we think in this manner we think according to those laws of thought that are required in order to produce the results we have in view; therefore all the forces of mind will be directed to produce those very results. In this connection we should remember that every mental process produces its own results in the human system; therefore we can secure any result desired when we place in action the necessary mental process.

You never think scientifically unless you think for a purpose; it is therefore purposeless thinking that you must avoid. And all purposeless thinking is wrong. Every process of thought that works at random is wrong because it leads to waste, destruction and retarded growth. For this reason all thoughts that we may create at any time that have no special purpose in view are wrong thoughts and are detrimental to the welfare of the individual. But here we must remember that wrong thought is not simply thought that has base motives; it is also thought that has no motives. A right thought always has a definite motive with some higher goal in view. In fact, to be right a thought must have a motive, and that motive must be constructive; that is, it must aim to build, and to build for something worthwhile. Wrong thought, however, is scattering and destructive and retards growth. This is the real difference between thought that is wrong and thought that is right. The same is true with other things. Everything in life that retards growth is wrong. Everything that promotes growth is right. If we are in doubt as to whether any particular thing is right or wrong we can readily discover where it belongs if we apply this principle; that is, if it promotes growth it is right, while if it retards growth it is wrong. We shall find that all true systems of ethics or morals will be found to harmonize perfectly with this idea.

The purpose of life is continuous advancement and all the laws of life are created for the promotion of advancement in all things and at all times. Therefore, to retard growth is to violate the laws of life while to promote growth is to properly employ those laws of life. When we go with the laws of life we move forward, but when we go against those laws we begin a life of retrogression. According to this principle nothing is wrong unless it retards growth and nothing can be right unless it promotes growth, because nothing can be wrong unless it is against the laws of life and nothing can be right unless it is in harmony with the laws of life. And the laws of life demand continuous advancement.

Since our object is advancement and progress in every way, and since thinking is the key to all results, it is evident that all thinking must be established upon the principle of continuous advancement. For this reason all thinking that in any way retards growth in any part of the human system must be discontinued, and all thinking must be so arranged or rearranged that it will tend to promote growth and advancement in every phase of human life. In other words, all thinking must be designed, and designed according to the laws that underlie the purpose we have in view. To apply this principle we should never think unless we have a purpose that we wish to promote through that thinking. Before we begin any process of thought we should determine clearly what we wish to promote at the time, and we should then employ that process of thinking through which the purpose in view may be promoted to the best advantage. In this manner every action of mind will become constructive and will build up something that we wish to have constructed. Neither time nor mental energy will be thrown away by aimlessness, and no chaotic states of mind will exist for a moment. All our mental processes will be arranged according to such a system of action as can promote progress, and all the various forces of mind will work together in the creation of that which we wish to realize and possess.

To think according to the laws of growth and to think for a definite purpose — this is the foundation of scientific thinking. This is the principle upon which to act when thinking for results, and whoever resolves to think in this manner only will soon find remarkable changes for the better taking place in every department of his life.

In training the mind to think according to the exact science of right thought, to think according to system, to think for a definite purpose and to think for results, there are four essentials that will be required and we shall proceed to give these essentials our best attention in their proper order. The first essential is to provide what may be termed the mental attitude of normal states of consciousness for all our thinking; that is, to promote only right states of mind whatever the process of thought may be, because such states are always wholesome and are invariably conducive to mental development. In addition, such states tend to hold the various energies of the mind in a working attitude which is highly important when our purpose is to work for results.

To train the mind to think only in the right states of mind we must learn to distinguish between right and wrong mental states, though this is a matter that becomes very simple when we understand that the difference between right and wrong states of mind is found in this, that the former tends to relate the mind properly to the laws, the principles and the powers of life, while the latter tends to prevent that relationship. When we are at variance with our sphere of existence or out of harmony with the world in which we think and live we can accomplish nothing, but when we are in harmony with that world we place ourselves in a position where we can accomplish practically anything if we learn the full use of all the powers we possess. Therefore, if we wish to accomplish what we have in view we must work with those laws and principles of life that govern the sphere in which our work is to be done. But wrong mental states will prevent us from working with the laws of life while right mental states have a tendency to bring us more perfectly into harmony with those laws. Wrong mental states are wrong simply because they prevent this necessary relationship, and they are wrong for no other reason. The first problem before us therefore is to distinguish between the two states of mind, to eliminate the wrong and to cultivate the right. But to distinguish between the two is not difficult when we know that right states of mind always produce harmony between ourselves and those powers in life that we must use in order to realize our purpose in life, and that wrong states of mind always take us away from everything that has quality, superiority and worth, or that can serve us in realizing the greater and the better. However, that we may all understand what mental states to cultivate in order to make our thinking more scientific, more exact, more effective and more conducive to the production of the results we desire, we shall proceed to give a brief description of the most important of these states, or what may be termed the normal and the true state of consciousness.

Thinking for Results

AMONG the right states of mind the attitude of peace naturally comes first because at the foundation of all true action we find a state of deep calm. No growth is possible in confusion nor can we enjoy the steps already taken while strife and disturbance prevail. But if we find that we are not in a perfectly peaceful attitude the matter cannot be remedied through a strenuous effort to secure peace. Peace of mind comes most quickly when we do not try to be peaceful, but simply permit ourselves to be normal. To relax mind and body at frequent intervals will also aid remarkably, but the most important of all is the attainment of the consciousness of peace.

There is a state within us where all is still, and as nearly all of us have been conscious of this state at different times we know that it actually exists. To cultivate the consciousness of this state is the real secret of attaining a permanent mental state of peace. When we become conscious of that state we enter what may be termed the permanent condition of peace and thereby realize the peace that passeth understanding; and when we are in that state of peace we know why it does pass understanding.

A further proof of this idea is found in the fact that the center of all action is absolutely still, and that from this center all action proceeds. In like manner there is an absolutely still center in your own mind, and you can become conscious of that center by turning your attention gently and frequently upon the serene within. This should be done several times a day and no matter how peaceful we may feel we should daily seek a still finer realization of this consciousness of peace. The result will be more power because peace conserves energy. The mind will be kept in the necessary attitude for growth and you will avoid all such ills and failures as originate in mental confusion. According to the law that we always become in the without as we feel in the within you will naturally become more and more conscious of peacefulness in your personality as you become more conscious of the calm that is within you. In other words, the same stillness that you feel within yourself when in the consciousness of peace, will unfold itself through your entire system and you will become peaceful in every part of mind and body.

Closely related to the attitude of peace we have that of poise, and this is an attitude that is simply indispensable. The attainment of peace tends to conserve and accumulate energy while the attainment of poise tends to hold that energy in such a way that not a particle is lost. Peace is a restful attitude while poise is a working attitude. In peace you feel absolutely still. In poise you feel and hold the mighty power within you ready for action.

The well poised mind is not only charged with enormous energies, but can also retain those energies in any part of the system and can direct them towards any effort desired. The poised mind combines calmness with power. Through the attitude of calmness it retains its touch with the depths within and is thus constantly supplied with added life and power. Through the attitude of strength it relates itself to the world of action and thus becomes able to go forth and do things. The attitude of poise, however, is not well developed in the average person as the art of being peaceful and powerful at the same time is an art that has received but little attention; but it is something that is extremely important and no one who desires to learn to think and act for results can afford to neglect this high art for a moment.

To proceed with the development of poise we should work, act, think and live in the consciousness of peace and in the consciousness of power; that is, we should aim to combine peace and power in everything that we feel or do.

Here we should remember two great truths; that is, that unlimited power is latent within us and that at the depth of our being everything is perfectly still. When you realize these great truths you will feel more and more that enormous energies are alive in your being, but you will find that they never force themselves into any particular line of action, and that they never run over on the surface. On the other hand, you will find that you can hold those energies in perfect repose or turn them into your work just as you wish. When you have poise therefore all those energies will also have poise. They will be as you are because they are your creations.

The effect of poise upon thinking is very great because the attitude of poise is the one essential attitude through which constructive work of mind or thought can be promoted. The object of exact scientific thinking is to bring about the results we have in view, but results follow only the true application of power, and power cannot be applied constructively unless it acts through the state of peace. We therefore understand why poise, the action of power in peace, is indispensable to every mode of thinking that aims to produce results.

Another mental state of extreme value is that of harmony; and as there is only a step from peace and poise to harmony we may readily acquire the latter when we have acquired the former. In the attitude of peace the mind finds its true self and its own supreme power. Through the attitude of poise this power is brought forth into action and is held in its true spheres of action, but it is only through harmony that this power can act properly upon things or in connection with things. Nothing comes from the application of power unless it acts directly upon something, but it cannot act upon anything with the assurance of results unless there is harmony between the power that acts and the thing acted upon. No action should be attempted therefore until harmony is secured between the two factors involved. In this connection we find that thousands of well meant actions lead to confusion, sickness and failure because no attention was given to the attainment of harmony. But the importance of attaining harmony before undertaking anything is realized when we learn that the real purpose of harmony is to bring the two factors concerned into that perfect relationship where they can work together for the promotion of the object in view.

To secure harmony it may be necessary for both factors to change their present positions. They may have to meet each other half way, but there can be no objection to this. Our object in life is not to stand where we are, but to do something; and if we can do something of value by changing our present position, that is the very thing we should do. In fact, we can even return with advantage to positions that we imagine have been outgrown if something of value can be accomplished by such a move. The one thing to consider, however, is the result. Any movement that leads to results is a movement in the right direction.

Harmony is not cultivated by isolation nor exclusiveness. There are many minds who think they are in perfect harmony when they are alone, but they are not. They are simply at rest and the sensation is somewhat similar to certain states of harmony. We are in harmony only when we are properly related to someone else or something else. There must be at least two factors before there can be harmony and those two factors must be properly related.

The best way to cultivate the mental state of harmony is to adapt yourself consciously to everything and everybody that you meet. Never resist or antagonize anything nor hold yourself aloof from anybody. Wherever you are aim to look for the agreeable side of things and try to act with everything while in that attitude. After a while you will find it an easy matter to meet all things and all persons in their world, and when you can do this you can unite with them in securing results that neither side could have secured alone.

To secure results two or more factors must work together, but they cannot work together constructively unless they are in harmony; that is, unless they are perfectly related to each other. To be in harmony, however, does not mean simply to be on good terms. You may be on good terms with everybody and not be in harmony with anybody. We are in harmony with persons and things when the two factors or sides concerned can actually work together for the promotion of some actual purpose. In the mental world this law is very easily discerned and its operations found to be exact. You may have a fine mind, but if the different parts of your mind do not harmonize and work together you will accomplish but little, and there are thousands of brilliant minds in this very condition. Then we find minds with simply a fair amount of ability who accomplish a great deal, and the reason is that the different parts of such minds are in harmony working together according to the laws of constructive action. And here we should remember that wherever two or more factors actually work together desirable results will positively follow. To agree with your adversary has the same significance. There is a certain side of every form of adversity to which you can adapt yourself. Look for that side and try to relate yourself harmoniously and constructively to the power of that side. You will avoid much trouble thereby and bring to pass scores of good things that otherwise would not have been realized.

To harmonize with the adverse does not mean that you are to follow or imitate the adverse. At all times we should be ourselves. We should change nothing in our own individuality, but should aim primarily to adapt the actions of our individuality, whether physical or mental, to those things with which we may be associated. Under all adverse circumstances we should remember that vice is virtue gone wrong and that the power in the one is the same as the power in the other; the good misdirected, that is all. But you are not to harmonize with the misdirection. You are to harmonize with the power that is back of the action and try to use that power for some valued purpose. Here we find a subject upon which volumes could be written, but the real secret that underlies it all is simple. Adapt yourself to everything and everybody with a view of securing united action for greater good. You will thus continue in perfect harmony, and you will cause every action that may result from your efforts to work directly for the production of the results you have in view.

Thinking for Results

THE three states of mind mentioned in the previous chapter will naturally lead us to a place where results can be secured, but how great these results are to be will depend upon the loftiness of our aim. Therefore a mental state will be required that will constantly center attention upon the high places of attainment, and such a state we find in aspiration. But here we must know the difference between aspiration and ambition especially when they act separately. When ambition acts aside from aspiration the aim of the mind will be to promote the personal self by calling into action only those powers that are now active in the personal self. Such an action, however, tends to separate the personality from the greater powers within which; will finally produce a condition of personal inferiority. We have seen this fact illustrated so frequently that it has become proverbial to say that personal ambition when in full control of the mind invariably leads to personal downfall.

It is a well known fact that no mind that is simply ambitious can ever become great, and the reason is that personal ambition prevents mind and consciousness from ascending into those superior states of thought and power which alone can make greatness possible. This ascension of mind and consciousness, however, invariably takes place through the attitude of aspiration, and therefore the force of ambition should always be inspired by the spirit of aspiration. Both are necessary and they must combine perfectly in every case if results worthwhile are to be realized.

The attitude of aspiration causes the mind to think of the marvels that lie beyond present attainment and thereby inspires the creation of great thoughts which is vastly important. There must be great thoughts before the mind can become great, and the mind must become great before great results can be secured.

Aspiration concentrates attention upon superiority always and therefore elevates all the qualities of the mind into that state. This being true every effort in life should be directed towards those possibilities that lie beyond the present attainment if we wish to cultivate and strengthen the attitude of aspiration. When we are simply ambitious we proceed as we are and seek to make a mark for ourselves with what power we already possess; but when we are alive with the spirit of aspiration we seek to make ourselves larger, more powerful and far superior to what we are now, knowing that a great light cannot be hid, and that anyone with great power must invariably reach the goal he has in view. The ambitious mind seeks to make a small light shine far beyond its capacity, and through this effort finally wears itself out.

The aspiring mind, however, seeks to make the light larger and larger, knowing that the larger the light becomes the further it will shine, and that no strenuous efforts will be required to push its powerful rays into effectiveness. But when the attitude of aspiration looks beyond the personal self it does not necessarily look outside of the self. The purpose of aspiration is to enter into the possession of the marvels of the great within because what is found in the within will be expressed in the without. Therefore, when we constantly rise above the personal self we perpetually enlarge the personal self, thus gaining the capacity to accomplish more and more until we finally accomplish practically everything we have in view. The attitude of aspiration therefore should never leave the mind for a moment; but we should on the contrary keep the mental eye single upon the boundless possibilities that are within us and deeply desire with heart and soul a greater and a greater realization of those possibilities in practical life.

The attitude of contentment may truthfully be said to be the twin sister of aspiration and its important function is to prevent aspiration from losing sight of what has already been gained. When contentment is absent the present seems more or less barren, and when aspiration is absent the present seems sufficient. But the present is never barren nor is it ever sufficient. The present is rich with many things of extreme value if we only train ourselves to see them. These things, however, are not sufficient to the advancing soul. Greater things are at hand and it is our privilege to press on through the realization of those greater things. We must therefore conclude that the true attitude of mind in this connection is to be content with things as they now are, and at the same time reach out constantly for greater things.

When contentment is absent the present is not fully utilized and we cannot attain the greater things until we have fully employed what has already been received. When aspiration is absent the present is used over and over again like the air in a closed room, and the result must be mental stagnation to be followed by failure and final extinction. When we look at this subject from another point of view we find that the mind that is not contented cannot be developed; nor can such a mind make the best use of the powers it may now possess. Every moment therefore should be filled with contentment and perfect satisfaction, but every moment should also be filled with a strong desire for still greater attainments and achievements. In such a state where contentment and aspiration are combined we shall find life to be a continual feast, each course being more delicious than the one preceding. We shall also find such a life to be the path to perpetual growth and continuous joy.

To cultivate the state of contentment we should live in the conviction that all things are working together for good, and that what is best for us now is coming to us now. The truth is that if we are trying to make all things work together for good, and live in the faith that we can, we actually will so order things in our life that all things will work together for good. And what comes to us every day will be the very best for us that day. When we live, think and act in this manner we shall soon find that the best is daily coming to us, and that the best of each day is better than that of the day preceding. The result will be perfect contentment, and the placing of life in that position where it can receive in the great eternal now all that the great eternal now has to give. In brief, when we so live that we permit the present moment to be filled with all the richness that it can hold, then we shall have the contented mind and the ever-growing mind, the mind that is proverbially described as a continuous feast.

The attitude of gratitude is closely related to that of contentment and is one of the greatest of all mental states; and the reason why is found in the fact that no mind can be, right nor think constructively unless it is filled with the spirit of gratitude. The fact is that new life is coming to us every day and with it new opportunities. Every moment therefore is richer than the one before; but if this coming of new life and new opportunities does not add to the richness and value of our own personal life there is a lack of gratitude. And the explanation is that where gratitude is lacking the mind is more or less closed to the many good things that are coming our way. The grateful mind, however, is always an open mind, open to the newer, the higher and the better, and therefore invariably coming into possession of more and more of those things.

The entire race is moving forward with the stream of continuous advancement; better things therefore are daily coming into the life of each individual. If he does not receive them the reason is that his mind is more or less closed on account of the lack of gratitude. For let us remember in this connection that the mind simply must be grateful for everything in order to be open to the reception of new things and better things. We simply cannot receive better things unless we are truly grateful for that which we already possess. This is the law in this matter, and it is a law that will bear the most rigid analysis. To give thanks therefore with the whole heart for everything that conies into life, and to express constant and whole-souled gratitude to all the world for everything that is good in the world — this is the secret through which we may open the mind to the great cosmic influx; that influx that is bringing into the life of every individual the richness and the power that complete life has in store for every individual.

But in order to be grateful in the best and most perfect manner we must have appreciation. We must be able to see the real worth of that which comes into life before we can express the fullness and the spirit of the grateful heart. The attitude of appreciation is also valuable in another direction. When we appreciate worth we always gain a higher consciousness of worth and thereby make our own minds more worthy.

To cultivate the mental state of appreciation we should eliminate all tendency to fault finding, criticism and the like, and we should make a special effort to see the worthy qualities in everything and everybody with which we come in contact. The result of such a practice will not only be a better appreciation, with a deeper insight into the superior qualities of life, but also the building of a more wholesome mind. Realizing the value of appreciation we should, whenever we discover a lack of appreciation in ourselves, proceed at once to remove the cause. We shall not hesitate in doing this when we find that a lack of appreciation also tends to give the mind a false view of things thereby preventing the acquisition of the best that life has in store.

Thinking for Results

The appreciative mind has a natural tendency to look upon the better side of things, but this tendency becomes complete only when the optimistic attitude is added. To be optimistic, however, does not mean to think that black is white or that everything everywhere is all right. The true optimist can also see the flaws and the imperfections in life, but he gives direct attention to the good side, the better side and the strong side. And having this larger view he always knows that the strong side is much larger and far superior to the weak side. He never becomes discouraged therefore because he knows that failure and wrong are only temporary, and that the right finally wins every time. In addition, he knows that he can aid the right to such an extent that the victory can be gained now.

The pessimist lives in the false and does not see things as they are. His conclusions are therefore worthless. For this reason we should never pay any attention to the words of the pessimist as we shall be misled in every instance if we do. Instead we should listen to the prophecy of the optimist, and then put all our ability and all our faith into the possibilities of that prophecy thereby making it come true, proceeding of course in the conviction that we can. The value of the optimistic attitude in scientific thinking therefore is very great; because to think correctly on any subject the mind must have the mountain top view, and we must think correctly if we wish to think for results.

Though the optimist may live on the sunny side, still the full value of life's sunshine cannot be gained until we add the attitude of constant cheerfulness. To be cheerful, bright, happy and joyous is absolutely necessary if we wish to think scientifically, think constructively and think for results. When we proceed to think for results we think for a purpose. We employ correctly the constructive mental processes so that we may work ourselves up to the goal in view. Growth and development therefore must take place all along the line of action, but no mental growth can take place without mental sunshine. Accordingly, we should resolve to be happy no matter what may transpire. We cannot afford to be otherwise. Sunshine will melt the most massive iceberg if the rays are direct and the clouds are kept away; and it is the same in daily life. No matter how cold, disagreeable and uncongenial your present environment may be, plenty of mental sunshine can change it all.

It pays to be happy. Cheerfulness is a most profitable investment and there are no riches that are greater than constant joy. This attitude is not for the few or for occasional moments because all the sunny states of mind can be made permanent in a short time by a very simple process. Make it a practice to go to sleep every night with cheerfulness on your mind and with a feeling of joy in every atom of your being. Through this practice you will carry the cheerful idea into the subconscious, and gradually the joyous state will become an established state in the subconscious mind. The result will be that the subconscious will express cheerfulness and wholesomeness at all times, and it will become second nature for you to have a sweet disposition, a sunny frame of mind and an attitude of perpetual joy. This method may seem to be too simple to be of value, but the simplest methods are usually the best. And anyone can prove through a few weeks of trial that this method will produce the desired results, and will through more continuous practice actually transform mind and disposition to such an extent that the mind will henceforth live in constant mental sunshine. And there are few things that are more important than this if we wish to train the mind to act and work in those attitudes that are necessary in order that we may proceed successfully in thinking for results.

THE attitude of kindness is one of the greatest among the right states of mind. Therefore to be kind to everybody and to feel kindly towards the whole of creation, this must be the attitude if the right use of mind and thought is to prevail. Kindness enlarges the inner consciousness thus promoting the enlargement and the expression of life. And it also creates the tendency to give one's best and there is nothing that brings forth the greater life and power within us so quickly and so completely as the giving of one's best in all things and at all times.

Both the soul and the mind, with all their powers and possibilities, tend to unfold themselves through the actions of the strong whole-souled attitude of kindness. In fact, no one can begin to unfold his larger life and receive the greater richness from within until he begins to give, through the attitude of kindness, all that which he already has in his personality. And the more one gives of the richness of one's own life, ability and power, the more he will receive from the limitless realms of the within. This is a law that no one, not even the most materialistic, can afford to ignore. But giving is not giving unless it comes from the heart, and it must invariably be an act of expression for some great purpose. Your expressions, either of thought or action, will not open the way for inner unfoldment unless you give richly through a fuller and larger expression, and in all such expressions you must feel kindly. The attitude of kindness is therefore indispensable to growth, mental unfoldment and constructive thinking.

The attitude of sympathy always acts in close connection with kindness, and though it is a most important state of mind it is also a much abused state. There are few people who sympathize correctly and there is possibly nothing that interferes with correct thinking as does misdirected sympathy. When we sympathize with anyone we enter into a certain unity of that one's mind and we almost invariably imitate to a degree the mind that we unite with in this way. Two minds with but a single thought will imitate each other in nearly everything and will actually grow to look alike. It is therefore very important to know with what we should sympathize. When you sympathize with a person in distress you will think the thought of distress at the time, and will reproduce in a measure the same state in your own mind, and possibly in your own life and personality. Many a person has failed in life because he has sympathized too much with the weak side and inferior side of those who have had misfortune. When you sympathize with a person that is sick your mind will create within itself a similar condition of disease, and this expression will express itself in your own body, a fact to which thousands can testify. We realize again therefore that it will not do to sympathize with anything and everything that may arouse our sympathy.

Why does it hurt to see a friend punished? Why do we usually feel bad when those of whom we think a great deal feel bad? Why is there a tendency of most minds to think and feel like the prevailing thought in their community? Why does a mob lose its head, so to speak, and proceed to think, feel and act precisely like the leader? Why do scores of incidents of a similar nature take place in our midst constantly? Sympathetic imitation explains such phenomena. And the law that underlies this phenomena is a law that we must understand thoroughly if we wish to master our own thinking and our actions wherever those actions may be expressed. When you sympathize with weakness you are liable to become weak. When you sympathize with disease you are liable to get the same symptoms and frequently the very disease itself. When you sympathize with the wrong you are liable to think that same wrong and possibly act it out in your own life. These are facts with which we are all familiar. It is therefore a subject of extreme importance. The law that governs sympathy is this, that you enter into mental unity in a measure with everything with which you sympathize, and that whatever you enter into mental unity with you tend to imitate and produce in yourself to a degree. Understanding this law we realize that we cannot afford to sympathize with everything, but on the contrary find it absolutely necessary to make a careful selection of those things with which we may sympathize.

When you sympathize with a person who is in trouble do not think of the trouble or the pain or the weakness, but think of that something within him that is superior to all pain and that can annihilate all the trouble in existence. Then remember the great statement that "he that is within you is greater than he that is in the world." Make it a practice never to sympathize with the inferior side, but only with the superior side. But this will not make you cold and indifferent as many suppose, for it is impossible for you to become mentally cold while being in touch with the very life of the soul itself which must be the very essence of tenderness, kindness and love. In applying this principle we find that the more perfectly you sympathize with the higher, the finer and the stronger side of man the more love you feel, the more tenderness you express and the more helpful you become in all of your efforts. Nothing is lost, therefore, but much is gained by training the mind to sympathize only with the true side of human life.

The man who is sick and in trouble does not want more tears. He has had enough of them. What he wants and what he needs is that sympathy that can banish all tears and that can reveal the way to emancipation, power and joy. This being true we must try to banish completely every form of morbid sympathy. It hurts everybody. It perpetuates weakness and keeps the mind in bondage to inferior imitations. In applying this higher form of sympathy do not tell the unfortunate that you are sorry. Tell them how to get rid of their sorrow. Then do something substantial to speed them on the way. This is sympathy that is worthy of the name.

Right thinking cannot be promoted so long as we sympathize in the old fashioned way. We cannot think constructively so long as we permit the mind to imitate the wrong, the weak, the inferior and the destructive. Here, however, we find a problem that we must solve because it is natural for the mind to imitate to a certain degree. We should therefore give the mind something to imitate that has quality and superiority. In brief, we should train the mind to imitate the strong, the worthy, the superior and the ideal, and thus cause all mental actions to produce the strong, the worthy, the superior and the ideal in ourselves. For the mind invariably tends to create that which we think of the most. The true attitude of sympathy will be promoted to a very great extent if we train ourselves to live in the upper story or rather the idealistic state of mind. There are two planes upon which the mind can dwell and they are usually called the idealistic and the materialistic. The ideal plane is the upper plane while the materialistic is the lower. In the idealistic all the tendencies of the mind move towards the qualities of superiority and worth; all the desires are for the higher and the better; all thoughts are created after the likeness of our higher conceptions of the perfect, the true and the superior. To live in such an attitude is to be an idealist and this is the meaning of idealism. An idealistic mind therefore is a mind that is constantly ascending, and thus taking a larger view and a more beautiful view every day of the richness and splendor of real existence.

In the materialistic attitude all the tendencies of mind move toward the superficial, the inferior and the imperfect.

Thinking for Results

In this attitude we usually think according to those false conceptions of things that have been handed down by the race, and all our desires are concerned principally with satisfying the needs of the body. The materialistic mind is the descending mind, the mind that is losing ground gradually, and that is daily being overcome more and more by its own perverted and materialistic thought habits. But to live in the upper story is to keep the mind concentrated upon the great possibilities that are latent within us and to desire with the whole heart the daily realization of more and more of the wonders that are in store for those who are steadily pressing on towards greater things. In the upper story we live with greatness. In the lower story we live with mistakes and inferiority. In the upper story we see that man is daily unfolding the greatness of the superman. In the lower story we see only the depravity or weakness of error and sin. In the lower story we are in partial or complete darkness. In the upper story we are in the full light. It is therefore easily understood why the mind must dwell in the upper story before right thinking can begin.

After beginning to live in the upper story the consciousness of superiority and supremacy will naturally appear, and these two states should be thoroughly developed. We should all train ourselves to feel that we are superior beings; not superior to others because we are all superior, but superior to everything that pertains to personal existence; superior to ills, pains, weaknesses, mistakes and failures; and superior to everything that is imperfect or undeveloped. Here we should remember that the consciousness of superiority does not produce vanity or egotism. When a person has really become conscious of the superiority of his true being he is above all small and questionable states of mind.

Thinking for Results

When you are superior you do not have to make any display of the matter to prove it. It will show in your life and in your work, and actions speak more eloquently than words. The principal reason why the attitude of superiority is so important is because it unites the mind with everything in your life and your thought that has quality, and thereby gives everything in your mind and personality the stamp of greater worth. And it is a well known fact that whenever we enrich our thought, or any expression of thought, we tend to enrich everything in our life and those things that we produce through our work.

The attitude of supremacy should refer to your own being only. To rule supremely in your own domain and not interfere with the domain of anyone else — this is the true purpose of self-supremacy. And the value of self-supremacy is realized not only in its power to give the individual self-mastery, but also in the fact that when the mind feels that it is superior it can more easily think its own thoughts and thereby prevent the practice of imitating false actions or ideas. It must therefore be quite evident that this state is absolutely necessary to scientific thinking and to the art of thinking for results.

The mind that recognizes its own supremacy is a strong mind and will therefore seek to extend its power wherever the enlargement of life can be promoted, but to accomplish this the mind must be positive; that is, every action of the mind should be filled, so to speak, with a thought current that tends to press on and on to the goal in view. The positive mind, however, does not force its way, but wins because it is strong, and every mind becomes strong when constantly filled with thoughts that are positive and determined. To the attitude of positiveness we should add those of push and perseverance because these two attitudes tend to promote the increase of the results that are already being gained; and there is nothing that succeeds like that which is constantly pressing on to greater success.

When we proceed to think for results we are invariably imbued with the spirit of advancement. Therefore to increase the power of this spirit the mind should cultivate the persevering attitude and should feel a strong desire to push forward into the ever enlarging realms of perpetual growth. But in this connection we must not forget courage and patience, nor the progressive attitude. It has been well said that we all could accomplish far more if we would only attempt more, but in the majority courage generally fails when in the presence of great undertakings. This, however, we cannot afford to permit. To the attitude of courage we should add the mental states of self-reliance and self-confidence and still greater gain will be realized. In fact, these two states are of such value that their importance cannot be described in words. They are not sufficiently developed in the average person, however, because he depends too much upon environments, opportunities and associates, and not enough upon himself. The great soul depends upon nothing exterior to himself. Such a soul makes opportunities to order and changes environments to comply with requirements. Such a soul turns adversity into a willing servant and makes every obstacle a new path to greater achievement. But no soul can become a great soul until faith in its own power has become unbounded.

The strong, positive mind may at times go beyond its own domain and may sometimes act in realms where it has no legal right, but this can be prevented through the attitude of nonresistance, another most important attitude in the art of constructive thinking. The attitude of resistance is always destructive and therefore interferes with the real purpose of right thinking. But it is not necessary to resist anything. That which is inferior will disappear when we produce the superior and not until then. It is therefore a waste of time and energy to try to remove wrong through resistance. The proper course to pursue is to build up the right and the wrong will disappear of itself. In this connection, however, it may seem to be difficult to continue in a non-resisting attitude when we are constantly in the presence of adverse conditions. But here we should remember that the mind that is constantly creating the larger and the better will hardly be aware of the imperfect in his life because the imperfect is constantly passing away with the ceaseless coming and upbuilding of the more perfect. Our purpose should be never to resist evil; though we should not on the other hand fold our arms and let things be as they are. While we are turning away from lesser things we should concentrate our whole attention upon the building up of the greater. This is a method that will give perfect freedom and continuous advancement to us all.

To the practice of nonresistance we should add forgiveness. Forgive everybody, even yourself. To condemn anything or anybody is a misuse of the mind. So long as we condemn the wrong the mind is forcefully directed towards the wrong. The mental picture of wrong becomes more deeply stamped upon the subconscious, and more thoughts and mental states will be created in the likeness of those impressions or pictures. These impressions will reproduce themselves in us and this is how we tend to create in ourselves what we condemn in others. The reverse of this principle is also true; that is, that we tend to create and build up in ourselves the good that we commend and appreciate in others.

To promote the cultivation of forgiveness we should become conscious of real purity, and the reason for this is readily understood when we remember the statement about the eye that is too pure to behold iniquity. Why the pure eye does not see evil is a subject too large to be discussed here. But we shall find that the more perfectly we develop the consciousness of purity the smaller and more insignificant evil becomes to us, and the easier it becomes to forgive everybody for everything. In the attitude of mental purity we look upon the mistakes of the world in the same way as we look upon the false notes that the child makes while learning to play. We want those false notes corrected, but we do not call them bad. We know that the child will learn to play perfectly later on, not by being punished or scolded, but by being taught thoroughly and persistently. It is the same with the mistakes of the human race, and those mistakes should be dealt with in the same manner.

One of the very important states of the mind is that of justice, or the consciousness of justice, and it is most necessary that we cultivate the habit of being just even in minute details. The just mind can readily direct its processes of thought and creation into those channels of action that are in harmony with the laws of life, while the mind that is not just will misdirect many of those processes and thereby produce all kinds of detrimental conditions of mind and body. In a state of justice everybody has his own. Therefore to be just is to so act that you never deprive anyone of his own nor fail to render to anyone that which is his own. To know what really belongs to you and what really belongs to others, however, may at first sight seem to be a difficult problem, but we cannot solve it by looking at external possessions. We become just by developing the consciousness of justice and not by measuring this to one and that to the other. To execute justice in the world, or in connection with any of our own actions, we must realize justice in our own soul because effects do not precede causes. And if all moral teachers hi the world would cease their criticisms of powers and systems and give their entire attention to the development of the consciousness of justice in the mind of the race, we should soon have an order of things which would be absolutely just to all. In our own thinking, however, the attainment of this consciousness of justice is so absolutely necessary that it should be given a most prominent place in all our efforts, because it is only through the consciousness of justice that all misdirection of thought and energy can be prevented.

There are three additional states of mind required to make this study complete, and these are refinement, receptivity and faith. But we need not take the time to give them special attention as we all understand their nature and importance. Faith and receptivity have special functions to perform in all kinds of mental actions and development, and the advancing process of the mind must of necessity be a refining process; otherwise growth would be an impossibility. The purpose of scientific thinking therefore cannot be promoted unless the entire system is permeated with the consciousness of refinement. And to attain this consciousness we should picture before us the most refined state of the ideal that we can possibly conceive, and keep this picture before us constantly with the deep desire to make it real.

The above is a brief analysis of the most important of the right mental states — those states that are needed to place the mind in that state of action that is absolutely necessary if we wish to think for results. We are now ready therefore to proceed with the real process of thinking.

Thinking for Results

EVERY normal person has a definite goal that he expects to reach; some purpose for which he is living, thinking and working; one or more objects that he is trying to gain possession of. But how to realize this ambition is the problem, and though he hopes to find the solution in some way, that way is not always as clear as he should wish it to be. A study of natural laws, however, both physical and metaphysical will readily reveal the secret.

When we study natural laws we find that aimless living is wasteful, deteriorating and detrimental both to the individual and to the race, and the same study reveals the fact that all the laws of nature are constructed for the promotion of progress and growth. Therefore to be natural we must move forward, and to move forward we must have a definite purpose. From this we conclude that the life with a definite purpose is the only natural life. And as it is natural, nature must be able to provide a way by which such a life can be perfected fully and completely. In other words, there must be a solution for every problem, and this being true, he who seeks the solution will certainly find it.

Nature is dual, physical and metaphysical. What we fail to find in the one, therefore, we shall certainly find in the other; and the study of the larger metaphysics gives us the solution for the problem under consideration. This solution is based upon the discovery that thought is the one power that determines the life, the position, the circumstances and the destiny of man, and that to use that power we must learn to think for results.

Whether the individual is to move forward or not depends upon what he thinks. His actions, his intentions, his motives, his plans, his tendencies, his efforts — all of these play their part, but they are all the products of thinking, and therefore are invariably like the process of thinking from which they sprang. Every thought is a power in the life where it is created and will either promote or retard the purpose of that life. Every thought you think is either for you or against you. It will either push you forward or hold you down. When your own thought is against you all your actions, efforts, tendencies, plans, intentions, and everything that is produced by thought or directed by thought will also be against you; and conversely everything that you do with muscle or brain will be for you when your thought is for you. This is a fact the importance of which is certainly great. And since it has been fully demonstrated to be a fact we cannot afford to give it less than our most profound attention.

Since it is natural to have definite aims in life, in fact absolutely necessary in order to be in harmony with the purpose of life, and since it is natural to move forward, it must be natural to have only such thoughts as are for you; thoughts that can push you forward and that will be instrumental in promoting the purpose you have in view. In other words, to comply with the laws of nature, physical and metaphysical, it is necessary to think in such a way that all mental action tends to produce growth, advancement and progress. In this connection we find that nature's laws do not conflict. One law declares that the individual must move forward constantly if he would be in accord with nature, and another law declares that our thoughts will either promote or retard the forward movement. Therefore when our thinking retards our progress we violate natural law and will consequently produce conditions that are detrimental.

To discriminate between right and wrong thinking, between scientific and chaotic thinking, and all thinking is chaotic that is not scientific, becomes very simple when we define the former as being in accord with natural laws, and the latter as being at variance with natural laws. Or to be more explicit, scientific thinking is the formation of all such mental actions, mental states and mental forces as have the power to produce in our efforts what nature has given all things in the human system the power to produce. It is the intention of nature that all things shall work for perpetual advancement of all things. Therefore a thought to be in accord with nature must have the inherent impulse as well as the power to promote advancement in its sphere of action.

To be scientific is to be in accord with nature; to work physically and mentally with nature, and to carry out the fundamental intentions of nature. And since all the actions of man are produced and directed by his thinking, he cannot work with nature unless his thinking is in accord with nature, and is designed and applied with definite results in view. In brief, thinking is scientific and designed when its purpose is to produce advancement, and when it has at the same time both the power and the knowledge to carry out that purpose.

Every intelligent person tries to live in accord with natural laws, but as a rule complies only with those laws that deal with the physical side of life. He therefore cannot be in perfect accord with nature because to obey one group of laws and ignore another group will produce nothing but confusion and ultimate failure. And what is important, it is not possible to comply perfectly with physical laws unless we understand metaphysical laws. Physical actions are both produced and directed by mental action. Not a muscle can move unless the mind moves. Therefore, if the mental action is not fully in accord with natural laws it will not be possible for the consequent physical actions to be in full accord with nature. It is not difficult to understand therefore why the majority of those who have tried to live in accord with nature, and tried to apply fully the powers and possibilities of nature, have not succeeded in as large a measure as their ambitions might desire. They have tried to bring physical actions into harmony with nature while their mental actions have been more or less at variance with nature. They have tried to make their actions scientific while their thinking remained unscientific. And here we have the cause of practically all the trouble, confusion and failure in the world.

The statement that nature's fundamental intention is the perpetual advancement of all things, may be questioned when we take note of the many processes of nature that appear to be destructive, and find that those processes invariably work in harmony with natural law. But when we look beneath the surface we find that the consuming process is necessary to the refining process, and that the decomposing process is indispensable to growth. That which destroys does not tend directly to build up, but the inferior must be removed before the superior can be constructed. The force of destruction, however, can be used in many ways. It can be turned into the gross actions of the sledge that tears down the present structure. Or it can be employed through the channel of transmutation which removes the present structure, not by tearing it down, but by changing it into something better. In the grosser forms of action destruction is usually separated from construction, and may or may not be followed by the latter, but in the higher forms of action destruction and construction are one. The inferior is destroyed by being immediately transmuted into the superior. And here we should remember that everything in nature regardless of its present condition can be transformed into something higher, finer and better because every process in nature can promote advancement, being created for that purpose. Therefore to be in accord with nature man must have the same purpose. He must live, think and work for perpetual advancement, constant growth and eternal progress.

Thinking for Results

In preceding pages it has been stated that the foundation of scientific thinking consists of thinking only in the attitude of right mental states, and the principal right mental states were enumerated and defined; and in this connection it may be added that the reason why such states of mind constitute the foundation of scientific thinking is based upon the fact that wrong mental states tend to pervert and misdirect the original intention of every process of thinking, while right mental states tend to hold in position, so to speak, or properly direct the original intention of every mental process. To think scientifically and to think for results is to think with a definite object in view; that is, to so think that every thought will aid in the realization of that object. Therefore it cannot be scientific to originate a mental process with a certain object in view and then permit that process to be misdirected, but this is what we continue to do so long as wrong mental states are permitted to act in the mind. A misdirected mental process always creates thoughts and mental actions that are foreign or adverse to the original intention of that process and are in consequence detrimental. Such thinking therefore does not only waste time and effort, but places serious obstacles in the way of our constructive and properly directed efforts. In the average mind we find mental states that are right as well as mental states that are wrong. The one group assists the forward movement of mind while the other not only retards or misdirects, but usually acts as an obstacle as well. This, however, we cannot afford to permit. The proper course to take therefore in the very beginning is to eliminate absolutely all mental states that are wrong and to shun them completely in the future. Should we be in doubt as to what states are wrong, we need only remember that every mental state is wrong that has no tendency to build, and that every state is right that does have a direct upbuilding tendency. And in eliminating the wrong states of mind the simplest method is to give so much attention to the creation and the strengthening of right mental states that not a single mental action is ever permitted to create or perpetuate wrong states. In other words, there will be no power with which to produce the wrong when all the power of the mind is used in building up the right.

We may proceed, therefore, upon the principle that right mental states constitute the foundation of scientific thinking, and that the very first thing to do in learning how to think for results is to train the mind to create, entertain, and perpetuate only right mental states. When we have established this foundation we may proceed with the first story of the superstructure. To this structure there are several stories, but the first one is to give every thought you think the tendency and the power to promote your own individual purpose in life; that is, every mental action, every mental creative process and every form of thinking should be so constituted that everything that transpires in the mind will work both fully and directly for your welfare and advancement. In other words, train your mind to think only thoughts that will push your work, and every thought you think can push your work if properly constructed. But the opposite is also true. Every thought you think can interfere with your work if not properly constructed. We realize therefore the importance of discriminating between the right and the wrong even in the most insignificant of our mental attitudes, because we want everything that takes place in our system to act to our advantage.

Before you can apply scientific thinking in your own life it is necessary to make a definite decision as to what purpose you wish to live, think and work for. And in most minds this purpose will assume a threefold aspect. The first will be to succeed in your vocation; the second will be a continuous development of the leading mental qualities; and the third will be the attainment of higher and higher states of ideal existence. To these three many may wish to add the development of one or more special talents, or the attainment of certain special objects, and these different things can easily be added without interfering with the full promotion of the general purpose. The idea is that you must clearly fix in mind what you wish to think and work for in the great eternal now. In the future, some or all of your plans may be changed, but you may do that when the future comes. While the present remains there must be something definite to work for now, and that something should receive your undivided attention. By doing justice to the present we shall be far better equipped for the opportunities of the future. In fact the very best way to prepare for the future is to be your very best in the present, and if you are your best in the present your future will certainly be better.

Whether you have a few objects or many that you wish to realize, place them properly in your mind giving each a special position before your mental vision, and then hold these objects constantly before you as the great goal for which you desire to live, think and work. Center all attention upon that goal, mentally moving in that direction every moment, and turning on the full current. No force of thought or action must go to the left or to the right. Every force you place in action in your system must aim upon that goal, and must proceed with the definite purpose of helping you reach that goal. In brief, you must actually live in every sense of the word for the purpose you have in view. That does not mean, however, that you must ignore the interest of others or become oblivious to the many phases of life that exist about you. The mind is complex and consciousness is capable of many grades of action; therefore you can in general be interested in everything that has worth. But all these other interests must be made a channel through which your fundamental purpose can be promoted, or rather an aid to the great plan for which you live, think and work. If you are a business man you need not ignore music, art or literature. The more you have of these the better for your business provided you employ them as forces of inspiration. Though it is necessary for you to concentrate your life upon your business, still you must constantly enlarge your mind, character and soul in order to insure increased success in your business. Your capacity for work and your power to improve the quality of your work must develop. And everything in life that has worth can be made to promote your own individual growth. In other words, be interested in everything that has quality and worth anywhere in life and use everything you gain through this interest for the making of your own life larger, richer and more successful.

It is not the narrow mind that succeeds. The mind that invariably realizes the greatest success is the mind that is broad, and at the same time has the power to focus the whole of its larger capacity upon the one thing that is being done now. When you constantly focus your mind upon that which you are living for and working for you are giving all your creative powers to those faculties and talents that are required in the realization of your objects in view. It is therefore evident that the larger your mind is, both in its capacity and power the greater will be the results. It requires ability and power to do things. Therefore the more ability and the more power you can apply in any line of action the more you will accomplish and the more rapidly you will advance in that direction. For this reason we do not wish to throw away ability and power upon those things that cannot promote our present progress. We do not wish to give thought and attention to plans that are of no use to us now. We may need those plans some day, but the plans that we can use now are the only ones that have a right to our present attention.

The idea is to think that you can, to think for results and to give your life in the present to that which can use your life in the present. This is not done, however, when we permit aimless thinking. And the amount of life and ability that is thrown away in this manner is enormous. Aimless thinking has the same effect upon your capacity and ability as punching holes in the boiler has upon the capacity of the engine. But the giving of attention to foreign or temporary plans is just as wasteful. When you decide upon a plan see it through. Give your whole life to it. Turn the full force of your whole mind upon it and keep at it until you are ready for some greater plan. You will thus build yourself up and prepare yourself for a greater plan, and when such a plan arrives, which it positively will, drop everything else and give this new plan the full force of your undivided attention.

Too many minds are constantly wishing they were in some other kind of work, thus diverting their attention every few moments from the work in which they are engaged now. The result is not only poor work, but they place themselves in a position where they can never find opportunity for advancement. If you want something better to do, do your present work so well that it becomes a stepping stone to something better. It is the man who thoroughly fills his present place that is asked to come up and fill a larger place, but no man can fill his present place to full capacity unless all the life and all the power that is in him is applied directly in producing results in that place.

Since thought is a definite power, with great constructive possibilities, the more thought we give to our work the more successful we shall be in that work provided our thought is scientific, designed and constructive. This is simple. On the other hand whenever we encourage aimless thinking or wishing for something else to do we are taking power away from our work thereby decreasing results. One of the first principles in thinking for results therefore is to give your whole attention to your present work; to give all your creative power to the building up of the purpose at hand; and to cause every mental action to act in such a way that it will act with the plans and for the plans you are now seeking to push through.

THE next question that will naturally arise is that of knowing what to think about our work and the objects we have in view. Every mental state becomes the mother of ideas; every idea can produce a tendency of mind, and every tendency tends to draw mental actions in its own direction. A false conception will produce false ideas, false ideas will originate false tendencies and false tendencies will lead the mind into mistakes. To promote any purpose, however, mistakes must be avoided as far as possible. Everything must be done correctly, and whatever is done should be done better and better every time. The way we think therefore of what we are to do or the objects we have in view will directly determine the results that are to be attained.

When you think about your work as being difficult you form a wrong mental conception; for the fact is that no work is more difficult than we make it, and we can relate ourselves to our work in such a way that we shall always be equal to the occasion. When you think about your work as difficult you will usually approach it in the attitude of doubt and fear, and no mind can do its best while in such states. Nor can you relate yourself to your work under such conditions because the false mental tendencies that follow such false conceptions will mislead many or all of your faculties. To think of your work as being completely under your personal control is correct because the possibilities within us are unlimited and we can make ourselves equal to any occasion. From this we are not to infer, however, that we can do now whatever our personal opinions may conclude that we can do now; for such opinions are not always based upon the whole truth in the matter. But the idea is that you can succeed in that work which your best judgment has decided upon, and that you can increase your success in that line more and more for an indefinite period. To think of your work as trivial, mean or burdensome is wrong because such an attitude of mind will tend to make you inferior, and there is no success for you while you are on the downgrade towards inferiority. To think of your work as ordinary or trivial is to think ordinary thoughts, and as such thoughts will decrease the power of your mind they will naturally interfere with your work and therefore be directly against you in their actions. To think of your work as drudgery, or as something disagreeable that is to be gone through with is in like manner a mistake; the reason being that such thinking prevents the mind from being its best and giving expression to its best. You cannot give your heart and soul to that which you despise, and you cannot do your best in any kind of work unless you give it your whole heart and soul.

If you want to think and work for results you must love your work, and you can, though such love is not to be sentimental, but rather the feeling of intense admiration for those lines of action that you know will lead to greater things. Think therefore of your work as a channel through which you are to reach the higher places of life because that is what your work really is if you approach it in the right way and apply its possibilities on the largest scale. To find fault with what you have accomplished is wrong as it tends to turn attention upon defects and inferiority. Every mind should constantly expect to do better and should with every effort try to improve upon what was done before, but no actual or chronic fault finding must be permitted. To find fault with what you have done is to belittle yourself; in brief, to place a wet blanket, so to speak, over your hopes and aspirations. Instead, you should think of your work as very good considering your present development, but you should set your whole heart and soul upon the attainment of something far superior. Think constantly of your work as being susceptible to perpetual improvement. Then proceed to make that thought come true, and you will positively succeed.

Thinking for Results

Every mental process that you turn into your work must be constructive. Your object is progress towards the goal you have in view. Therefore, every process that you place in action whether in mind or personality must be a building process. But your desire to make those processes constructive will not alone make them so. The idea of constant enlargement must be the very soul of every thought, and the whole of your mentality must live and act in a state of expanding consciousness. In the growing mind there is an interior ever increasing feeling of the consciousness of enlargement and expansion which we should cultivate extensively, and in this feeling every process of thinking should move.

The thought that you put into your work will increase or decrease your capacity, and will consequently either promote or retard your progress. And here we should remember that the thought you put into your work is the thought you think while you work. While you work you are actually giving a part of yourself to that which you are doing, but if you are giving your life and power correctly you will receive more than you give; that is, the reaction will be greater than the action. In order to give correctly of your life and power in this manner, or rather to think correctly while at work, every mental action in expression at the time should be permeated with the spirit of expansion, improvement and advancement. In brief, you should feel that the effort you put into your work is actually developing yourself. And this is precisely what is taking place in every mind that thinks scientifically, constructively and according to a definite purpose while at work.

Your thought about the progress of your work is very important and such thought should always be that of success. If you are determined to succeed your work is already a success, and it is strictly scientific to think of it as such. When the seed is good and has been placed in good soil we can truthfully say that a good harvest will be forthcoming. In like manner, you can truthfully say that you are a success when all the elements needed to produce success have been placed in action in your own mind and personality. Too many minds, however, do not recognize success until they see the physical results and for this very reason the physical results are frequently limited or of inferior worth; the reason being that the real spirit of success was absent during the actions of that process through which the physical results were being produced. But the cause of success has the same right to recognition as the effect of success, and if the cause is recognized in the beginning the effects will become much larger because the process will contain a much larger measure of the spirit of success. When we give conscious recognition to a cause we increase its power. When you have selected a work and have resolved to put your whole life into it you are already a success in that work, and it is perfectly right for you to think of yourself as a success. The cause of that success has been created; therefore that success already does exist. And by giving it faith, encouragement and mental power it will continue to grow, and will finally produce all kinds of rich harvests or tangible results in the external world.

When a powerful cause has been created the effect is inevitable, provided it is not destroyed during its process of expression. Wrong thought, however, has a tendency to destroy every constructive cause that may have been placed in action in the mind. Therefore we must think correctly, harmoniously and constructively of every process of thought or action all along the line; that is, we should give every good cause definite recognition as an individual power and give it full right of way in our world. To create a good cause and then ignore it is to deprive it of life during its infancy, but this is the very thing we do when we proceed in the belief that we may succeed some day. Say instead, and say it with all the power of mind and soul, I AM SUCCESS NOW. Every true effort is successful because it not only has the power to produce success, but is actually working out successful results; and if it is encouraged, pushed and promoted it will positively express the success desired in real life. To push or promote a true effort we should think of it as being already an individual power for success, because that is what it is, and by dealing with it as such we turn our creative powers into its sphere of action which means that the desired results will invariably follow.

The progress of anything will necessarily depend upon the methods employed. Therefore, the way we plan for greater achievements and the methods we employ in promoting our advancement, are matters of extreme importance. Every plan should be directly related to the purpose which it is intended to promote, and every method we employ should be based upon the laws required to carry it out. It is also important to increase the capacity of every new plan as much as possible. In formulating the best plans and methods, however, the laws of life should be thoroughly understood especially those laws that act in the metaphysical field because all physical action to be effective must be preceded by effective mental actions. But in addition to having the right methods, the right plans and the knowledge of constructive action, physical and mental, we must also have a powerful faith if we wish to work and think for results. When we plan for greater things and have faith in greater things we shall certainly see those greater things realized. In fact, the power of faith in the promotion of any plan or purpose is so great that no one can afford to give it otherwise than the most thorough attention. Though faith in one of its phases is what may be termed a mental attitude, an attitude with an upward look, still it is in its most important phase a positive mental force. The mental force or action of faith is always elevating, expanding and constructive. Therefore, to have faith in yourself and in your work is to cause all the powers of your mind to become elevating, expanding and constructive in all their actions. Faith always tends to build and it builds the loftier, the perfect and the more worthy. Doubt, however, retards and retreats; it is a depressing mental state that we cannot afford to entertain for a moment. But such a state can be removed at once by cultivating faith; and as we proceed to get faith we should by all means get an abundance of faith for in all efforts that aim for great results we cannot have too much faith.

It has been said that faith and science can never harmonize, because according to some they are antagonistic, and according to others they act in domains that are wholly dissimilar. But no matter what the views of the past may be on the subject the fact is that there is nothing more scientific than faith, and also that there is nothing that will aid the mind more in becoming scientific and constructive than a thorough realization, as well as expression, of the spirit of faith. The more familiar we become with real faith the more convinced we become that faith is indispensable in every effort we make, physical or mental, if the best results are to be secured. In fact, faith must be made the very soul of every thought, and the living spirit of every mental action. For this reason we realize that no greater step forward can be taken than to give faith the first place in life if our purpose in life is to think and work for results.

Thinking for Results

MAN is as he thinks and his thoughts are invariably created in the likeness of his mental conceptions of those things of which he thinks about habitually. Therefore as man improves his mental conceptions of all things he will improve himself in the same measure. To improve these mental conceptions attention should always be concentrated upon the ideal of everything of which we think. That is, all thinking should move toward the greater, the larger and the superior. Whatever we think about we should always think about its ideal side, its larger side and its superior side. Everything has two sides, the limited or objective side and the unlimited or subjective side. When we consider only the limited objective side of those things we think about our mental conceptions will be small, superficial and materialistic. But when we consider the unlimited subjective side of those things our mental conceptions will be larger, finer and of far superior worth.

The capacity, the power and the brilliancy of the mind depends entirely upon its mental conceptions. If the mental conceptions are formed in the likeness of the external, common or the ordinary, the mind will be inferior in every respect, and vice versa. It is therefore of the highest importance that every mental conception be as high, as perfect and as ideal as it is possible to make it. And to bring this about it is necessary to train the mind to concentrate attention upon the ideal side of everything and to think with the larger, the greater and the superior always in view.

When thinking about persons no mental conceptions should be formed of the mere external or personal side. The superior man alone should receive direct attention. To look through the person, so to speak, and view the inner possibilities, and all the worthy qualities that we know to exist back of the imperfect manifestation — this is the correct and the scientific way to think about the people we meet. When we analyze the inferior things we see about a person and permit those things to affect our minds we form inferior and detrimental conceptions in our own minds. When we think a great deal about the smallness we imagine we see in others we tend to breed smallness in ourselves. But when we think only of the larger and the better side of others we cause our minds to rise in the scale and thus gain power and understanding we never had before. In this connection the law is that when we look with deep interest for everything that is superior in others we actually develop the superior in ourselves.

When we think of the body we should not think of it as common flesh as the majority do, because the physical form will tend to express the crude and the common when we think of it in that way. When your mental actions are low, crude and coarse your body will have an ordinary earth-earthy appearance, but when those actions are highly refined your body will express a more refined appearance to correspond. All such actions constitute, or are produced by, the thoughts we think. Therefore all our mental actions are as crude or as fine as our thoughts themselves. To be scientific in this, however, we should think of the body as a great temple with millions of apartments, each one furnished most gorgeously with nature's own wealth and beauty, and this is what the body really is. Every cell of the body when viewed under a microscope is like a crystal palace, and the body is composed of millions of such. We should always think of the body as a divinely formed structure, as an ideal creation, and we should mentally view its perfect elements, its forces and laws in this manner as they perform their daily miracles. We should think of the body as it is in its true inner self, as it is in its fine and delicate structures and we should not think of those imperfections in its appearance which our own crude mental actions have produced; for when we form in mind the highest conception possible of the ideal physical form we will not only cause the body to grow more beautiful every year, but we will also enrich the mind with thoughts of high and superior worth.

When we think of the mind we should not think of its flaws or undeveloped states, but try to realize how great and wonderful the mind really is, and then hold attention upon our highest conception of true greatness. When all our mental activities move towards this lofty idea of a brilliant and prodigious mind we shall steadily develop our own mind up to that superior state; for according to a well known metaphysical law we mentally move towards the ideals we persistently hold in mind. Therefore by directing our attention upon the greater side of the mind we shall actually arise into mental greatness thus tending directly to develop superiority in our own minds. This is the path to mental greatness, but it is so simple that few have found it.

When we think about life we should always view the sunny side of personal existence and the real life of interior existence. Instead of viewing life as a burden or as a misery to be endured now, that glory may come in the future, we should think of the unbounded possibilities that real life has in store here and now. Our mind should be concerned with the real life itself and should seek to form the very highest conceptions possible of such a life. There is no greater subject for thought than life when we look at life as an eternity of rich and marvelous possibilities. And to view life in this way will not only elevate and enlarge the mind, but will also give us the conscious realization of a continuous increase in life. And as life increases everything in mind and personality will increase to correspond. A great life produces a great mind and a high soul, but to attain the greater life we must enlarge our view of life. And this we do by turning all attention upon real life itself, and the marvelous possibilities of real life. Realizing these facts we should never think of that which is small when we have the capacity to think of that which is great. And we all can think of the great. There is a beautiful and a wonderful side to all life, and the possibilities of all life are unbounded. We therefore understand the value of training ourselves to take the correct view of life, for to think of the larger and the more beautiful side of all life is to enlarge and beautify the life that is in us.

The same principle should be observed in all our thought about nature, and to learn how to enter into that perfect communion with nature where we can see her real beauty and her wonderful power, is to apply a faculty that deserves the highest state of cultivation in every mind. Those mental conceptions that are formed while we are in perfect touch with the true in nature are of exceptional worth and will add largely to the power and superiority of mind. Therefore when we think of nature all attention should be concentrated upon the ideal, the beautiful and true side. When we see what may seem to be flaws it is wisdom to pass them by and never permit them to impress our minds. Even a weed should be thought of with respect because it is also a product of natural law, and it is our privilege to transform the weed into something that has real beauty and worth. But here it is highly important to remember that our power to perfect anything in nature can only increase as we think less of its flaws and more of its hidden splendors.

When we come to the subject of our own personal life and experiences we cannot apply too well the principle of scientific thinking, because what we think of the experiences of today will largely determine what experiences we are to have tomorrow. What we receive from life passes through the channel of experience and every channel tends to modify that which passes through. The subject therefore is vitally important. As frequently stated before, scientific thinking is thinking that produces the larger, the better, the greater and the superior; thinking that promotes progress; thinking that produces results. And such thinking is scientific because it is in harmony with the purpose of life which is to advance constantly in the producing of greater and greater results; consequently to think scientifically about experience every mental conception formed by experience should be formed in the likeness of those facts that will be found back of the experience.

Every experience can teach us something we do not know; therefore instead of deploring the experience we should receive it with joy and proceed at once to look for the truth it has come to convey. No experience will be unpleasant if we meet it with the one desire to know what it has to teach; and what is better still when we think of experience as a messenger of truth we will form only lofty mental conceptions of all experience. We will thus not only gain much new truth, but we will enrich the mind with these many superior conceptions. In the usual way we meet unpleasant experiences with a heavy heart, and we meet the pleasant ones with the thought of personal gratification. Those mental conceptions that we form while thinking of our experiences in the usual way will therefore be ordinary and frequently detrimental. In the meantime, the new truth that those experiences could have conveyed will remain unlearned and undiscovered.

The reverses and misfortunes of life are usually looked upon with regret, and are deplored as so many obstacles in our way, but such thought is not conducive to good results. Reverses come because we have failed to comply with the laws of life, therefore instead of regretting the experience we should use it as a means of finding wherein we have failed. And having done this we may proceed once more with the positive assurance of gaining increased success. Misfortunes may also be employed as builders of character because there is nothing that strengthens the mind and the soul so much as to pass through reverses without being mentally or morally disturbed. The spiritual giant can pass through anything and gain good from anything. To him misfortunes are not disagreeable; they are simply opportunities to bring out greater life and power, to learn more laws, to gain a better understanding of things, and thus achieve still greater things when the next attempt is made. But though we may not have attained such a lofty state we can at least pass through reverses with our minds fixed constantly upon the high goal in view. The result will be greater moral stability, greater mental power and the turning of fate in the direction we ourselves desire to move.

That knowledge and power is gained through pain is a well known belief and it is one of those beliefs that contains much truth; and it is also true that when we have learned the lesson the pain came to teach the pain disappears. When the pain is felt attention should at once be directed upon that finer and larger life that lies back of the personal man. We feel pain because the outer forces are not in harmony with the more perfect life within; therefore to remove the pain this harmony must be restored. To restore this harmony we should proceed to gain consciousness of the finer forces of the inner life because when we become conscious of the inner life, which is always in harmony, the disorder of the outer life will disappear.

The more we think of the pain the more conscious we become of the discord in the outer life and the more difficult it becomes to gain consciousness of the harmony of the inner life. Therefore to think scientifically about pain is to take the mind beyond pain into the inner realms of life where perfect harmony reigns. The result will be freedom from pain and the discovery of a new interior world. When we take this higher view of pain, reverses, misfortune, troubles and the like we gradually work ourselves out of the lower and the confused, and will ere long get out of them entirely. It is therefore evident that when we think scientifically about the ills of life we proceed directly to rise above them and will therefore meet them no more. This is perfectly natural because when your thoughts are high you will rise in the scale; you will leave behind the inferior and the wrong and you will enter into the possession of the superior and the right.

When we think about ourselves we should always think about the unlimited possibilities of the within. Attention should be directed upon the larger self, and every thought should be formed in the likeness of the highest mental conceptions that we can form of the superior. We may, however, recognize the existence of flaws in our nature; in fact, it is necessary to know where the weak places are in order to remove them; but the mind should never hold its attention upon those weak places. The mental eye should never look upon the imperfect, but should look through it and direct its vision towards the ideal. And here we find the reason why the average person does not improve as he should. The fact is he thinks of himself as he appears to be in the limited personal self. He patterns his thought after the small life that he can see in the outer self. And as man is as he thinks he will therefore not rise above the quality or the nature of his own thought. No one can rise any higher than his thoughts. Therefore, so long as your thoughts are like your present limited personal life you will never become any more than you are now. The mind, however, that transcends its present states, talents and qualities and tries to gain mental conceptions of the larger and the superior will steadily rise and become as large as those new conceptions that have been formed, and may later rise still higher thus reaching greater heights of consciousness, ability, and power than was dreamed of before.

In the world of feeling the thorough application of the law of scientific thought is extremely important, the reason being that we generally live upon those planes where our feelings are the strongest. All our feelings therefore should be transformed to the highest planes of thought and living that we can possibly think of. But since feelings deal principally with forces, whether in mind or personality, it is in the world of force that we shall have to direct our attention if a change of feeling is to be made. And this is done very simply by training the mind to always try to feel the finer and the more powerful forces that are back of every state, condition or action. Whenever anything takes place in your system try to feel the finer forces in that part of the system where the action is taking place. This experience may not give you any new sensation at first, but you will gradually become conscious of a whole universe of finer life and action within yourself. Then your mind will be living in a much larger world and in a much richer world. These finer life forces that you feel within yourself are the powerful creative energies of the subconscious, and it is these energies that are so valuable in the development of the mind and the reconstruction of the body. Therefore, whenever you exercise the sense of feeling try to feel the higher and the finer that is in you. You will soon succeed and the results will not only add enjoyments, both to mind and personality, but will also give you the mastery of new and powerful forces.

An expanding and ascending desire should be back of every action of the mind, and all efforts to gain the conscious realization of the new should aim at the very largest mental scope and realization possible. Every desire should desire the largest, the purest, the most refined and the most perfect expression that present mental capacity can be conscious of. This will add remarkably to the joy of living and will have a refining effect upon the entire system. The most refined expressions of desire give the greatest pleasure, whether the channel of expression be physical, mental or spiritual. But no desire should be destroyed. The proper course is to refine it and turn it into, channels through which the forces back of that desire can be wisely employed now. When we refine our desires those desires will never lead us into wrongs or temptations because the fact is that a refined desire never desires to do wrong. On the contrary, every desire that desires higher and higher expressions will, through such a desire, tend to enter into the right, the more perfect and the superior. In this connection, we should remember that all ascending actions are right actions, that all descending actions are wrong actions, and that this is the only difference between right and wrong.

Every mental aim should have the greater in view, and every plan that is formed should embody the largest possibilities conceivable. Too many minds fail because their plans are so small and their aims too low; but the larger and the higher is invariably the purpose of scientific thought — thought that thinks for results. Every mental force, therefore, should be an aspiring force and should have the power to spur us on to greater efforts and higher goals. This is extremely important as we shall know when we learn that all forces are creative. When all the forces of your system are trained to aspire, everything that is being created in your system will be created more perfectly and you will steadily advance. In like manner, when every mental action is constructive, everything that may be placed in action in your mind will tend to build you up and will tend to work for the purpose you have in view. Mental actions that have no particular aim are usually destructive, but every action of the mind can be made constructive if we make it a point to always think for results. The first step in this connection, and the only really important step, is to have a strong desire for mental construction constantly held in mind, and to give this desire increased attention when our mental actions are especially strong. In all our efforts our object should be greater things, and to realize this object no building power in mind or personality must be idle or misdirected. On the contrary, everything within us should be trained to work for all those definite results that we have in view, and all actions of mind and body should be so perfectly directed upon the production of those results that everything we do under any circumstance will tend to work constantly and directly for those results. It is when we proceed in this manner that our thinking is right, designed and scientific, and it is such thinking alone that we can employ when we aim to think for results.

Thinking for Results

TO make the right use of thought we must make it a practice to think that which is inherently true. Therefore whatever we think about we must formulate our thoughts according to the truth which we know to exist within that of which we think. When we think about life we must think of life as it is in itself and not as it appears to be in the personal existence of someone who does not know how to use life. There are people who make life a burden, but life in itself is anything but a burden. On the contrary it is a rare privilege. Therefore, to think of life as a burden is to take the wrong view of life. It is to think the untruth about life. It is to view life from the standpoint of one who has misapplied life. Accordingly what we judge is not life, but a mistaken opinion about life. Our thought in the matter will thus be foreign to life and will naturally mislead us when we try to apply it in connection with real living. When we think about life we must think about real life and not about some illusion that we might have of life. The average person's thought about life, however, is simply an opinion about his misunderstanding about life and therefore his thinking is never designed, constructive nor scientific. Life itself is a joy, a rich blessing and it means so much that an eternity of mental growth will be required to comprehend its entire meaning. Life is not something that comes and goes; it is something that always is. Neither is life something that can be produced or destroyed. Life is inexhaustible and indestructible and contains within itself a definite and eternal purpose. We should therefore view life according to this idea. And when we gain this right idea of life we can become more deeply conscious of real life and thus gain possession of more life. This is extremely important because it is only as we gain added life that we can gain added ability and power. When we gain a correct conception of life we also enter into harmony with the purpose of life which means to enter the path of continuous advancement along all lines, the result of which will be perpetually increased in all things.

Thinking for Results

When you think about yourself view yourself as you are at your best and not as you appear when in the midst of failure. You never fail when you are at your best and you are true to yourself only when you are at your best. Therefore if you wish to think the truth about yourself think about yourself as you are when you are true to yourself and not as you appear to be when you are false to yourself. Scientific thinking does not recognize weakness of mind or body because you yourself are not weak, and you would never feel weak if you were always true to yourself. Thoughts should never be formed in the likeness of a weak condition because such thinking will perpetuate the condition of weakness. When weakness is felt think the truth about yourself; that is, that you are inherently strong and the weakness will disappear. Form your thought in the likeness of yourself as you are in your real and larger self; that is, as you are when you are true to your whole self — full of life, strength and vigor. And your thought will become the thought of strength conveying strength to every part of your system.

In the right use of thought we never permit ourselves to say that we cannot. On the contrary we continue to believe and say, "I can do whatever I undertake to do and I AM equal to every occasion." This is our firm conviction when we have come to that place where we really know what is in us, and it is a conviction that is based upon actual scientific fact. Unlimited possibilities are latent in every mind; therefore man is inherently equal to every occasion and he should claim his whole power at all times. If he does not make himself equal to every occasion the cause is that he fails to express all that is in him. But the greater capacity that is within anyone cannot fully express itself so long as thought is created in the likeness of weakness, doubt and limitations. Therefore the right and scientific use of thought becomes the direct channel through which the greatness that is within man may come forth and act in real life.

Thinking for Results

Man is not naturally in the hands of fate for the truth is that fate is in the hands of man. Man may appear to be controlled by a destiny that seems distinct from himself, but the real truth is that he himself has created the very life and the very tendency of that destiny. The destiny of every man in his own creation, be it good or otherwise, but so long as he thinks he is in the hands of this destiny he will fail to intelligently employ his own creations, and will accordingly originate adverse circumstances. Many have speculated as to the real cause of adverse circumstances, bad luck and the like, but the cause is simply this, that when man finds himself in adversity he has neglected to direct, consciously and intelligently, the forces which he himself has placed in action; and this neglect can invariably be traced to the belief that we are all controlled more or less by what we call fate. For this reason the sooner we eliminate that belief absolutely the better.

No man will attempt to control the forces of life so long as he thinks he is unavoidably controlled by those forces; but if those forces are not intelligently controlled, their action will be aimless and we shall have that confusion which is otherwise termed adversity. Every word, every thought and every action gives expression to certain life forces, and what those forces will do depends first upon their original nature and second upon how they are directed in their courses. The sum total of all the words, thoughts and actions expressed by man will constitute the forces of his destiny, and the result of those forces will constitute his fate. What those forces are in the beginning depends upon what man created them to be, and what those forces will unitedly produce will depend upon whether they are directed by man himself or left to act aimlessly. But man can make his words, thoughts and actions what he wishes them to be. He can direct them intelligently into channels of constructive and perpetual growth. It is therefore simply understood how man is unconsciously the cause of his fate, and how he can consciously and intelligently create his own fate. To create his own fate, however, he must make the right use of thought; that is, he must think for results.

To think scientifically about the people we meet it is necessary to apply the same principle which we apply to our true thought about life. We must think of people as they are in themselves and not as they appear to be while out of harmony with existence. When we are judging man we should judge the real man and not his mistakes. The mistakes of the man do not constitute the man any more than the absence of light constitutes light. The usual way, however, of judging man is to look at his weak points and then after comparing these with his strong points call the result the man himself. But this is as unscientific as to combine black with white and speak of the result as pure white. The weaknesses that we find in man may disappear in a day. They frequently do, while his virtues and superior qualities may double in power at any time. Then we have another man, and we say he has changed, which is not strictly true. The real man has not changed. The real man is already unbounded in life and power and does not have to change. The change that we see is simply this, that more of the true worth of his real being has been expressed.

Our thoughts about other people are more or less deeply impressed upon our own minds; therefore we cannot afford to think anything wrong about anybody. The better we understand life the more convinced we become that the average person is doing the best he knows how. For this reason we shall be training our minds to think the whole truth about the human race when we take this view, and what is highly important, such a view will tend to keep our own minds wholesome and clean. Then when we add to this the larger view of man himself, in his true glory and power, our thought about man will become as we wish it to be, strictly scientific.

In thinking for results all circumstances should be viewed as opportunities because that is what they are in reality. And to think correctly we must think of things according to what there really is in them. No circumstance is actually against us though we may go against a circumstance and thus produce a clash. A circumstance is usually similar to an electrical force. It may destroy or it may serve depending upon how it is approached. The power, however, is there and we are the ones to determine what that power is to do. Our relation to anything in the external depends upon how we view the circumstances involved. When we think of circumstances as adverse we become antagonistic to those circumstances and in consequence produce discord, trouble and misfortune. But when we think of circumstances as opportunities to take advantage of and control, we relate ourselves harmoniously to the power that is contained in those circumstances. Thus by entering into harmony with that power we will perpetuate more and more of it until we have made it our own altogether.

When disappointments appear it is not scientific to feel depressed nor to view the experience as a misfortune. To the advancing mind a disappointment is always an open door to something better. When you fail to get what you want there is something better at hand for you; that is, if you are moving forward. Therefore to every advancing mind so called disappointments may be viewed as prophecies of better things. If you are not moving forward a disappointment indicates that you have not made yourself equal to your ideal. But the fact that you have felt disappointment proves that you have seen the ideal, and to see an ideal indicates that that ideal is within your reach ready for you to possess if you will press forward steadily and surely until the goal is reached. Therefore no matter what your condition may be in life a disappointment indicates that there is something better at hand for you if you will go and work for it. For this reason, instead of feeling depressed you should rejoice, and then press on with more faith and enthusiasm than ever that you may meet your own at the earliest possible moment.

These thoughts are not presented simply to give encouragement or cheer. The fact is they are thoroughly scientific and based upon two well established laws in metaphysics. The first law is that no person can feel disappointed unle.ss he has had a perception of something better. And the second law is that whoever is far enough advanced to perceive the better has the capacity to acquire that something better, though he must make full use of the power at hand. Too many minds that see the ideal simply dream about it and feel depressed because the ideal has not been reached, while in the meantime they do nothing to work themselves up to that ideal. Instead such minds should take a scientific view of the entire subject and then press on towards the goal before them. They positively will succeed.

When we look upon a disappointment as a misfortune the depressed thought that follows will take us down and away from the open door of the better things, and will in consequence prevent us from realizing the greater good which was in store. We shall then have to give much time and effort to the bringing of ourselves back again to the gates of the ideal we had in view. But such tactics we cannot afford to employ if our object is to work and think for results. We conclude therefore that whatever conies or does not come the best way is always to smile and press on.

It is scientific to recognize only the sunny side of everything and to expect only the best results from every effort, because the sunny side is the real side and the substantial side, and our thinking should be concerned only with the substantial, or with that which has real or possible worth. Failure is an empty place, so to speak, or a condition involving a group of misdirected actions. To think of failure therefore is to produce a mental tendency towards misdirected or abortive actions, and at the same time create thoughts that waste energy. To dwell mentally on the sunny side, however, is to turn all the actions of the mind towards the construction of greater worth in the mind; and accordingly the habit of dwelling upon the sunny side will invariably tend to develop brilliancy of mind, clearness of thought and greater intellectual capacity.

The principal reason for this is found in the fact that such a mind deals almost entirely with the larger, the greater and the limitless of the potential. Mind therefore naturally expands and develops and steadily gains in power, comprehension and lucidity along all lines. To act in harmony with this principle we should expect the best results from every effort because the best results do exist potentially in every effort; and to be scientific we must think of things as they really are in themselves and not as they appear while in the hands of the incompetent. It is not our purpose to dwell mentally upon the absence of results, but to give all our thought and attention to the right use of those powers within us that actually can produce results.

To think scientifically about the health and the wholeness of mind and body is one of the most important essentials of all because health is indispensable to the highest attainments and the greatest achievements. The principle, however, is that the real man is well, and that you yourself are the real man. When you are thinking about yourself as you really are and since you, the real YOU, the individuality, are always well, your thought of yourself is not right and constructive unless you think of yourself as absolutely and permanently well. Every condition in the personal man is the result of habits of thought. Therefore when you think of yourself as being absolutely and permanently well you will through that mode of thinking give absolute and permanent health to the entire system. This is a law that is as strong as life itself. And we are not making extravagant statements when we declare that if this law were universally employed disease would be practically banished from off the face of the earth. This law is the absolute truth and every student of modern metaphysics knows that it is the truth. That its power is invincible no one can deny. Therefore the wise course to pursue is to apply this law thoroughly under all sorts of circumstances and never lose faith in its effectiveness for a moment.

In training ourselves to think for results we must constantly bear in mind the great fact that man invariably grows into the likeness of that which he thinks of the most. Therefore, think constantly of what you want to become and your life will daily grow in that direction. Think constantly of health, power, ability, capacity, worth and superiority and the powers of your being will gradually and steadily produce all those qualities in your own system. But all such thinking must be deep, persistent and of the heart. It is that thinking which is in touch with the under currents of life that shapes human destiny; therefore all such thinking should always be as we wish to become. No thoughts should ever enter the mind that do not contain in the ideal the very things that we wish to attain or accomplish in the real. But to train ourselves in this mode of thinking is not difficult. It is only a matter of deciding what we want in life; then to think the most of those things and make such thinking deep, persistent, positive and strong.

Thinking for Results

TO train the mind to think for results there are four essentials that must be provided. The first is to carry on all thinking in the attitude of right mental states. The second is to think only such thoughts as will push your work and that will constantly promote your present purpose in life. The third is to employ only such creative processes in the mind as will tend directly to produce the larger, the better and the superior. And the fourth is to think only the real truth about all things; that is, to fashion all thought according to the most perfect mental conception that can be formed of the real in everything of which we may think. The first three essentials have been fully considered in the preceding pages. We shall therefore conclude by giving our attention to the fourth. And in doing so we must prepare ourselves for thought that is somewhat deeper than the usual.

To begin we must realize that there is a vast difference between what seems to be true and what really is true, and that all thinking to be right, wholesome, constructive and scientific must deal directly with that which really is true. To illustrate we will consider the being of man. Viewed externally man seems to have many imperfections, to be limited in all things and to be more or less in the hands of fate. But when we consider, not the present conditions of the personal man, but the possibilities of his marvelous interior nature, we find that imperfections are simply greater things in the process of development. We find that there is no limit to his power and inherent capacity, and we find that he is strong enough, if he applies all his strength, to overcome any fate, to change any circumstance and to positively determine his own destiny.

When we examine other things we find the same to be true; that is, that there is more in everything than what appears on the surface. And therefore what appears to be true of things when viewed externally is not the whole truth;

in fact, it may frequently be the very opposite of the real truth. The right use of thought, however, must concern itself with the real truth, or the inside facts in the case; therefore, in thinking for results we must fashion our thoughts according to what really is in those thoughts of which we may be thinking.

In dealing with the inside facts of any case, condition or object the question always is: "What are the possibilities; what can be done with what is in the thing; and what results can be gained from the full use of everything that this circumstance or that object may contain?" And it is highly important to answer this question as fully and as correctly as possible because we are as we think and our thoughts are always like the things we think about. Besides we must be conscious of the real interior possibility of those things with which we deal in order to secure the greatest results. If we think only of the imperfections and the limitations that appear on the surface our thinking will be inferior, and we will become ordinary both in mind and personality. But if we think of what is really true of the greater possibilities of all things we will think far greater thoughts, and we will think inspiring thoughts — thoughts that will stir the mind to greater ambition and greater achievement, and the mind will accordingly enter more and more into a larger, greater and richer world. In consequence our mental powers along all lines will steadily increase.

To think what is really true about all things is therefore to think of the greater powers and possibilities that are in all things; and to think the truth in the broadest sense is to direct the mind upon the whole of life, with all its possibilities, and to deal mentally with all the richness, all the power and all the marvelousness that can be discerned in everything pertaining to life. Or to state it briefly, you have begun to think what is really true when your mind has begun to move constantly towards the vastness of the greater things that lie before us. And here we must remember that there is no end to that vastness; no limit to the greatness that is inherent in life. Therefore, we may go on and on indefinitely thinking more and more truth about everything; and as we do we shall continue to enrich and enlarge both the talents and the powers of the mind.

It is therefore evident that when we think the truth about all things, that is, think of what is really possible in all things, we will cause the mind to enlarge and expand constantly, because as we think of the larger we invariably enlarge the mind. And the real truth about all things grows larger and larger the further we advance in the pursuit of truth. And the importance of such a mode of thinking becomes more and more evident as we realize that an ever enlarging mind is an absolute necessity if our aim is to think for results.

When we proceed to think the truth about things we naturally think of the true state of affairs within those things. We think of the power itself and not of its past use. Therefore, such thinking will invariably keep the mind in a wholesome and harmonious condition. That which is true of the real nature of things must be good and wholesome, and therefore to think of that which is true must necessarily produce wholesome conditions in the mind. And here it is well to emphasize the fact that the mind that is wholesome and harmonious is far more powerful than the mind that is not. Such a mind therefore may secure far greater results, no matter what its work or purpose may be.

To think what is really true about everything will for the same reason prevent the formation of detrimental and perverted states of mind, and will also prevent the misdirection of mental energy. This is a fact of great importance to those who aim for results, because in the average mind the majority of the energies placed in action are either misdirected or applied in such a way as to be of no permanent value. Another fact that needs emphasis in this connection is that the thinking of truth will tend to bring out all that is in us. And the reason is that when we think of what there really is in everything the mind becomes more penetrating as well as more comprehensive in its scope of action. The result therefore will naturally be that our own mental actions will penetrate more and more every element and power that is in us, and thus arouse more and more of everything that is in us. In other words, the mind will proceed to act positively upon everything that exists in the vast domain of our own mental world, conscious and subconscious, and will actually think into activity every power and faculty we possess.

When we think the real truth about everything in life, including our own self, we invariably focus attention upon the best, the largest and the richest that exists in everything. And this we must do if our purpose is to secure greater and better results the further we go in our progress toward attainment and achievement. Your mind, your thought, your ability, your power, in brief, everything of worth in your system, cannot be fully and effectively applied unless your attention is constantly concentrated upon the greater; unless you are mentally moving towards the greater; unless you are giving your whole life and power to the greater; and to this end your attention must constantly be focused upon the best and the greatest that you can possibly picture in your mind.

When you think the truth you think of what can be done. You do not think of weakness, obstacles or possible failure; nor do you consider what may be dark, adverse or detrimental in your present circumstances. Instead you think of the tremendous power that is within you, and you try to turn on the full current of that power so that what you want to accomplish positively will be accomplished. But in turning on that full current you make a special effort to make every action in your system constructive, whether it be physical or mental, because in working for results you want all that is in you to work thoroughly, continuously and directly for those self same results. We realize therefore the importance of training the mind to think the truth according to this larger view of the truth in order that the best use, the fullest use and the most effective use of every power of mind and thought may be applied; and we shall find as we proceed that the art of thinking the truth in this manner can be readily mastered by anyone whose desire is to make his life as large, as rich and as perfect as life can be made.

To restate the principles and ideas upon which the right use of the mind is based we need simply return to the four essentials mentioned in the beginning of this chapter. We proceed by placing the mind in certain mental states called right mental states because the mind has more power while acting in such states, and can act more effectively while acting through the wholesome constructive attitudes of those states. We continue by thinking only such thoughts as will tend to work with us, and give their full force to the promotion of our purpose. We avoid thoughts and mental states that are against us and permit only those that are positively and absolutely for us. We place in action only such mental processes as tend to create the larger, the better and the superior in ourselves because our object is not simply to secure results now, but to secure greater and greater results; and to promote this object we must constantly develop the larger, the better and the superior in ourselves. Lastly we make it a special point to think the real truth about all things; that is, we form our mental conceptions, our ideas and our thoughts in the exact likeness of the great, the marvelous and the limitless that is inherent in all life.

We aim to fashion our thoughts according to everything that is great, lofty and of superior worth so that we may think great thoughts because we are as we think. When our thoughts are small we will become small, weak and inefficient; but when our thoughts are great we will become great, powerful and efficient. This is the law, and as we apply this law as fully and as effectively as we possibly can, we shall positively become much and achieve much, and the object we have in view — the securing of greater and greater results — will be realized. Therefore in all our thinking we focus all the actions of mind upon the unbounded possibilities that are inherent in ourselves, that are inherent in all things, that are inherent in the vastness of the cosmos.

We turn all our thoughts upon the rich, the limitless and the sublime so that we may live constantly in a larger and superior mental world — a world that we are determined to make larger and larger every day. And as we live, think and work in that ever-growing mental world we insist that everything we do shall, with a certainty, build for that greater future we now have in view; and that every action of mind and body shall be a positive force moving steadily, surely and perpetually towards those sublime heights of attainment and achievement that we have longed for so much while inspired by the spirit of ambition's lofty dream.

www.ingramcontent.com/pod-product-compliance
Lightning Source LLC
Chambersburg PA
CBHW031400290426
44110CB00011B/216